# GUITAR CHORDS I

## Practical Diagrams for Beginners

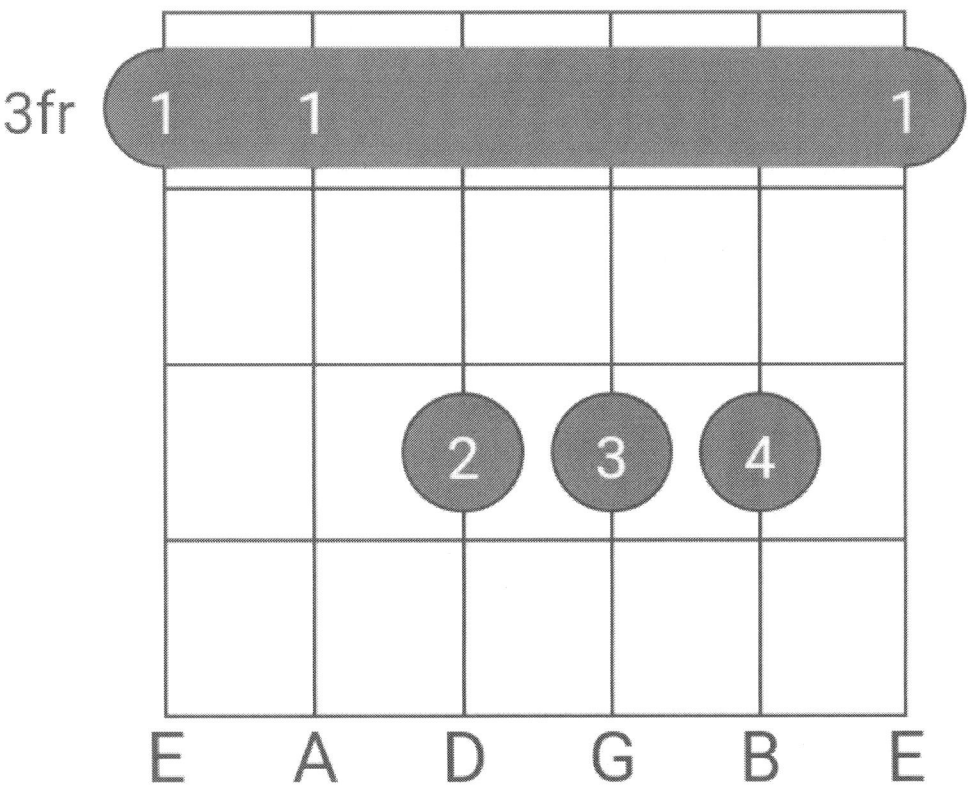

**Peter Music Publishing**

All Rights Reserved **2021**

# CONTENTS

**How To Use Diagrams** ..................................................................................................**2**

**C** - Major and minor, Diminished, Sus2 and Sus4, Augmented, Dominant 7, Maj7.....................**4**

**C# / Db** Major and minor, Diminished, Sus2 and Sus4, Augmented, Dominant 7, Maj7..........**13**

**D** Major and minor, Diminished, Sus2 and Sus4, Augmented, Dominant 7, Maj7....................**22**

**D# / Eb** Major and minor, Diminished, Sus2 and Sus4, Augmented, Dominant 7, Maj7..........**31**

**E** Major and minor, Diminished, Sus2 and Sus4, Augmented, Dominant 7, Maj7....................**40**

**F** Major and minor, Diminished, Sus2 and Sus4, Augmented, Dominant 7, Maj7....................**49**

**F# / Gb** Major and minor, Diminished, Sus2 and Sus4, Augmented, Dominant 7, Maj7..........**54**

**G** Major and minor, Diminished, Sus2 and Sus4, Augmented, Dominant 7, Maj7...................**67**

**G# / Ab** Major and minor, Diminished, Sus2 and Sus4, Augmented, Dominant 7, Maj7..........**76**

**A** Major and Minor, Diminished, Sus2, and Sus4, Augmented, Dominant 7, Maj7....................**85**

**A# / Bb** Major and minor, Diminished, Sus2 and Sus4, Augmented, Dominant 7, Maj7..........**94**

**B** Major and minor, Diminished, Sus2 and Sus4, Augmented, Dominant 7, Maj7..................**103**

All Rights Reserved **2021**

# HOW TO USE DIAGRAMS

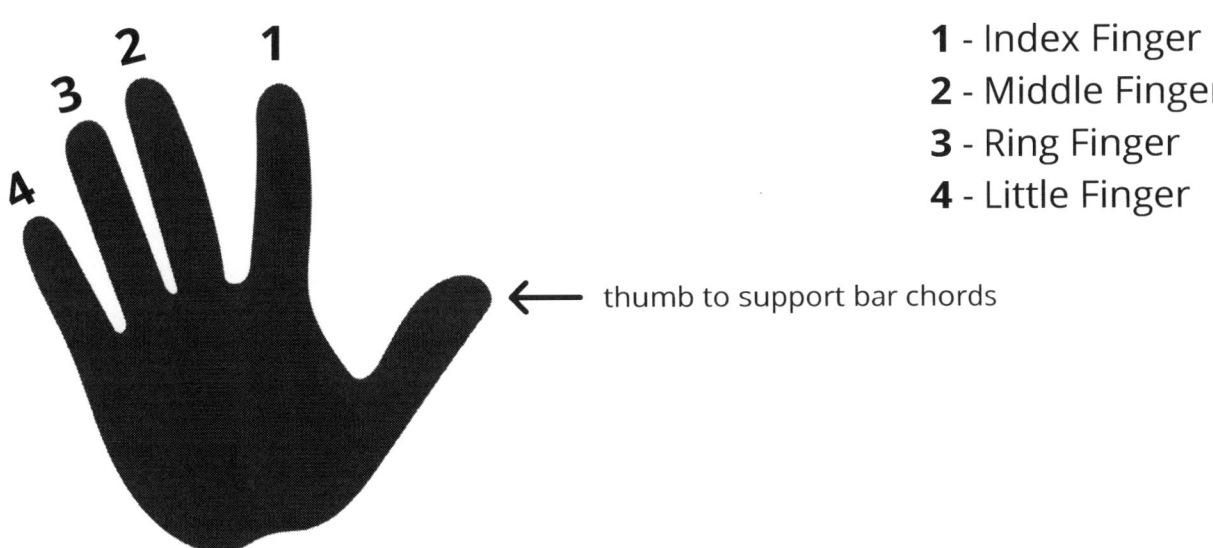

**1** - Index Finger
**2** - Middle Finger
**3** - Ring Finger
**4** - Little Finger

← thumb to support bar chords

LEFT HAND DESIGNATIONS

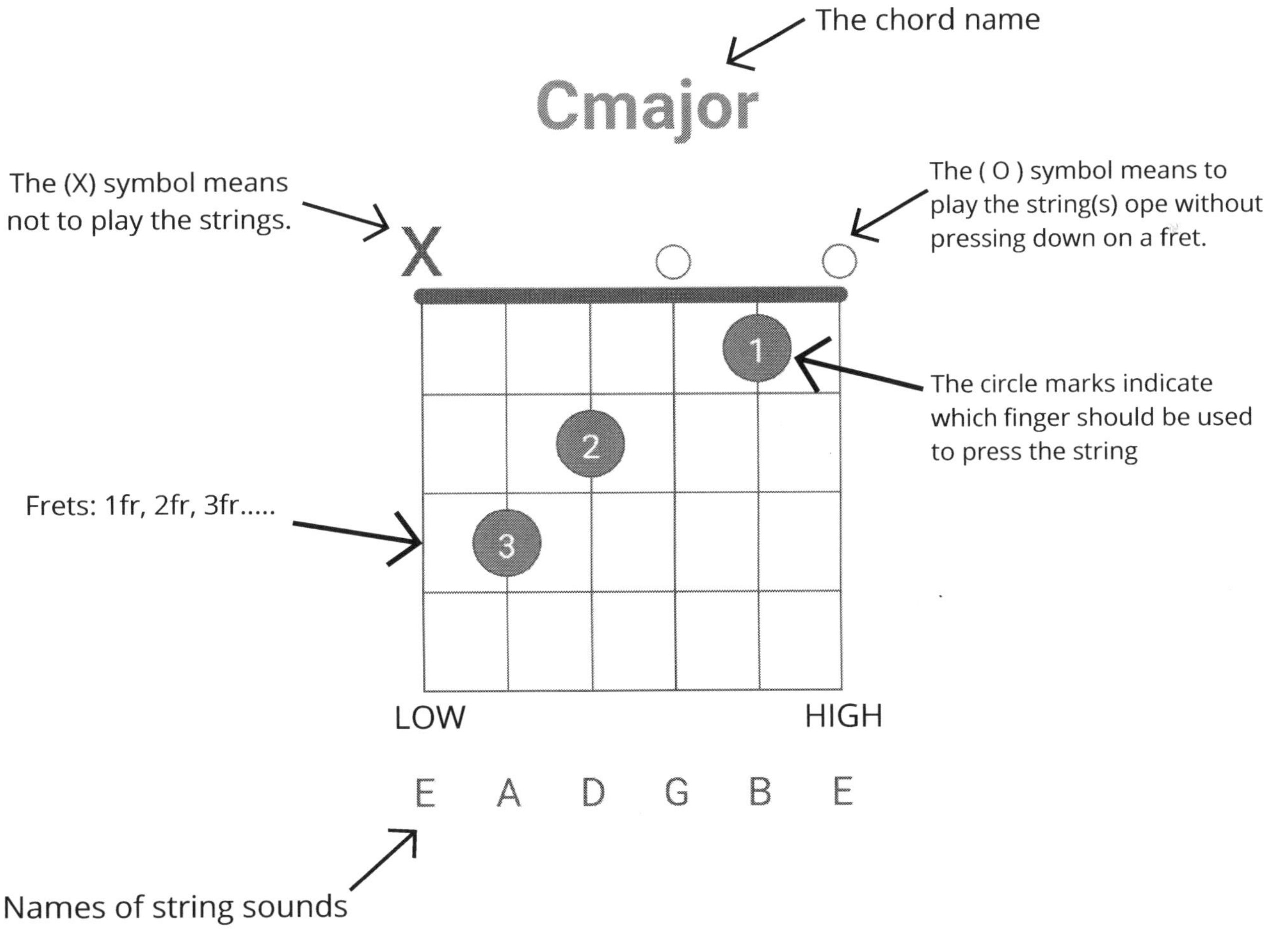

The chord name

**Cmajor**

The (X) symbol means not to play the strings.

The ( O ) symbol means to play the string(s) ope without pressing down on a fret.

The circle marks indicate which finger should be used to press the string

Frets: 1fr, 2fr, 3fr.....

LOW         HIGH

E   A   D   G   B   E

Names of string sounds

# HOW TO USE DIAGRAMS

Chords diagram are arranged chromatically from C - C# - D - D# - E...

Chords for Guitar book was written by a professional, it was created for beginners who are learning chords and for people who want to have all chords in one book. Maybe you already play, but you miss other chords that would diversify your repertory?
If so, this book will be perfect for you!

## Every CHORDS is written in 4 different ways

Where a bar appears between notes, the specified finger should hold down the notes across the strings shown.

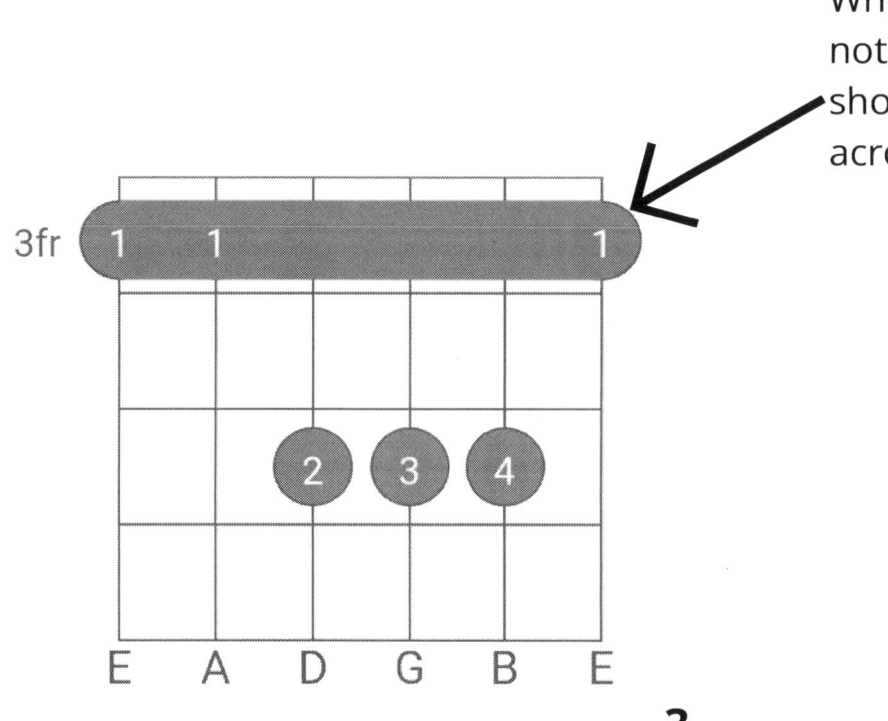

# C Major

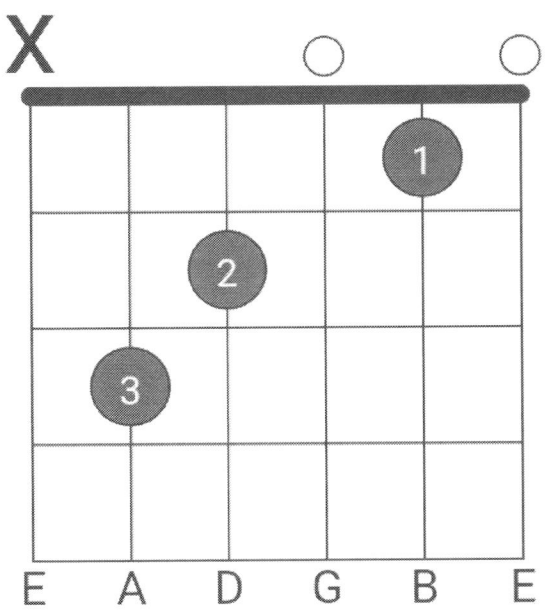
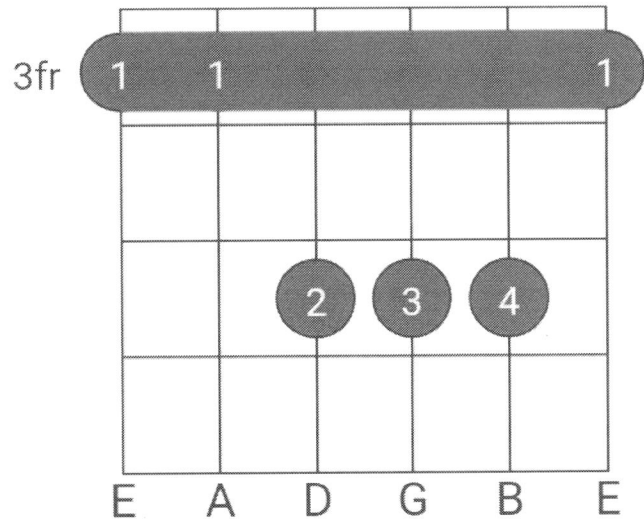
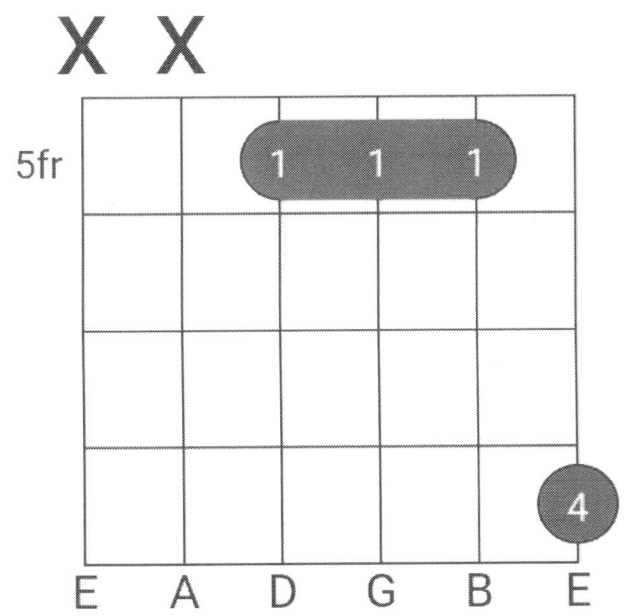
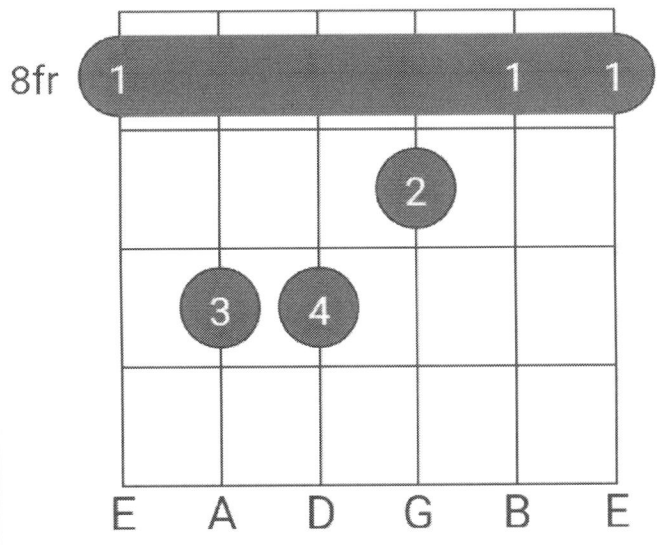

# C minor

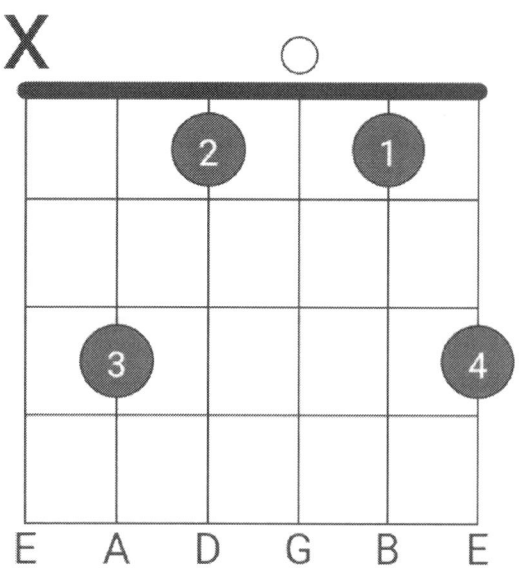
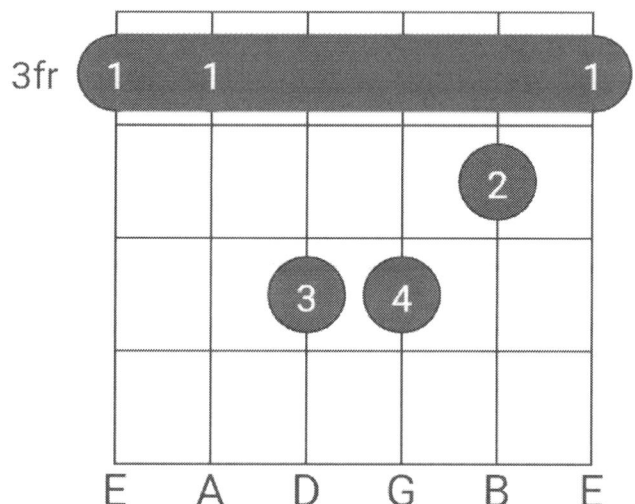
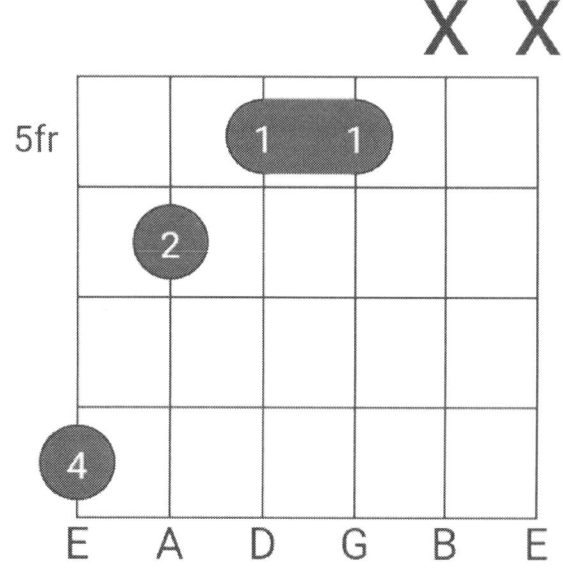
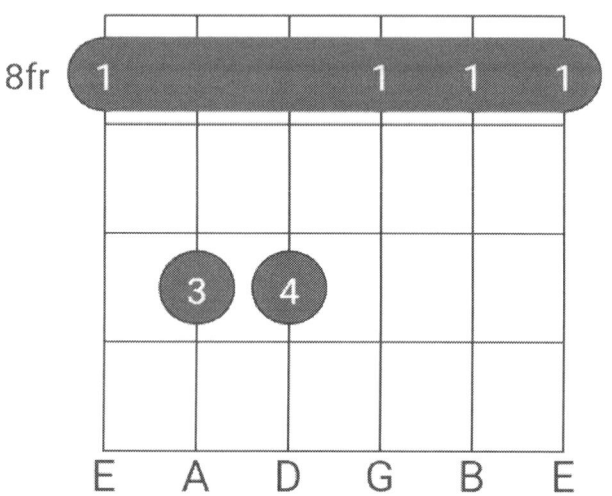

# C dim

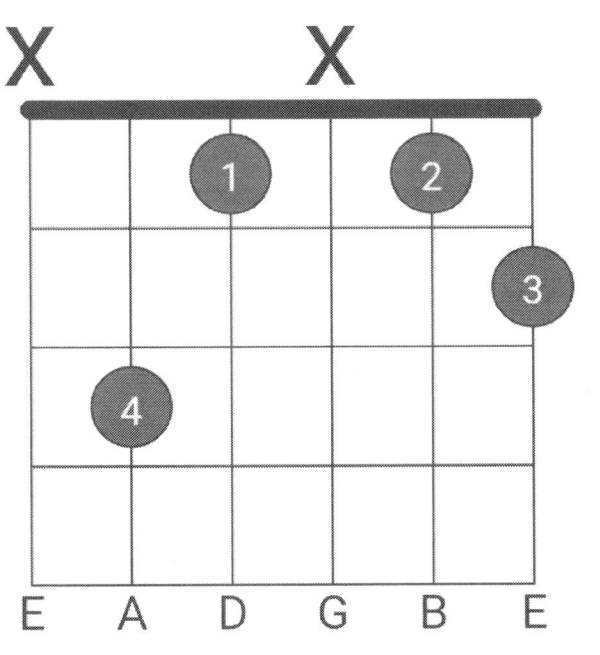
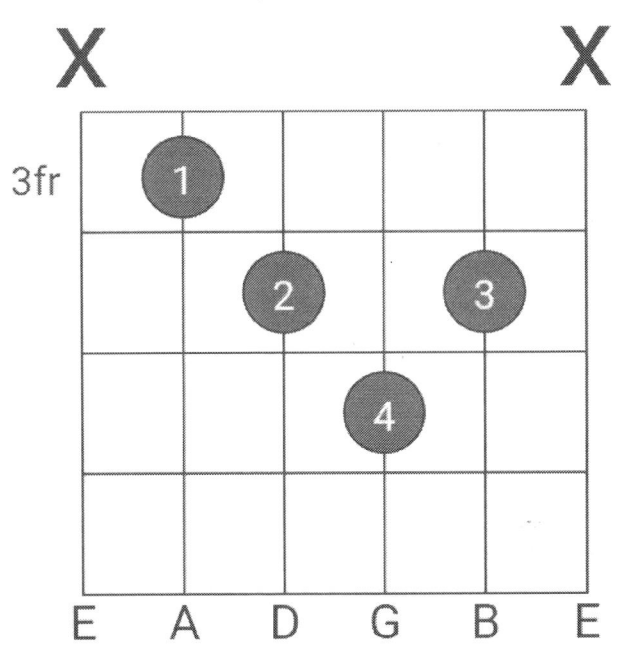
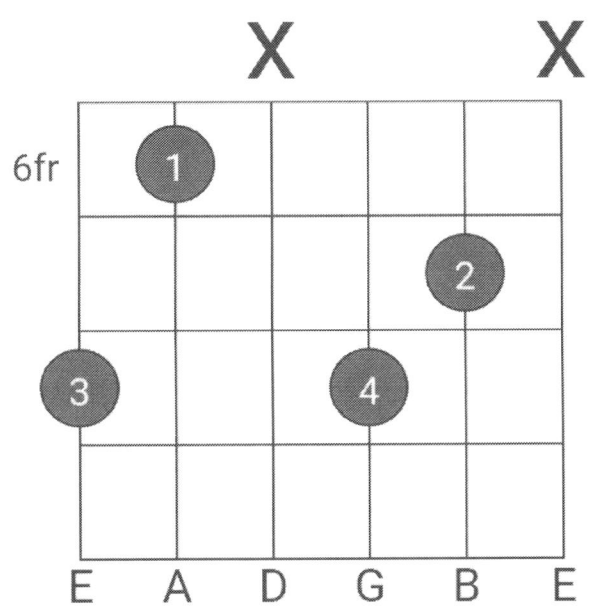
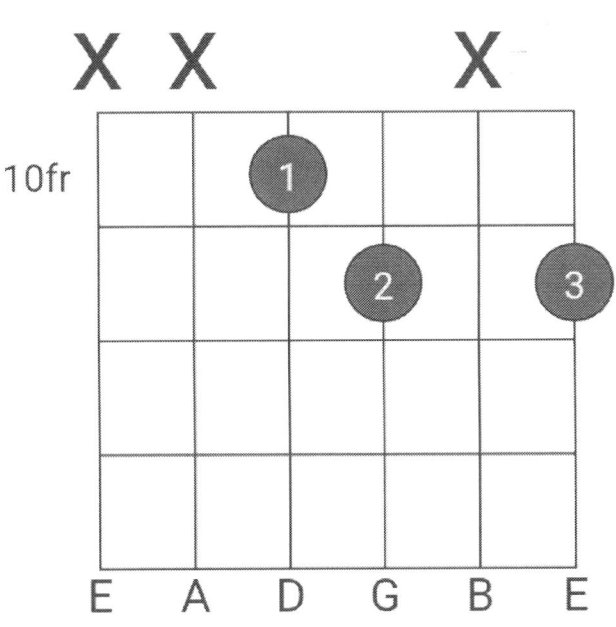

# C Sus2

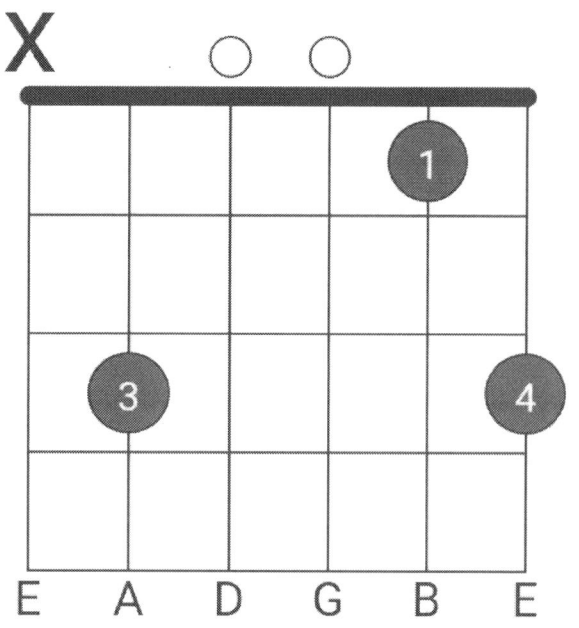
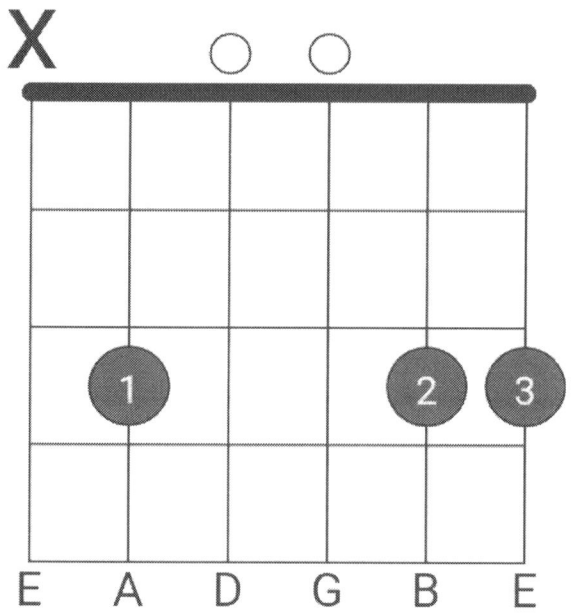
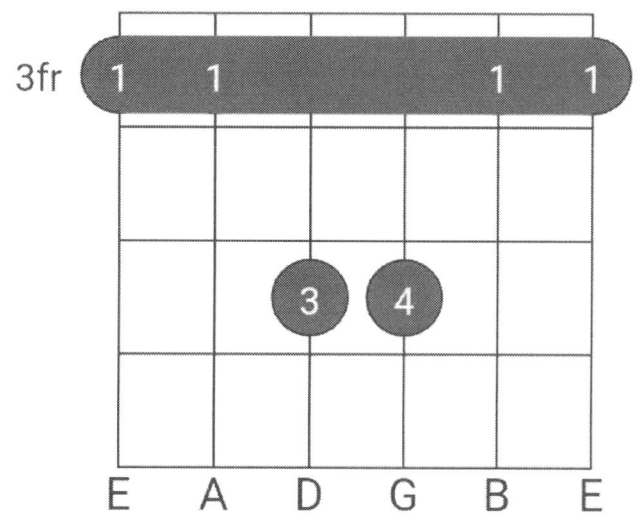
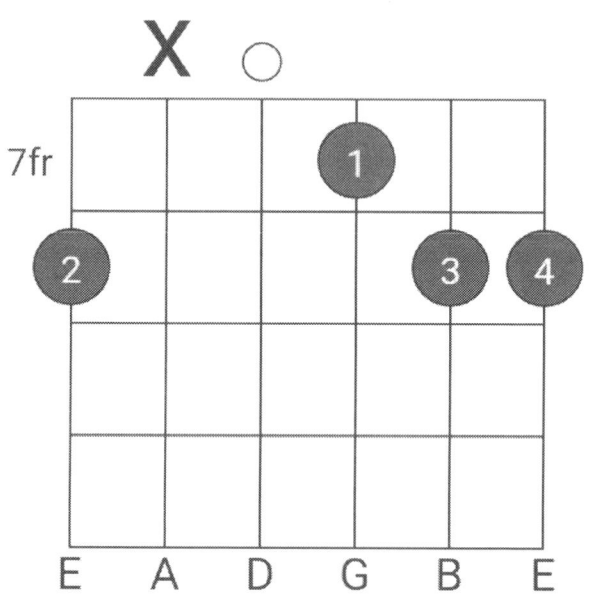

# C Sus4

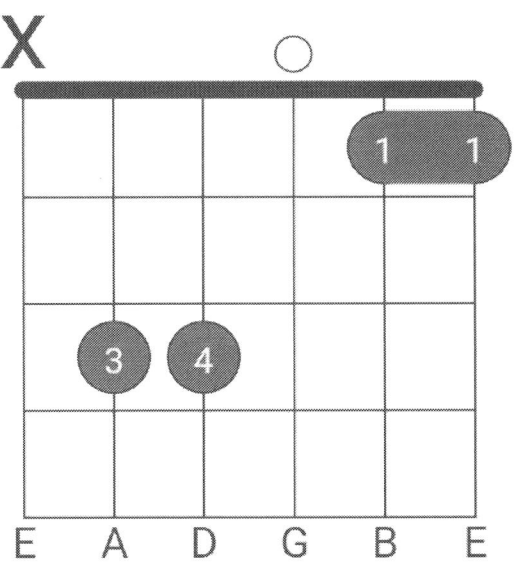
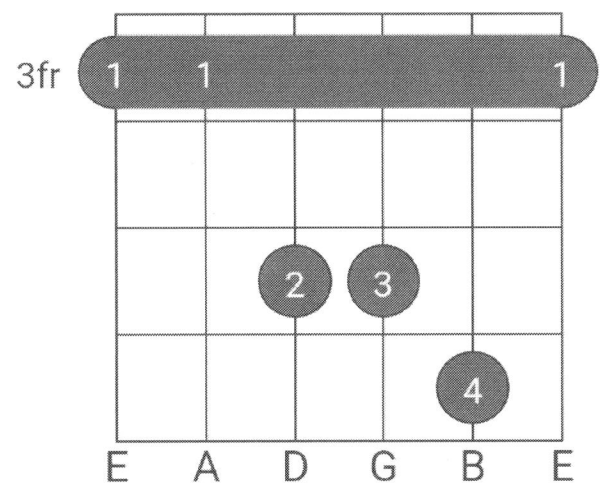
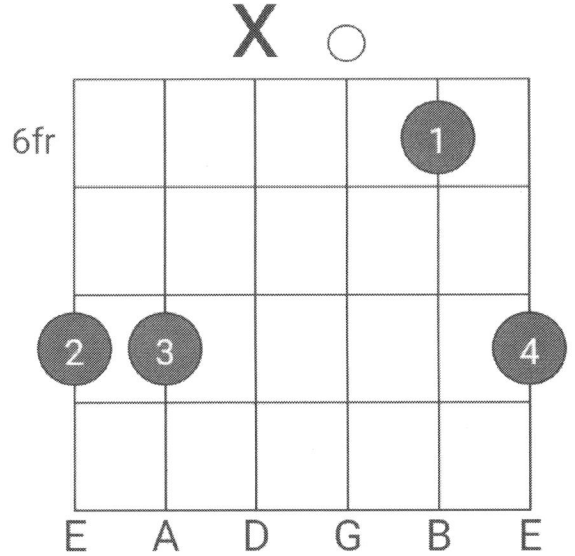
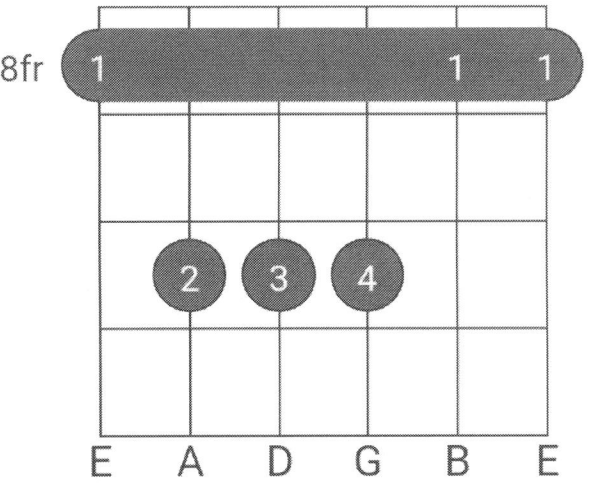

# C aug

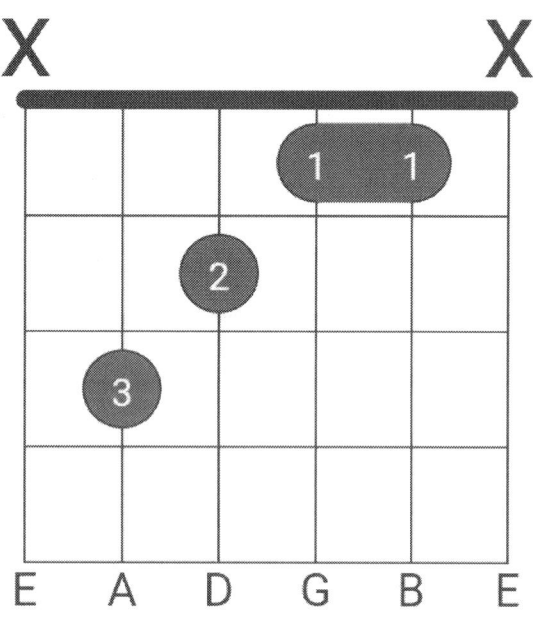
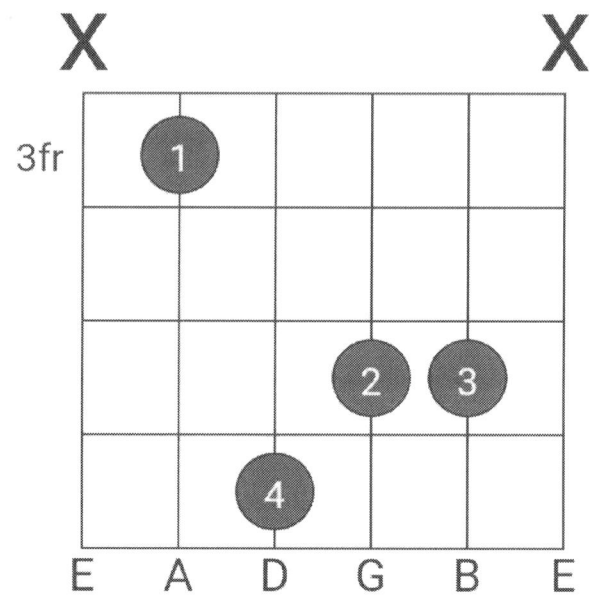
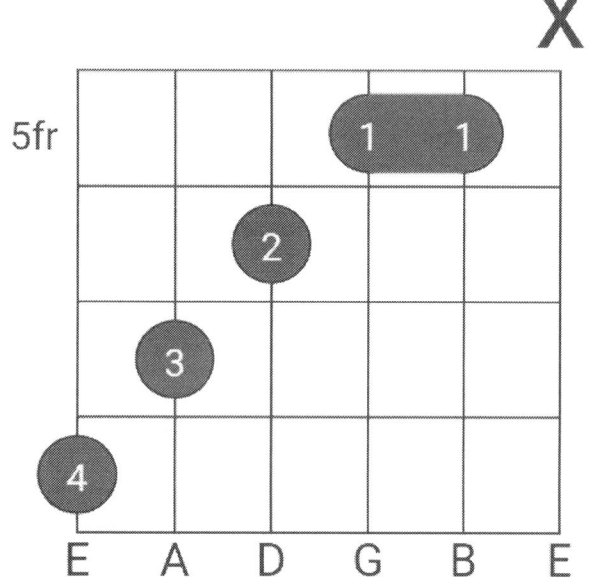
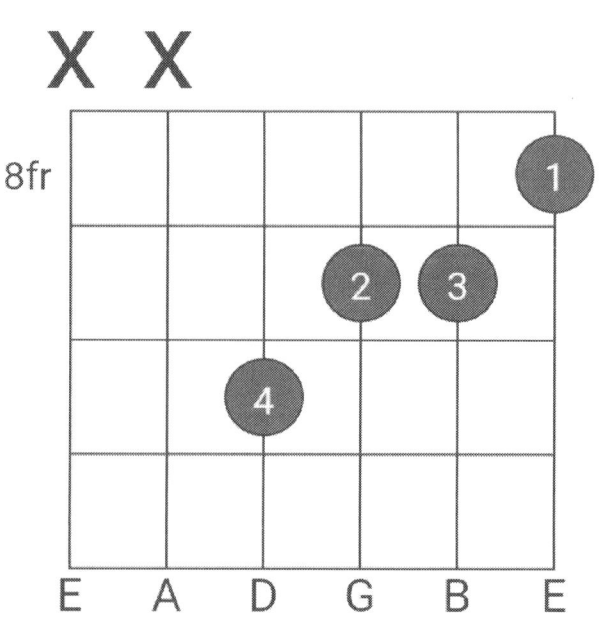

# C7

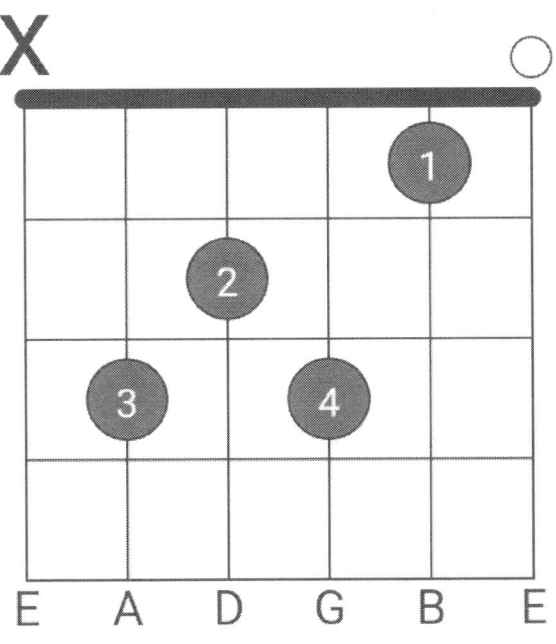
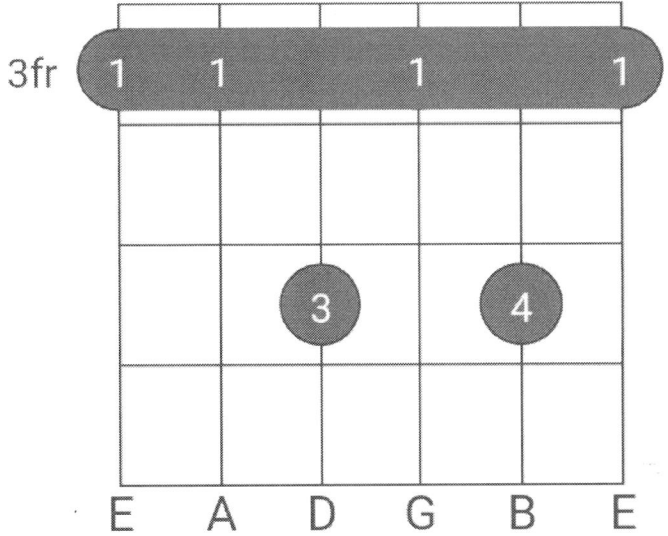
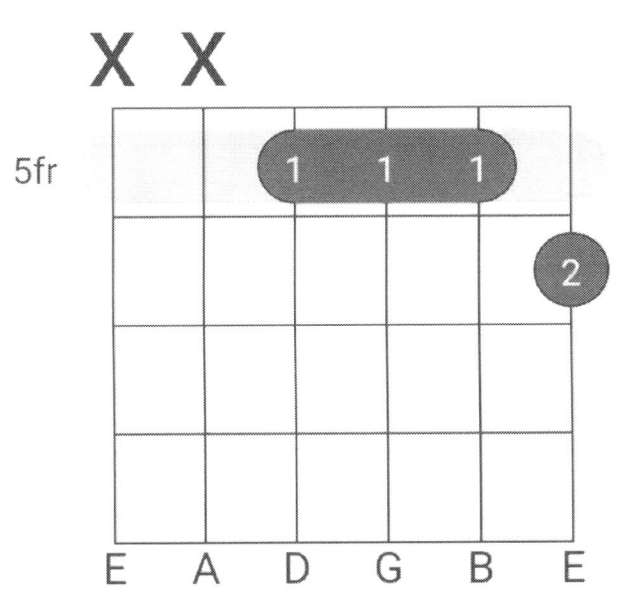
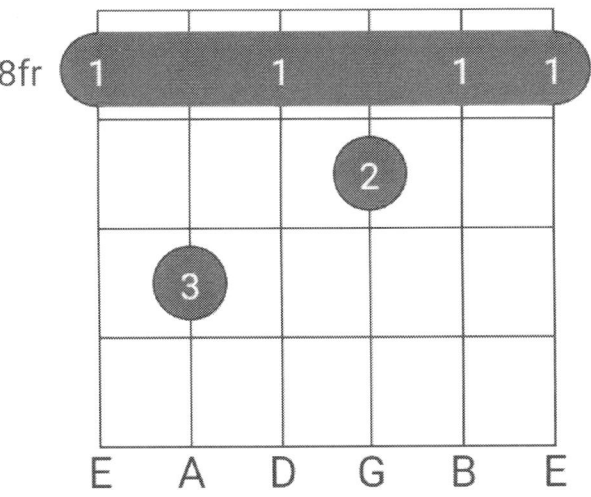

# C maj7

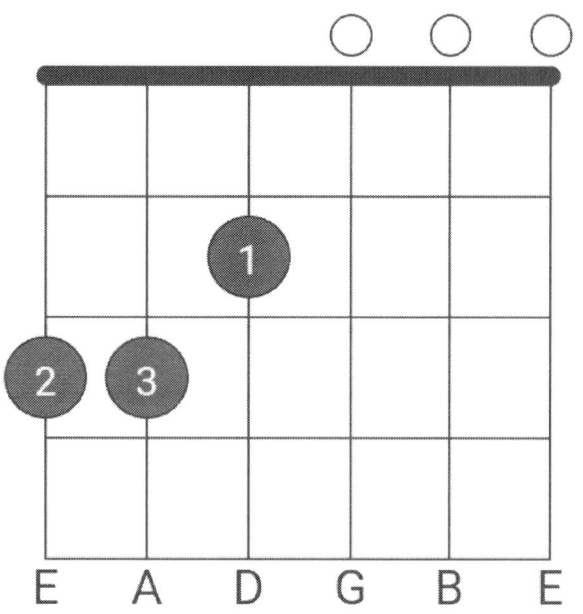
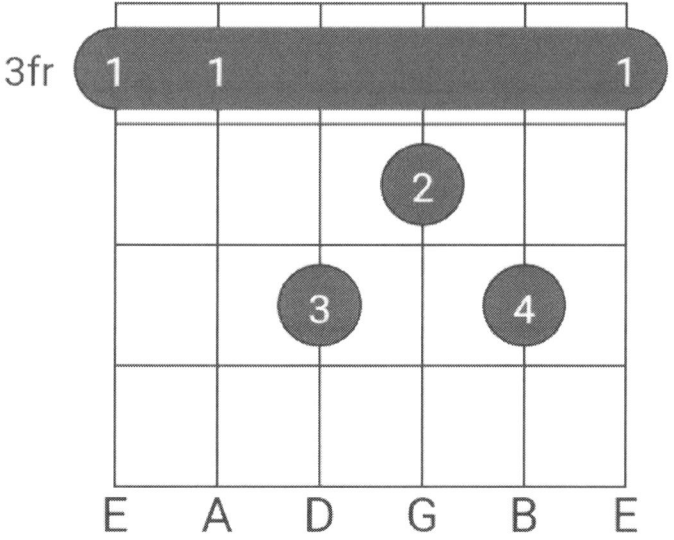
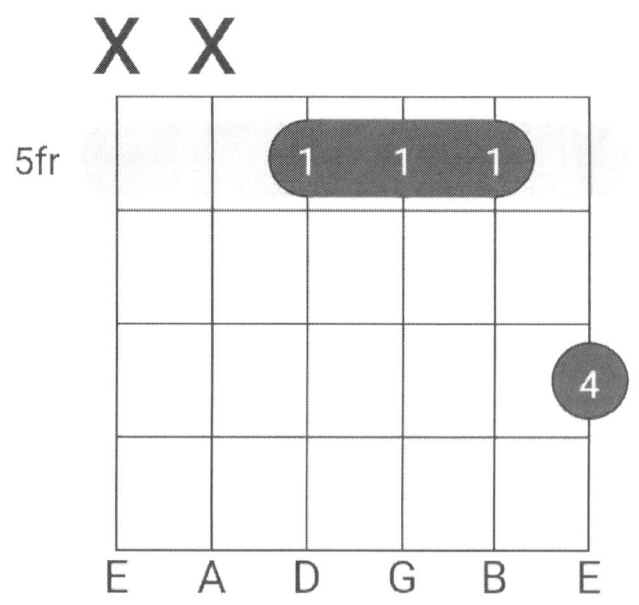
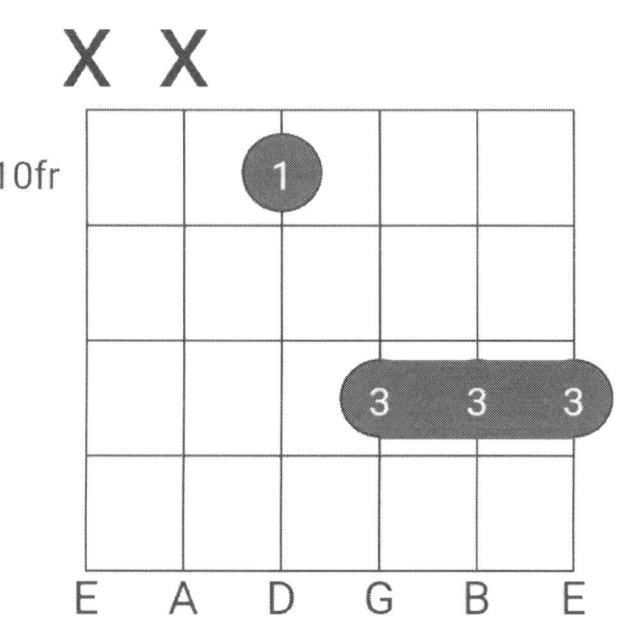

# Cm7

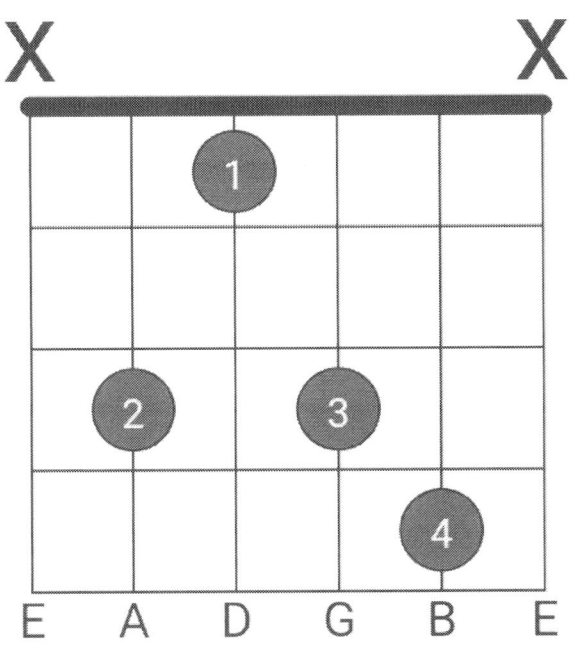
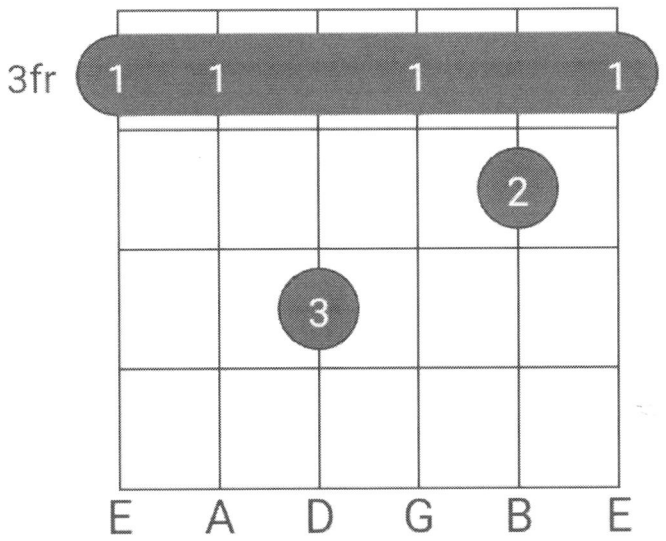
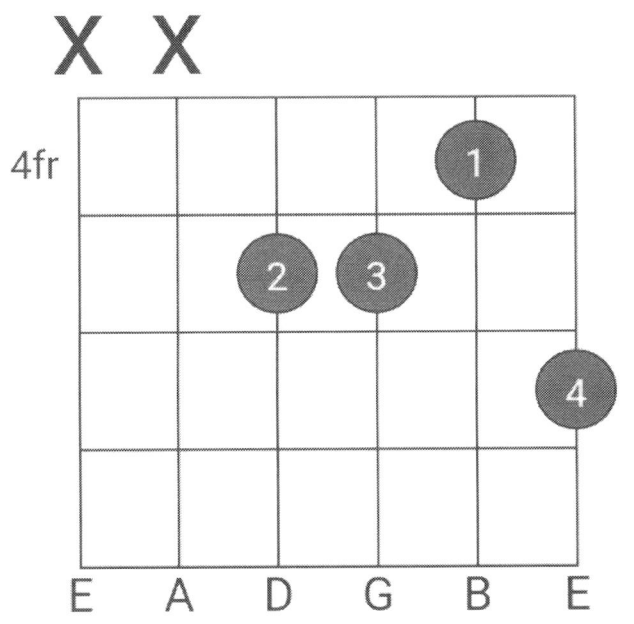
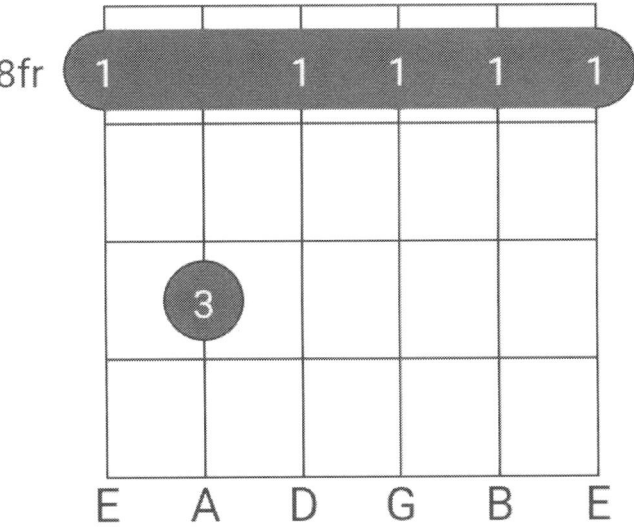

# C# / Db Major

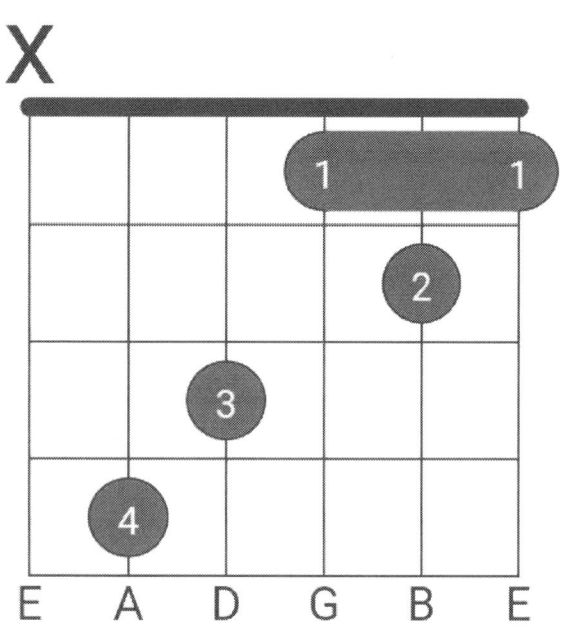
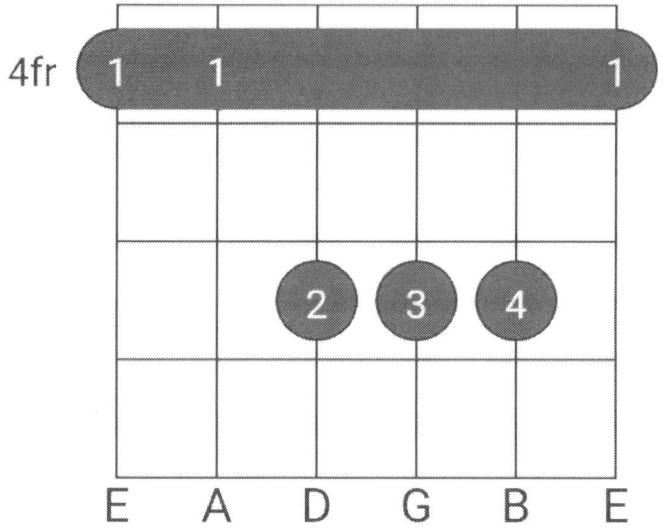
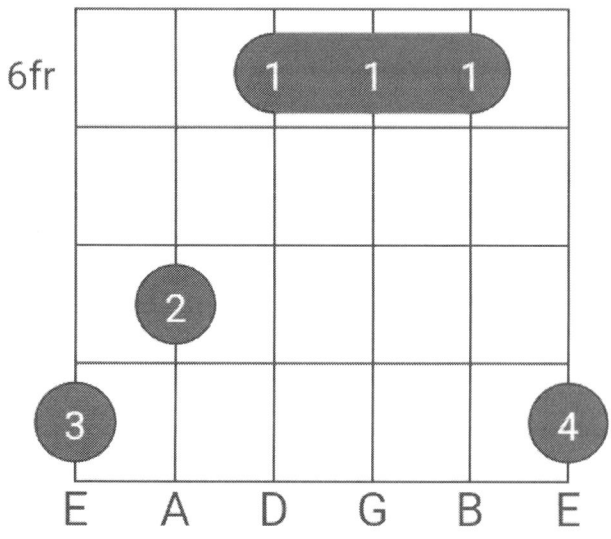
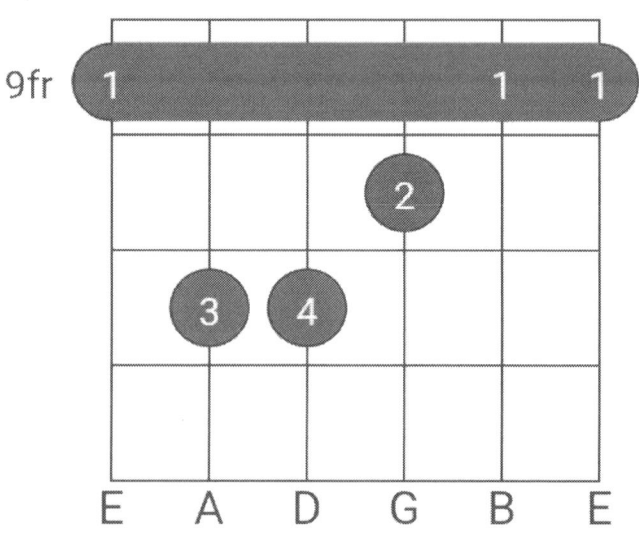

# C# / Db minor

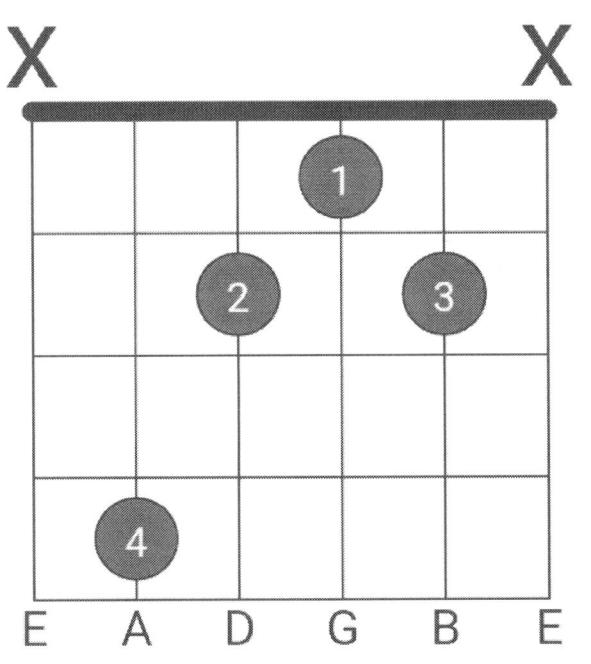
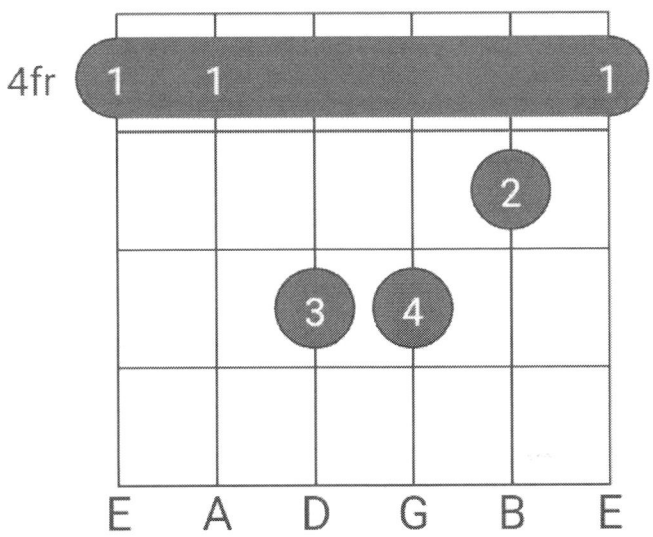
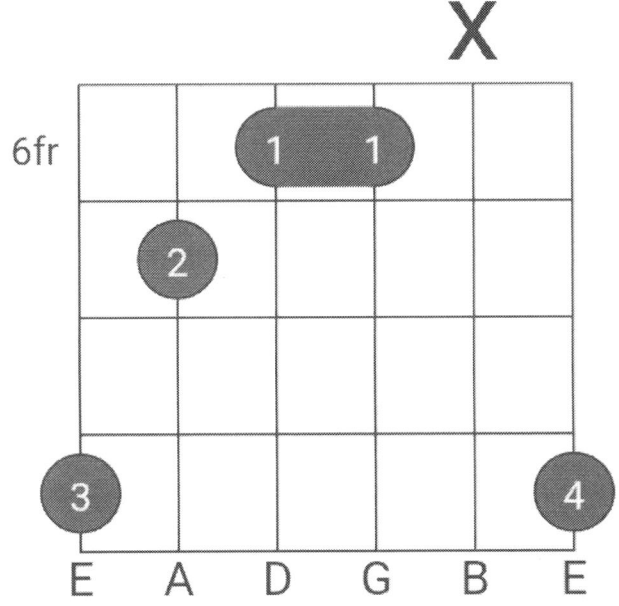
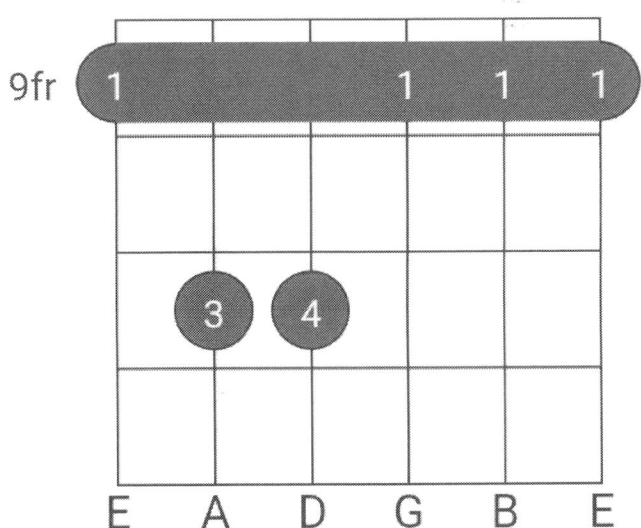

# C# / Db dim

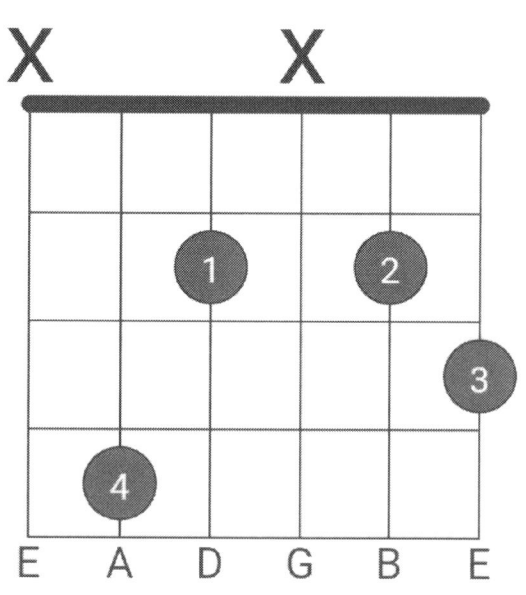
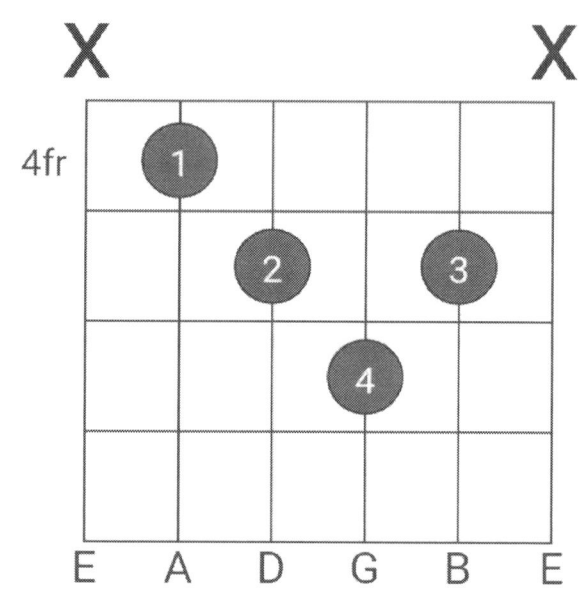
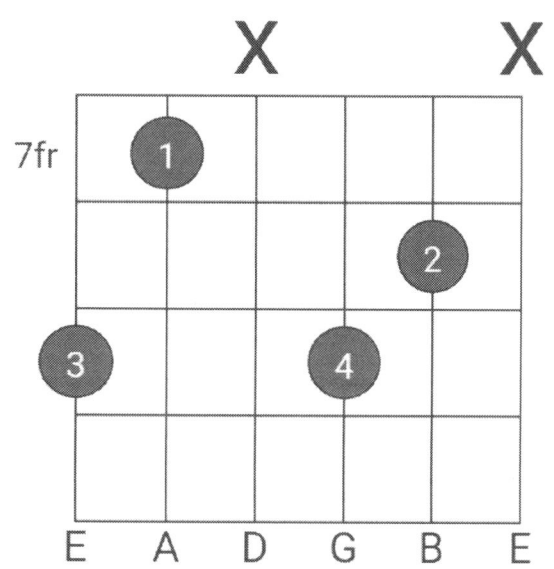
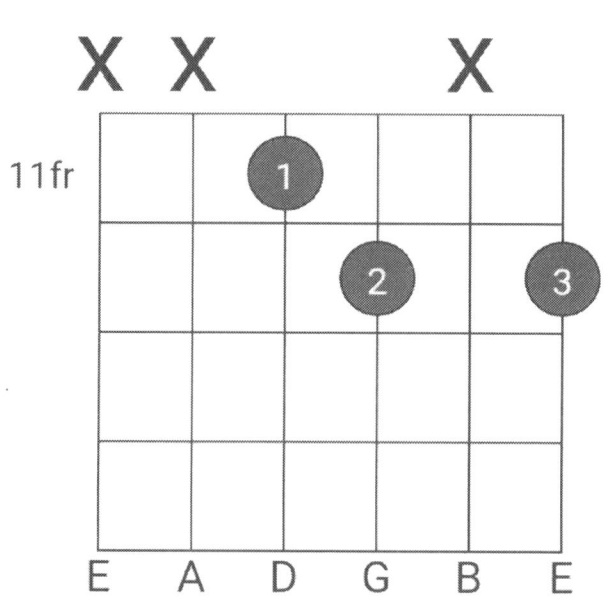

# C# / Db Sus2

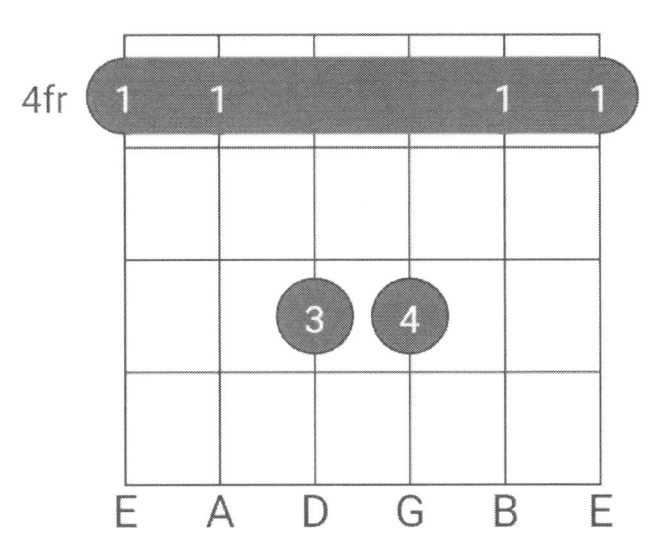
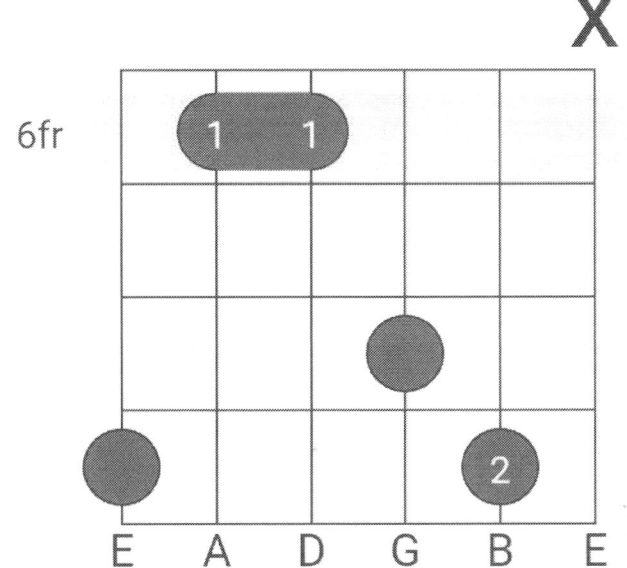
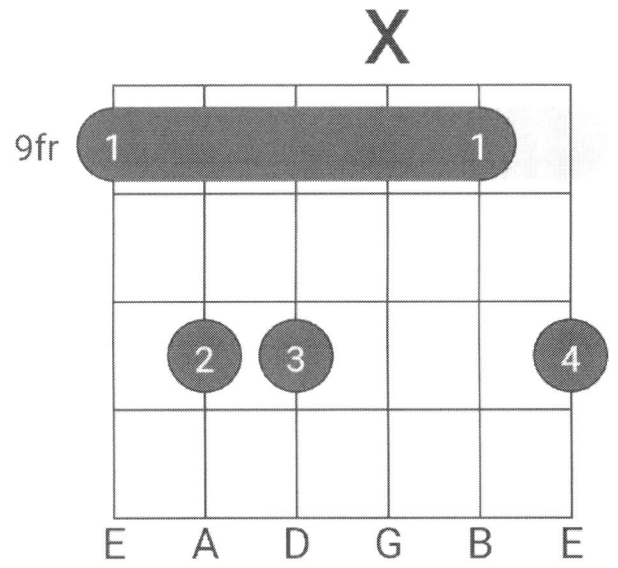
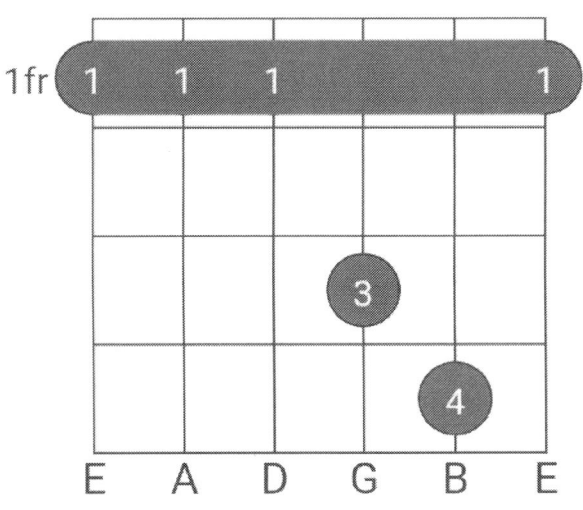

# C# / Db Sus4

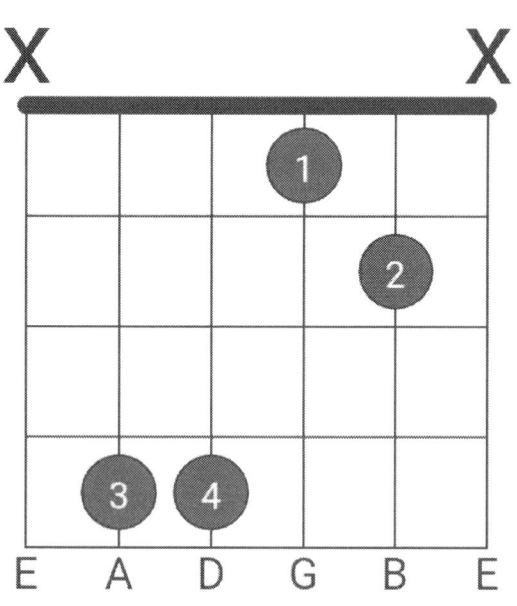
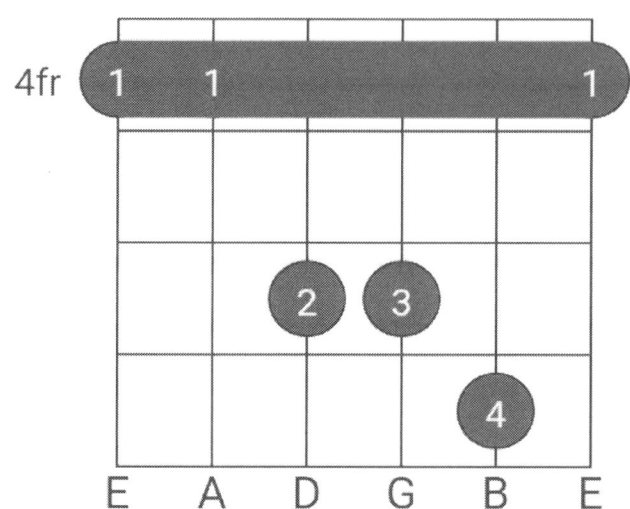
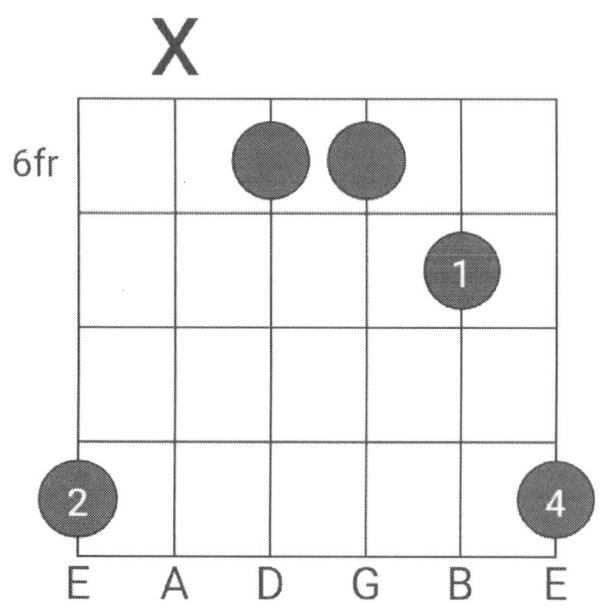
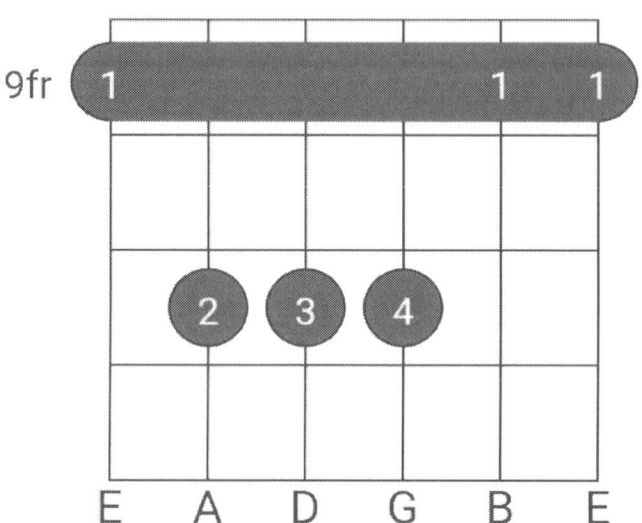

# C# / Db aug

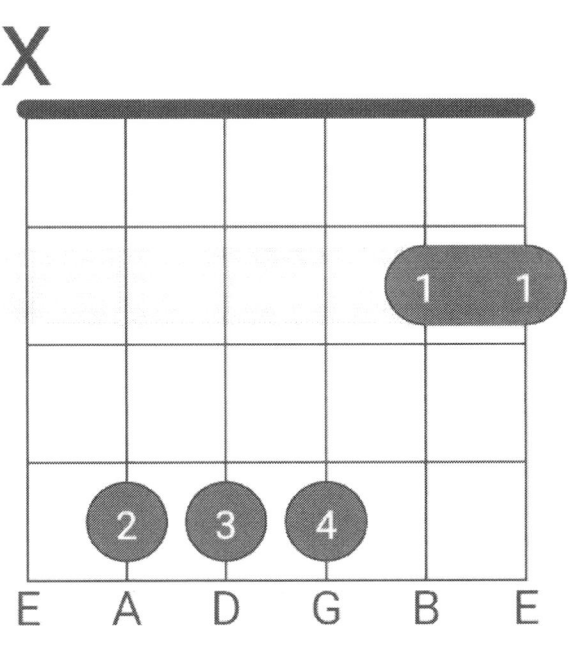
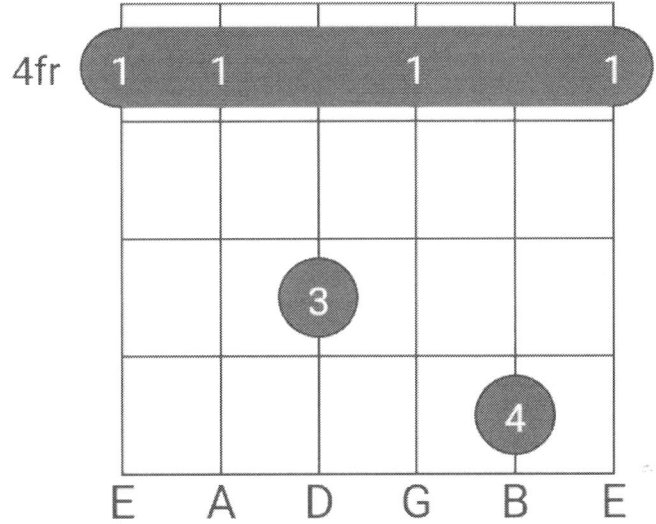
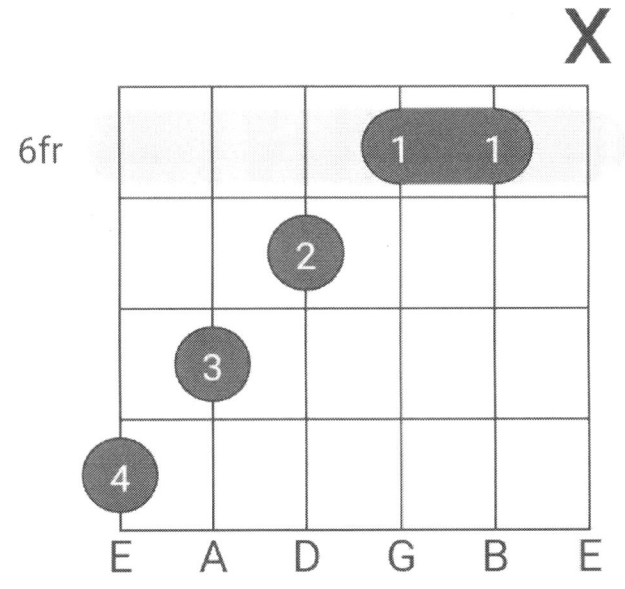
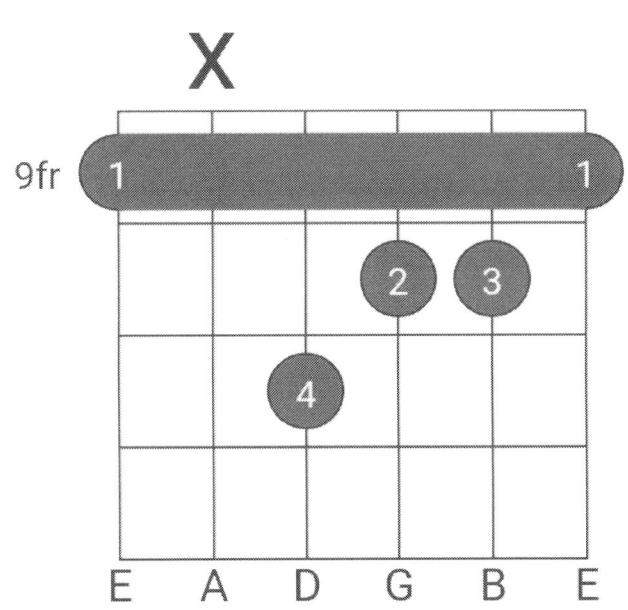

# C# / Db7

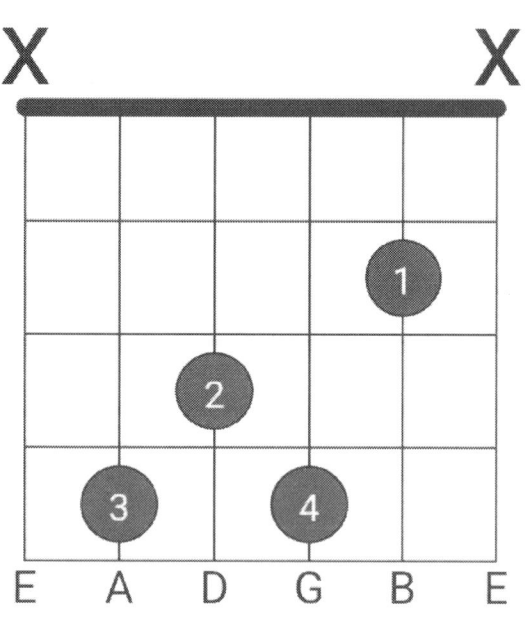
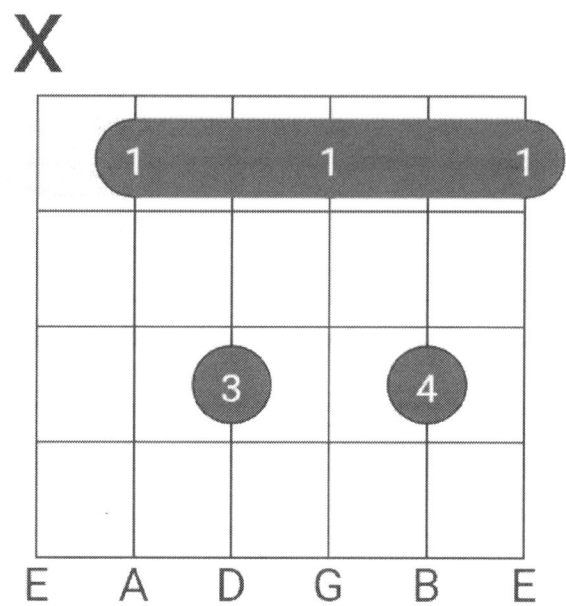
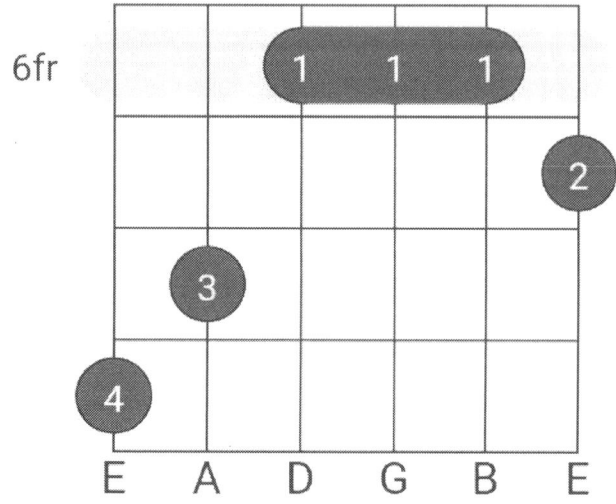
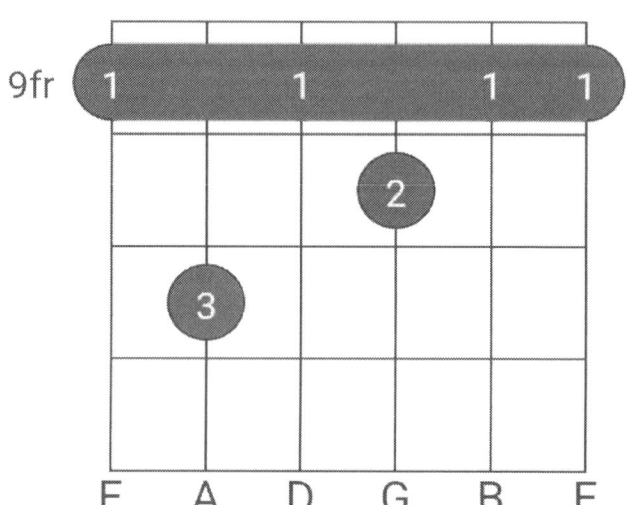

# C# / Db maj7

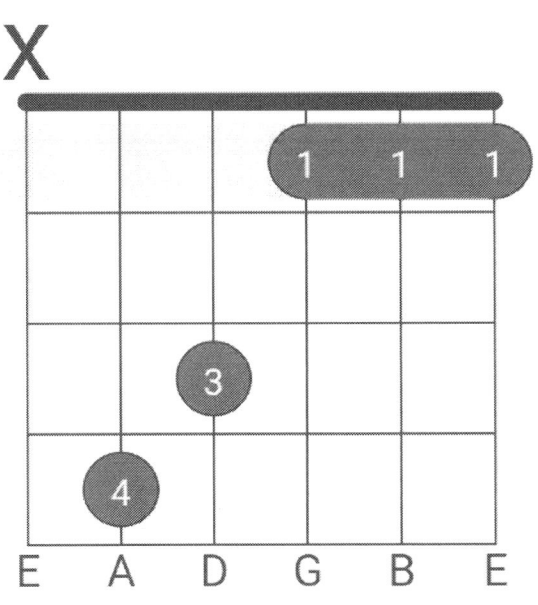
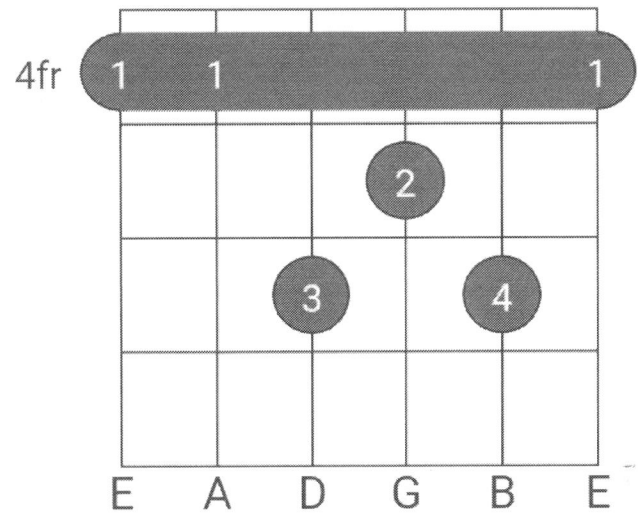
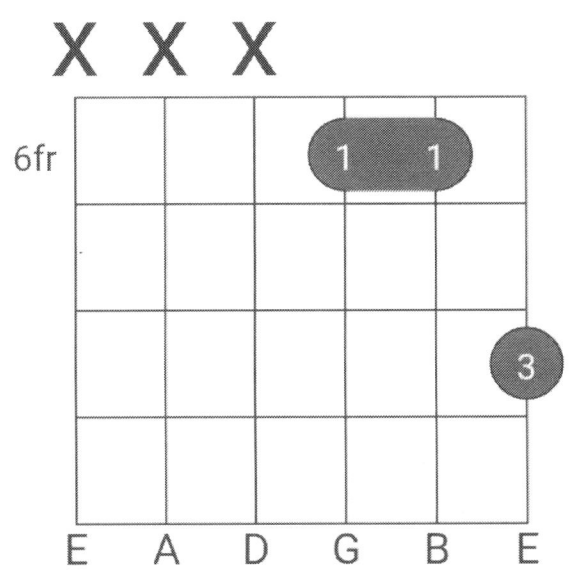
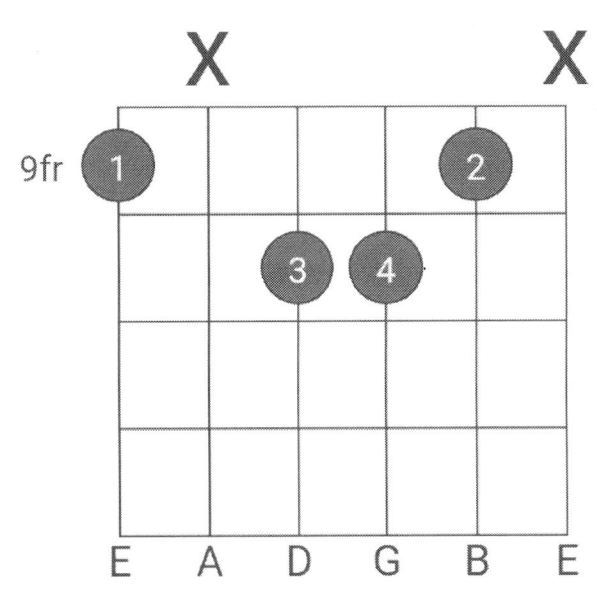

# C# / Db m7

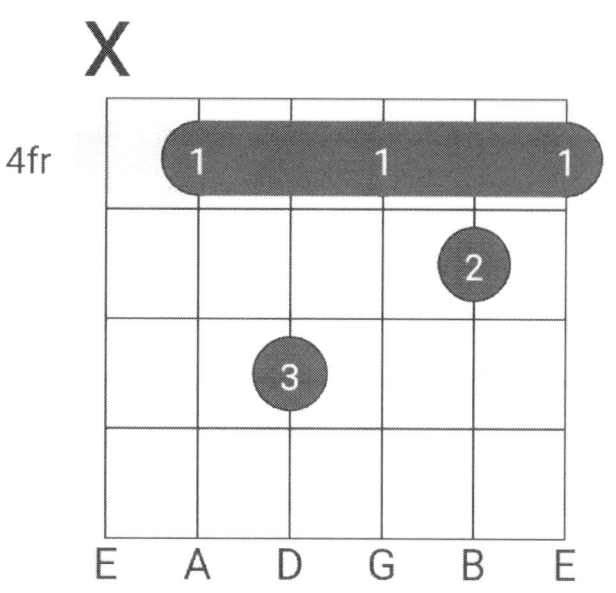
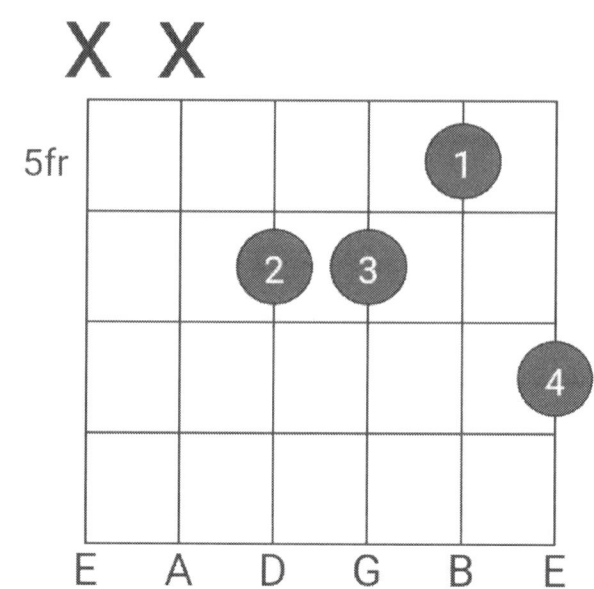
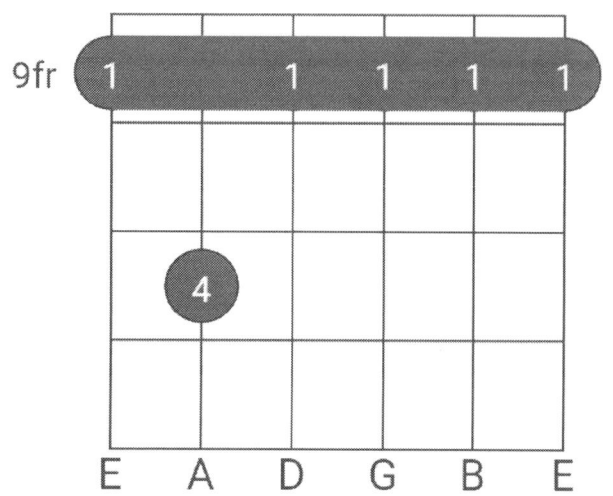
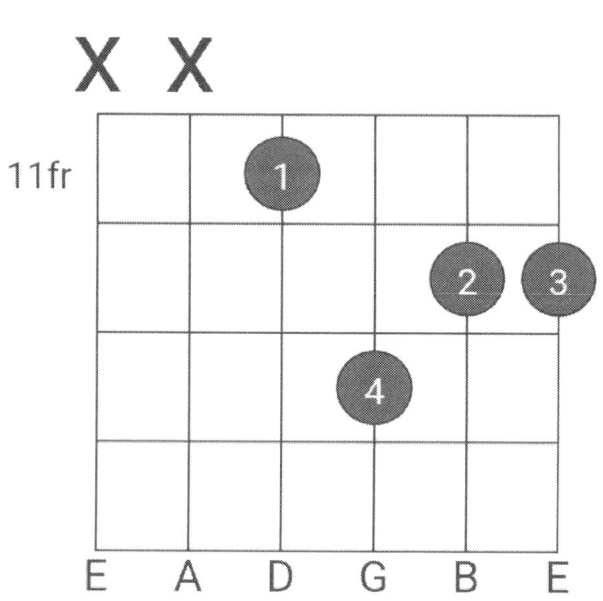

# D Major

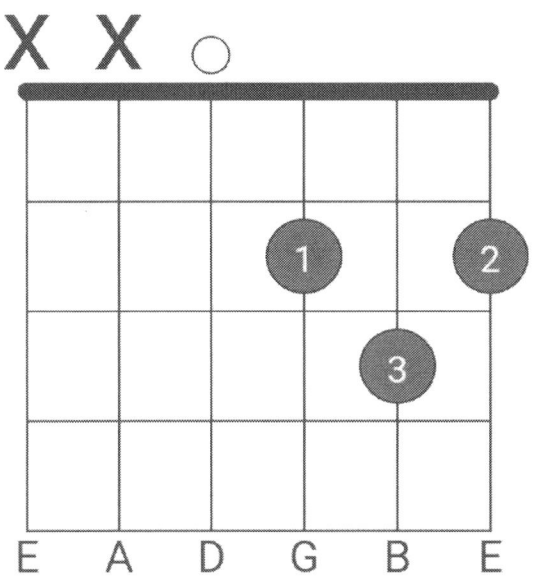
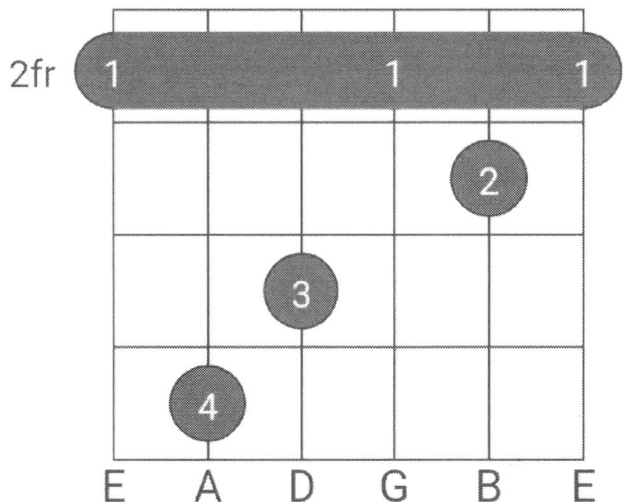
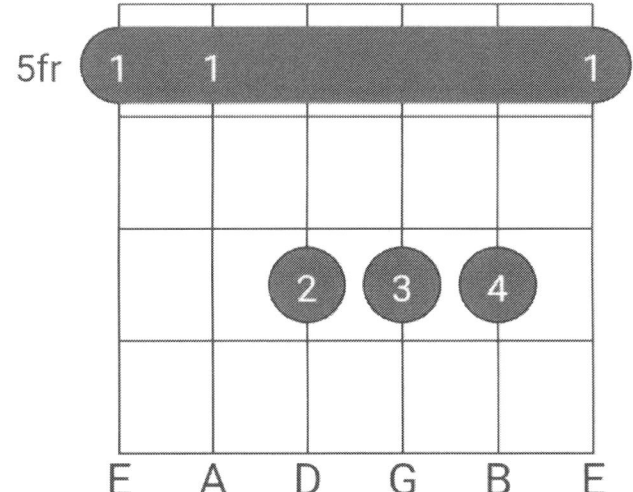
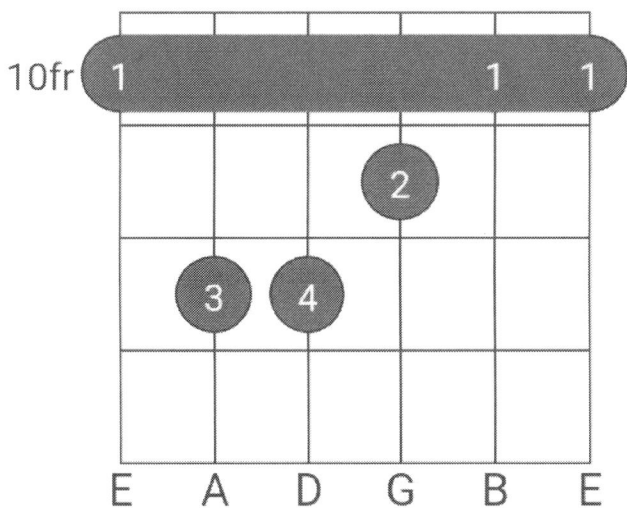

# D minor

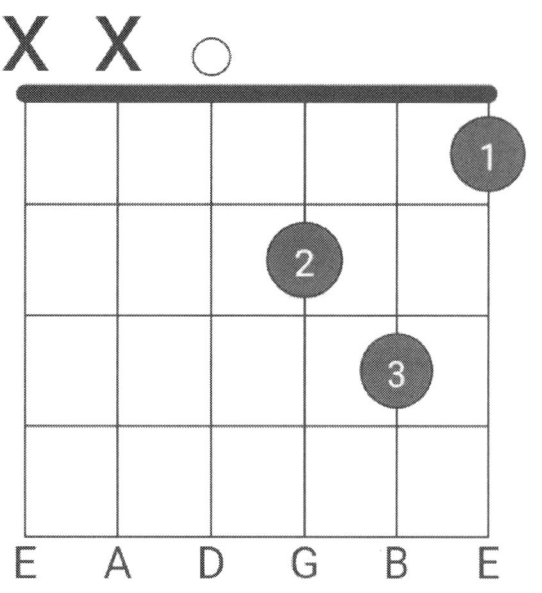
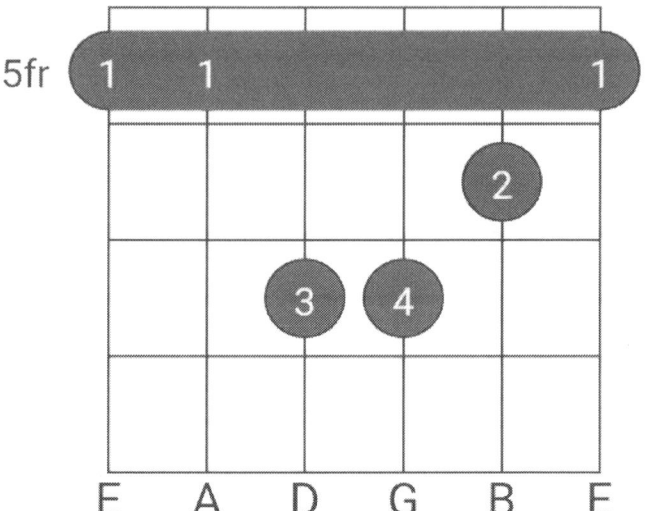
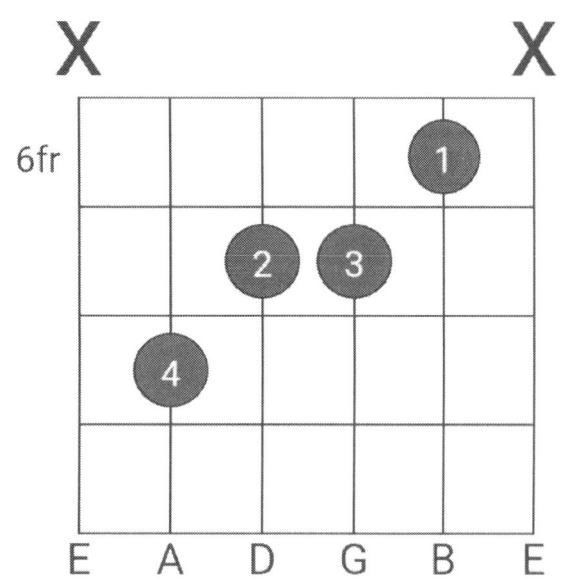
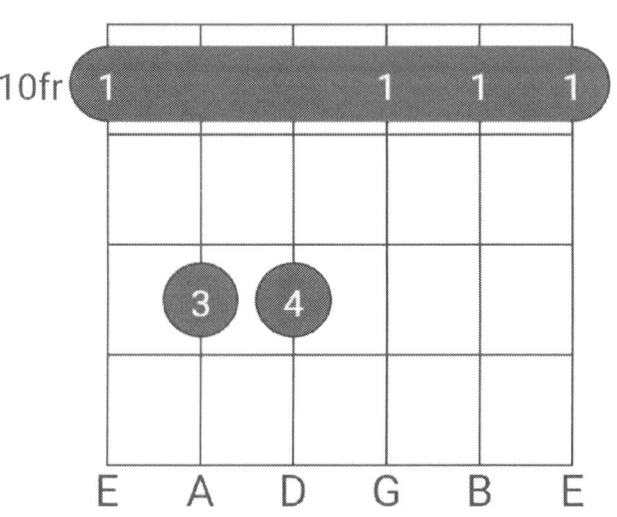

# D dim

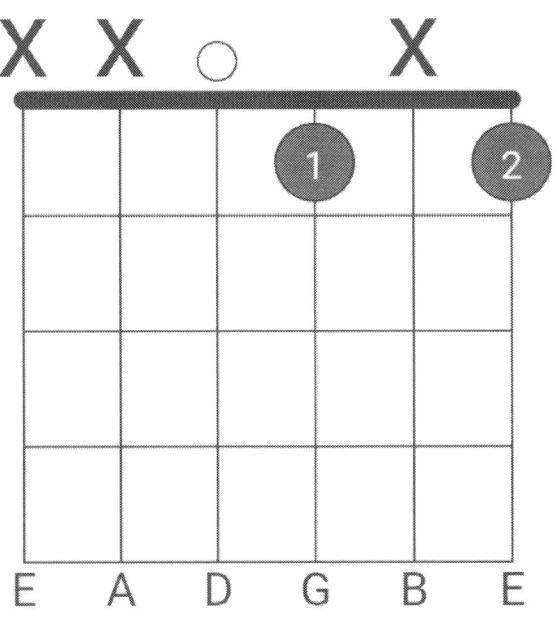
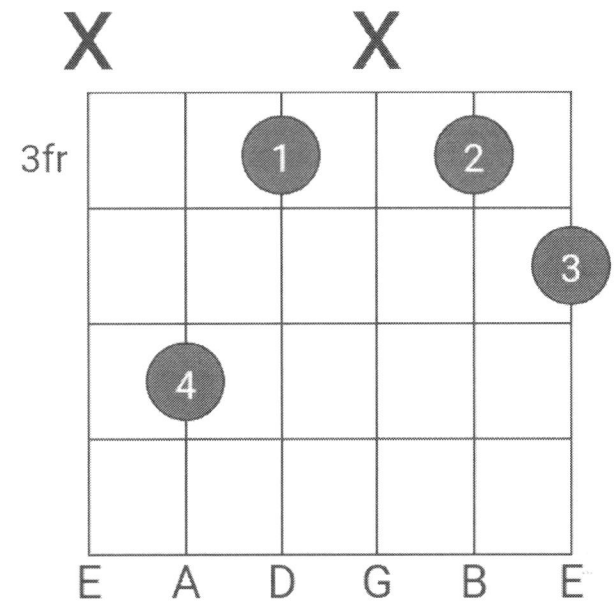
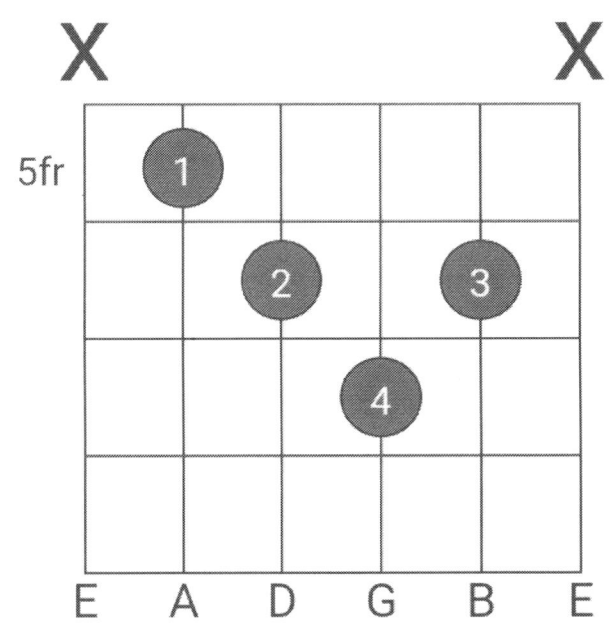
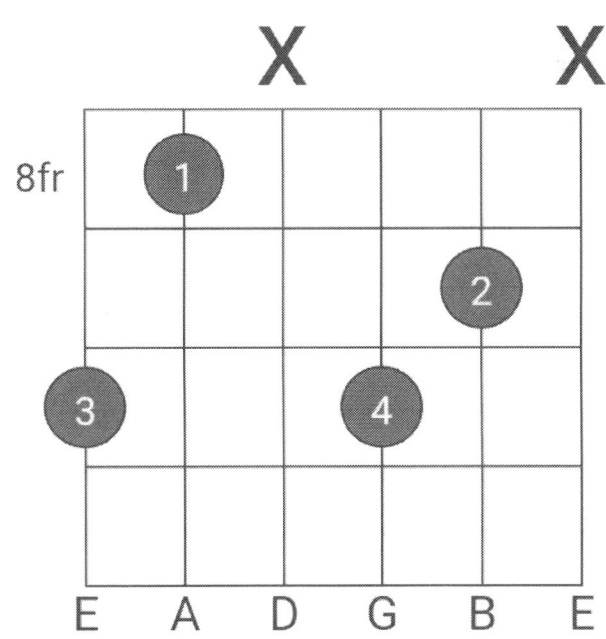

# D Sus2

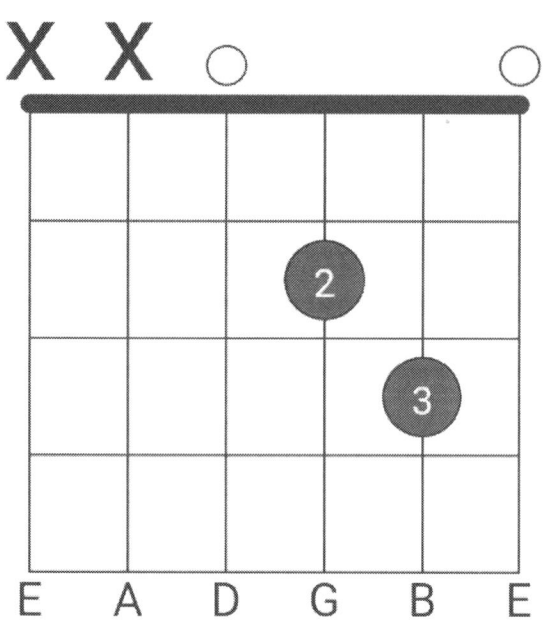
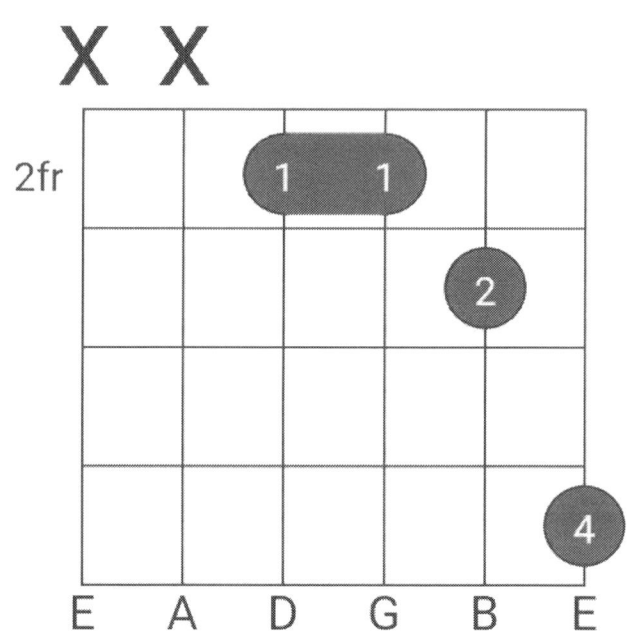
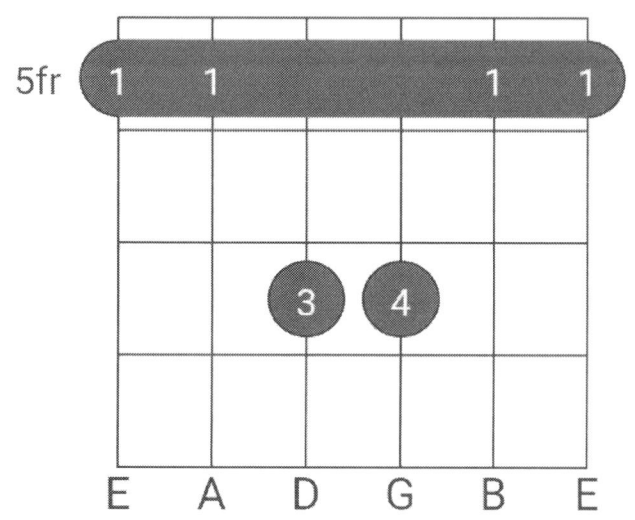
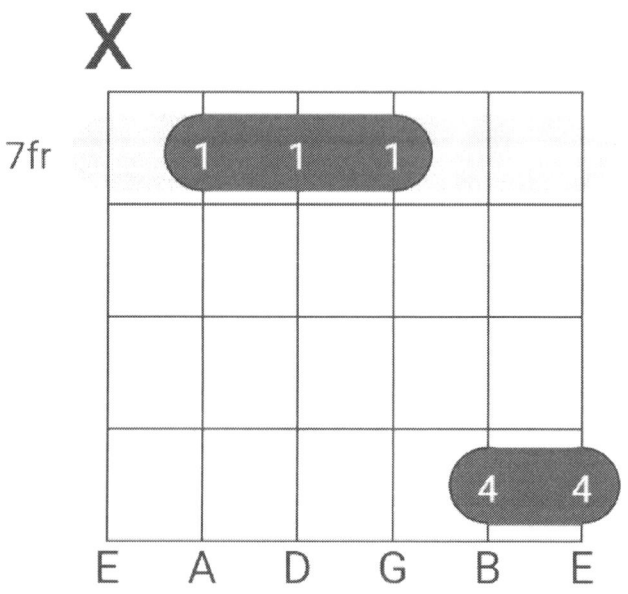

# D Sus4

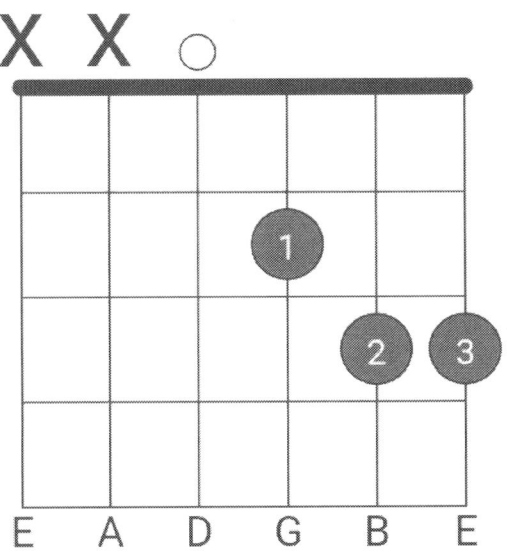
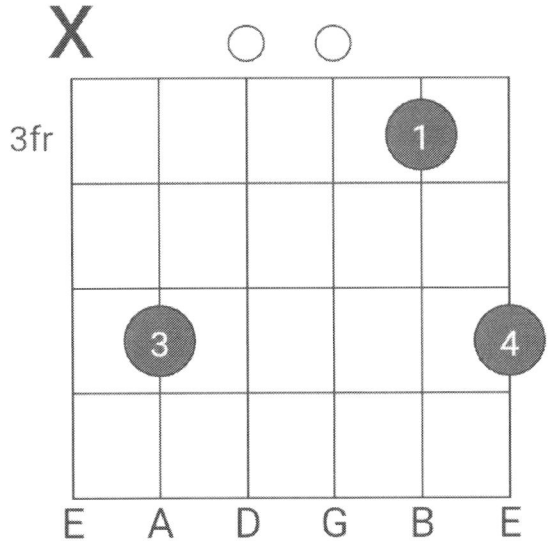
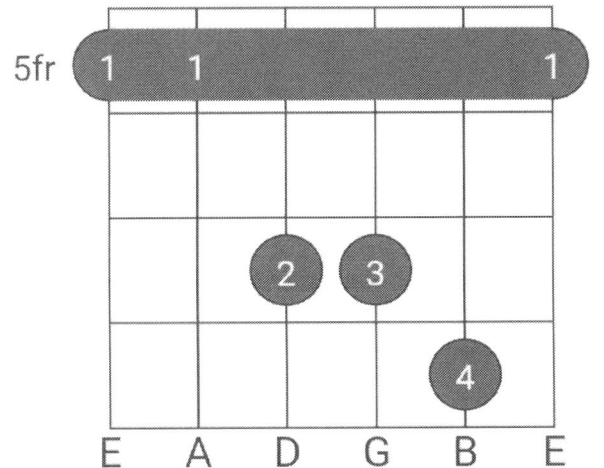
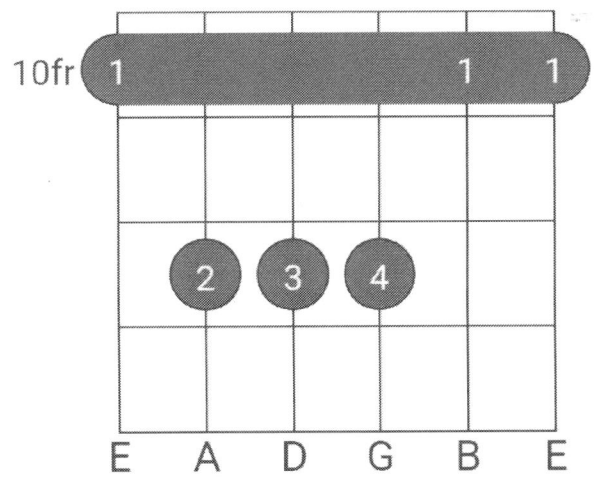

# D aug

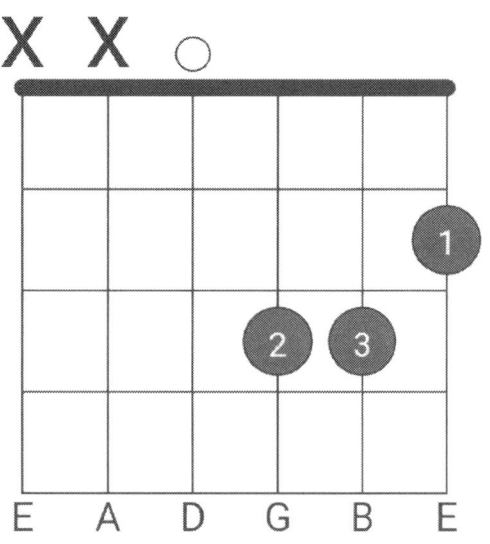
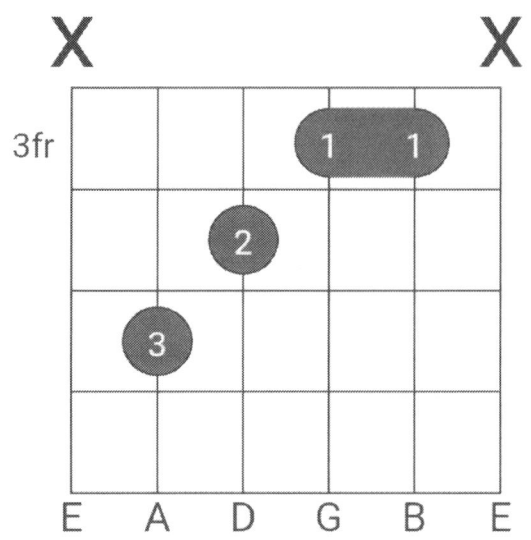
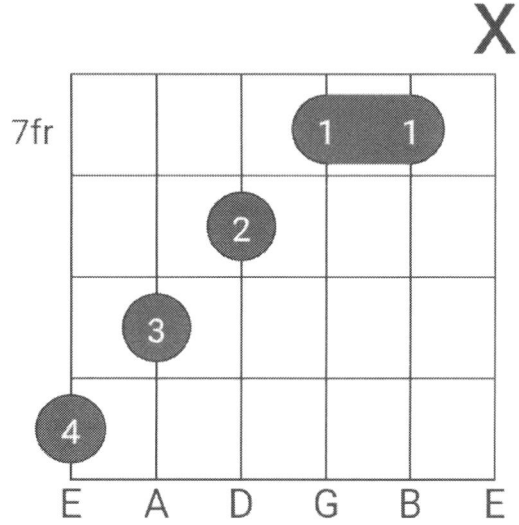
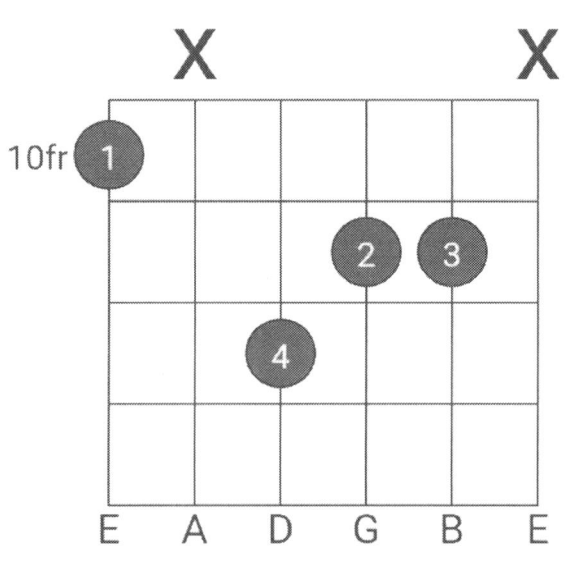

# D7

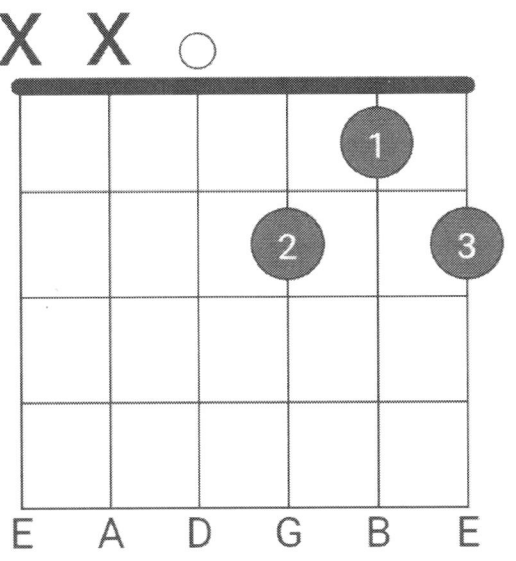
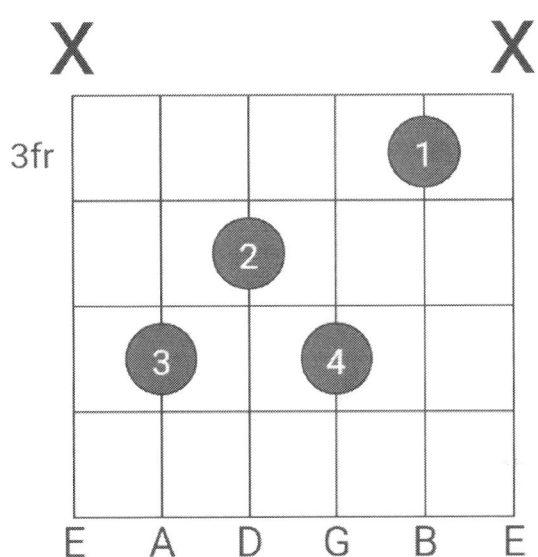
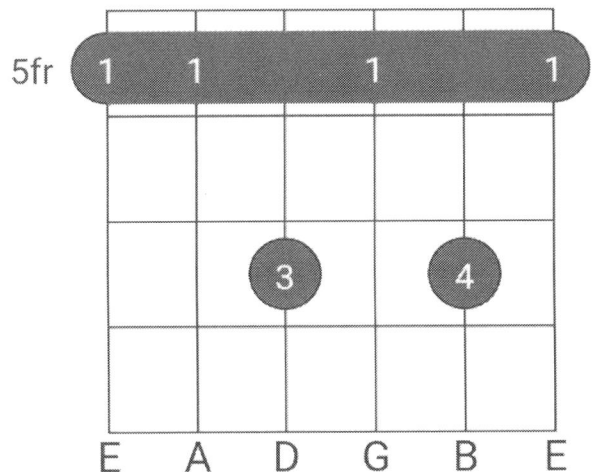
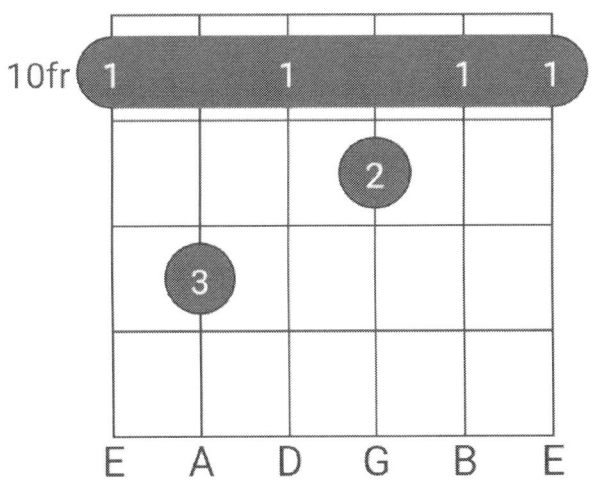

# D maj7

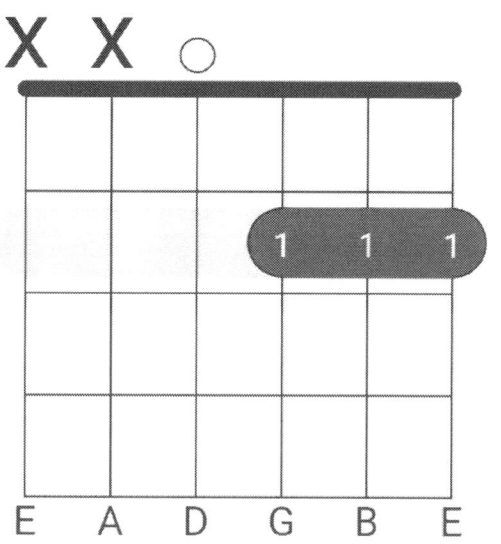
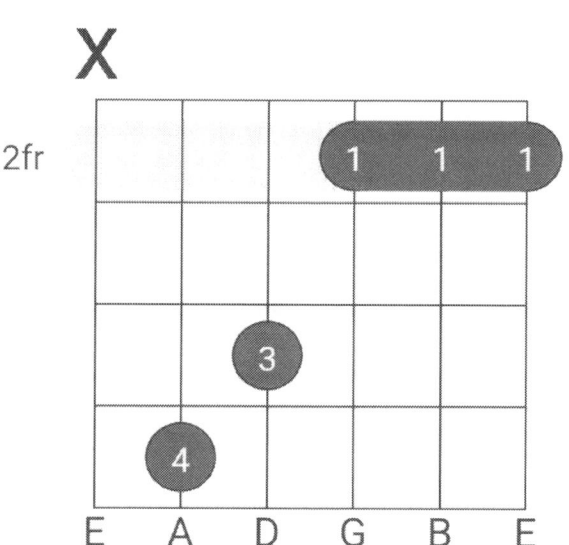
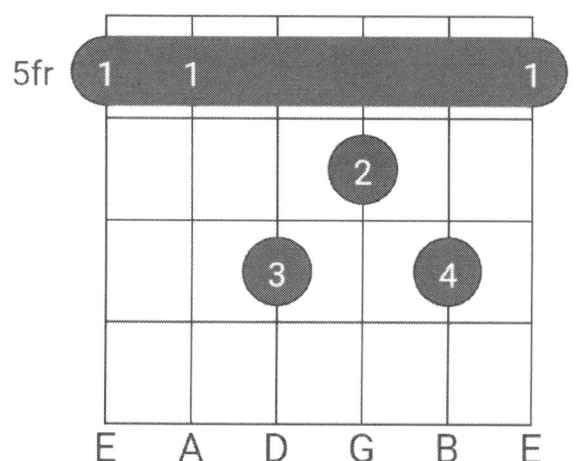
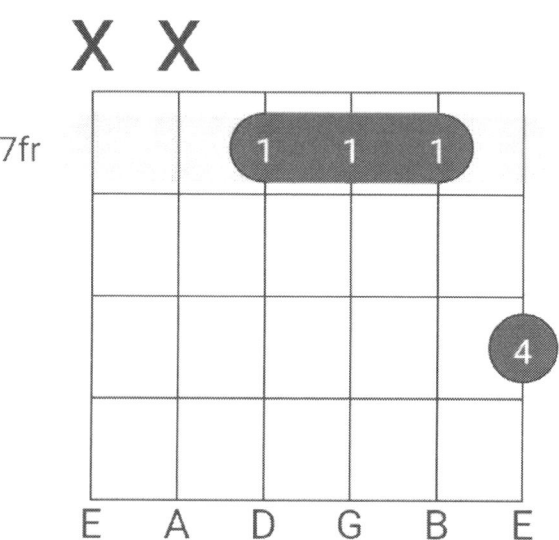

# Dm7

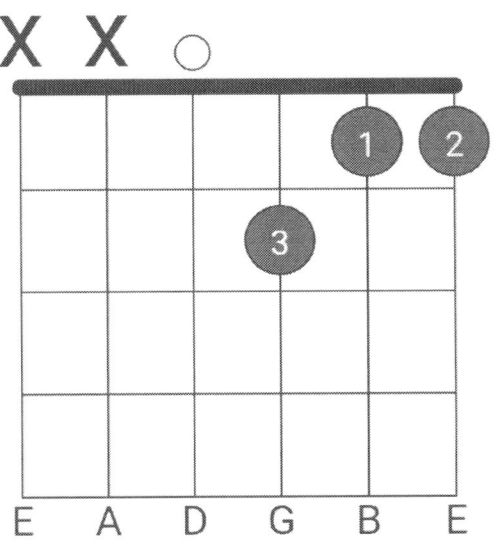
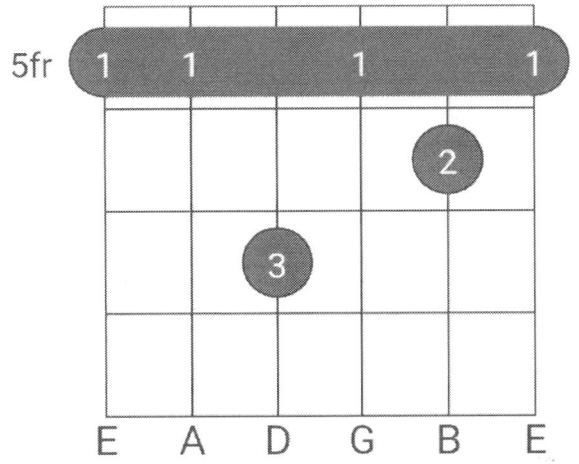
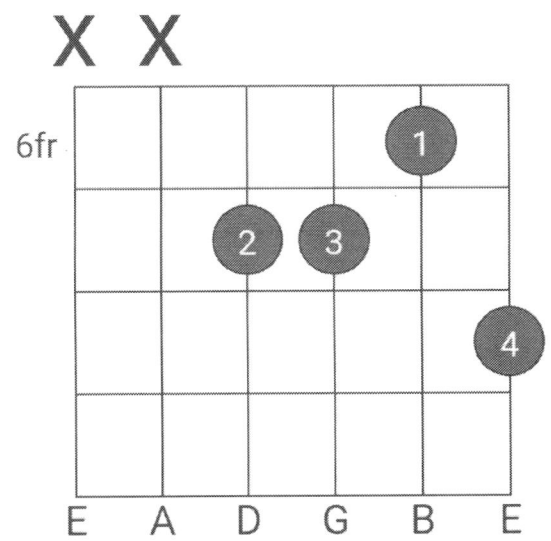
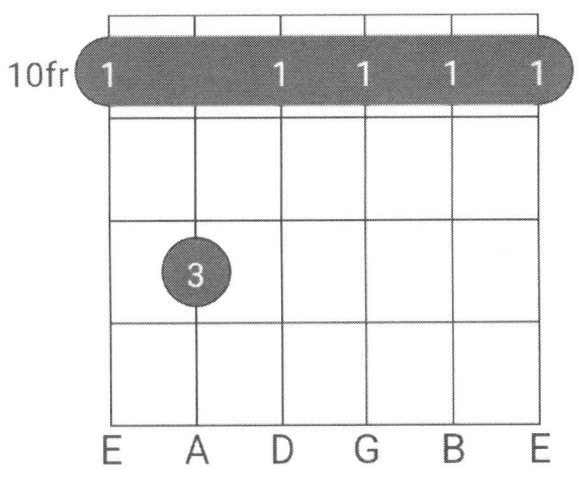

# D# / Eb Major

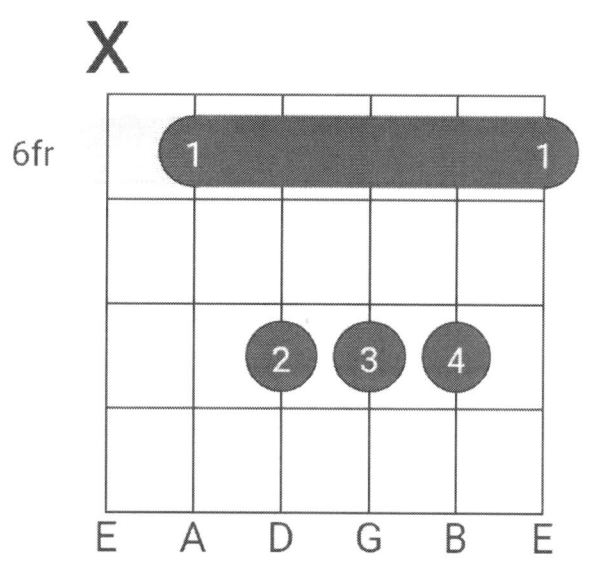
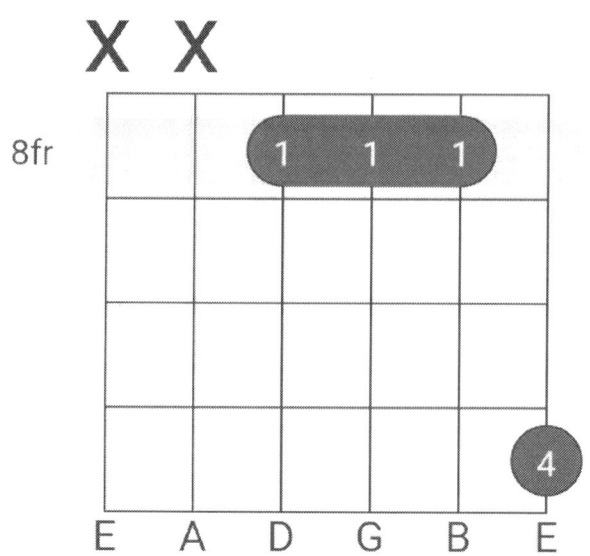
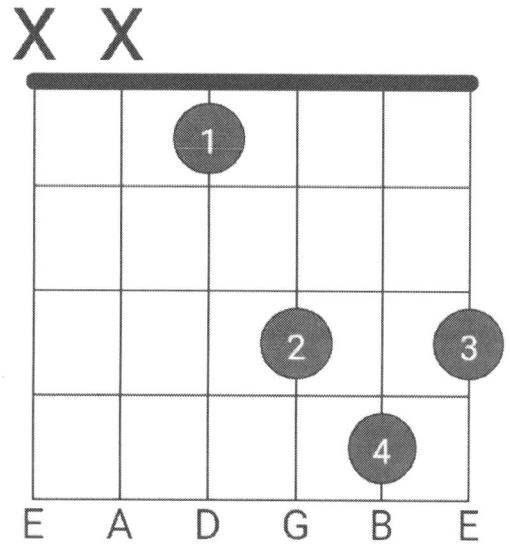
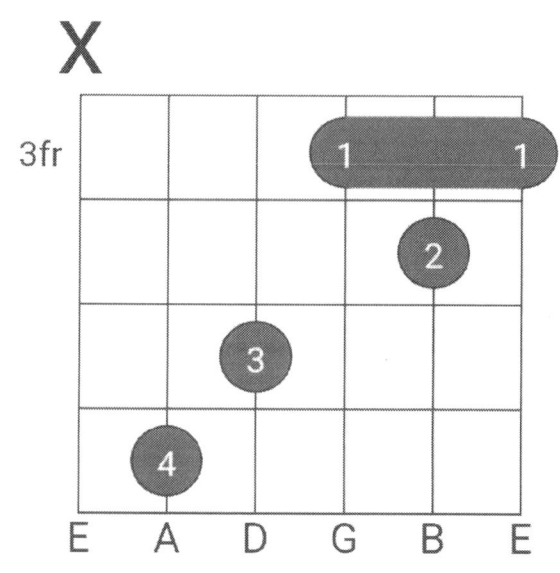

# D# / Eb minor

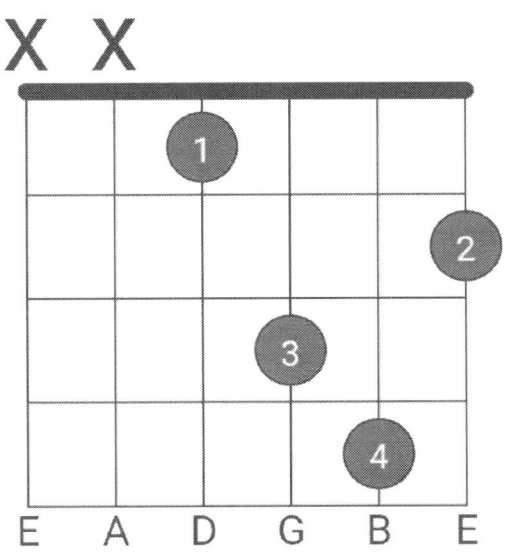
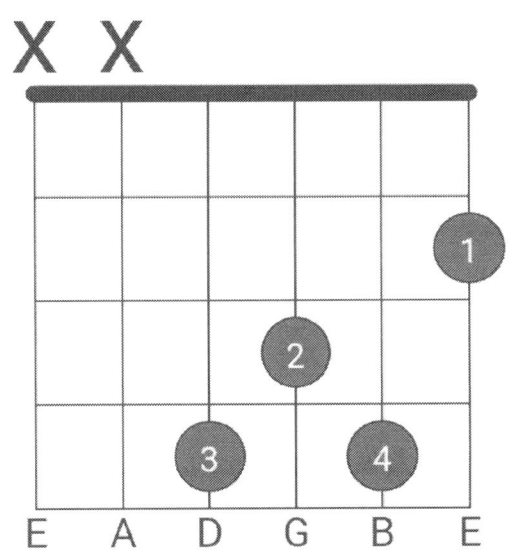
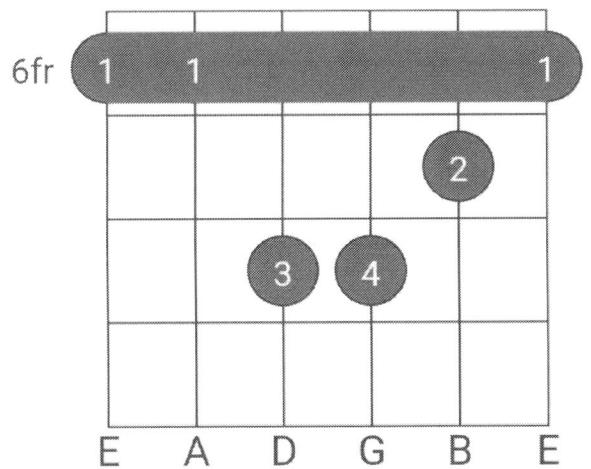
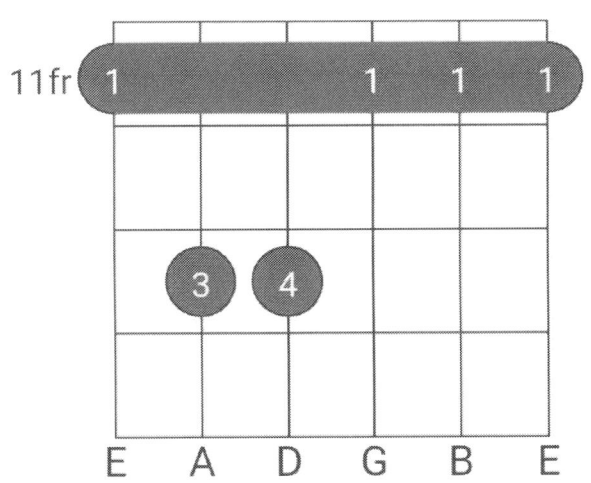

# D# / Eb dim

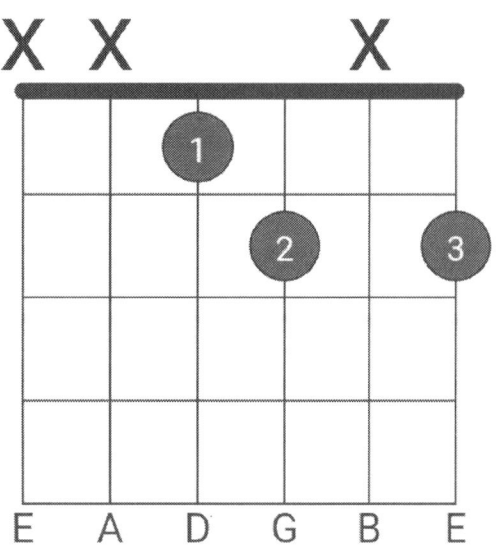
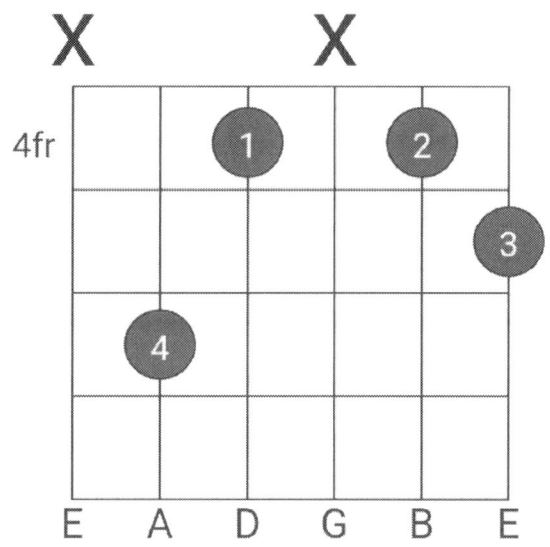
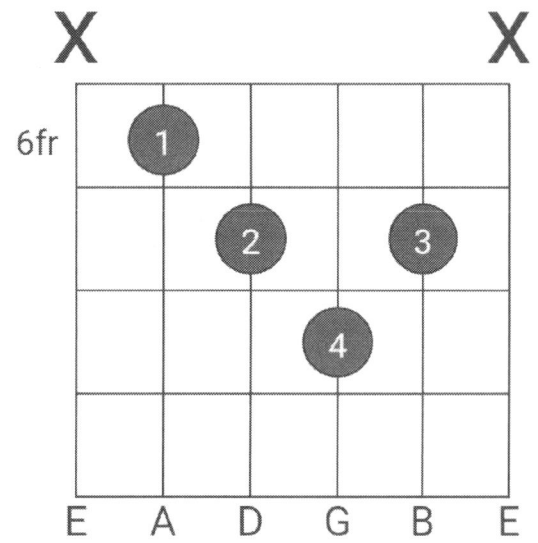
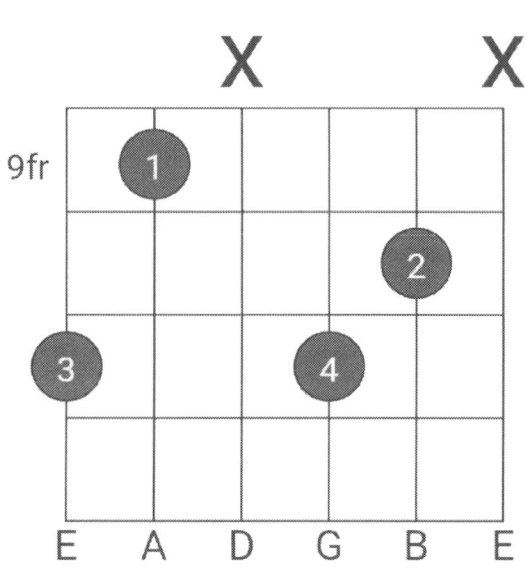

# D# / Eb Sus2

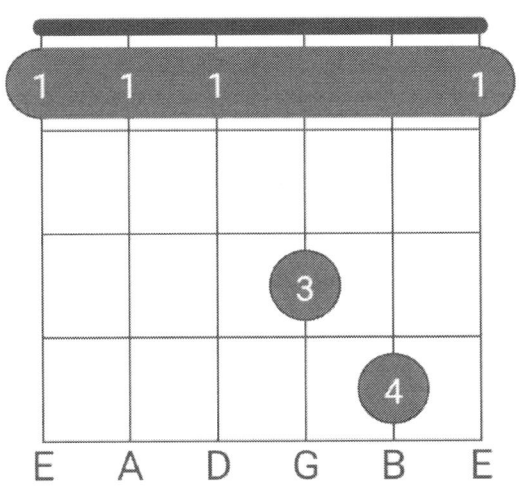
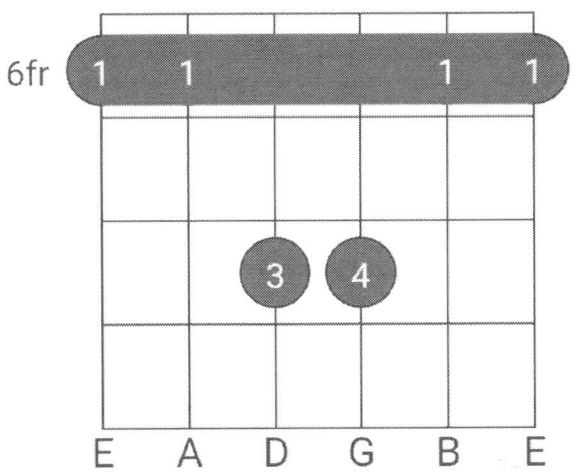
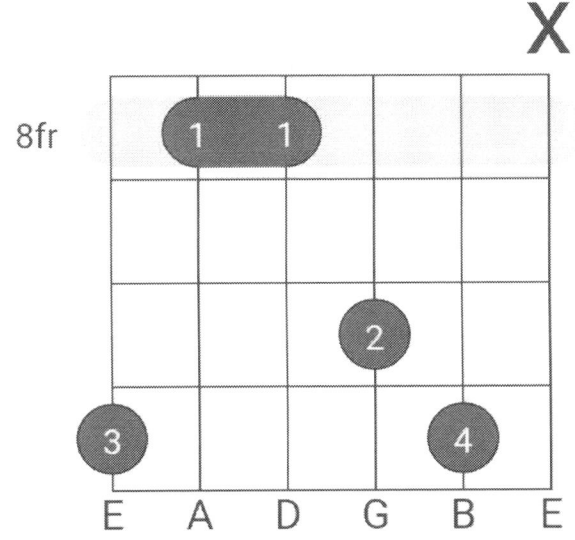
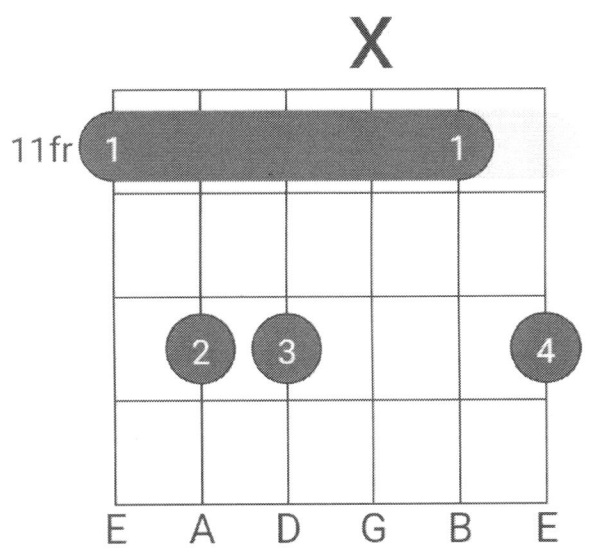

# D# / Eb Sus4

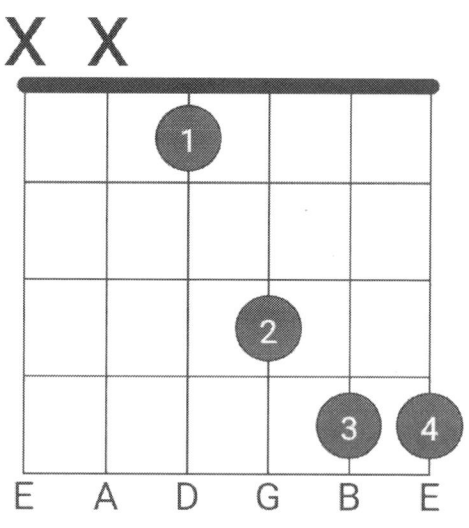
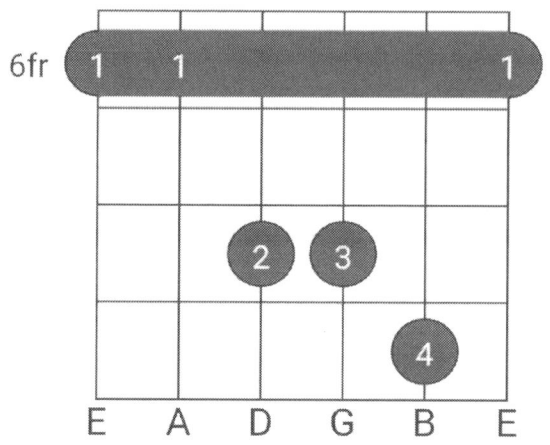
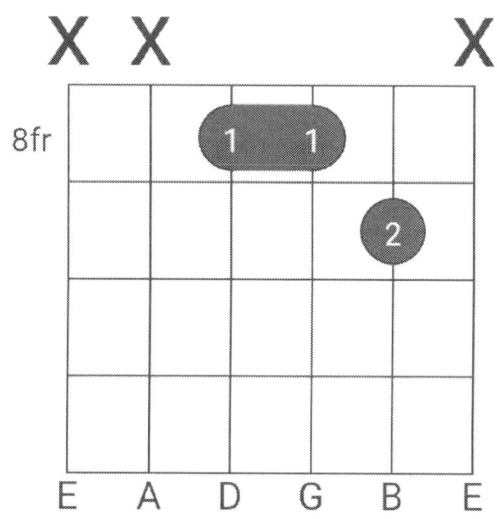
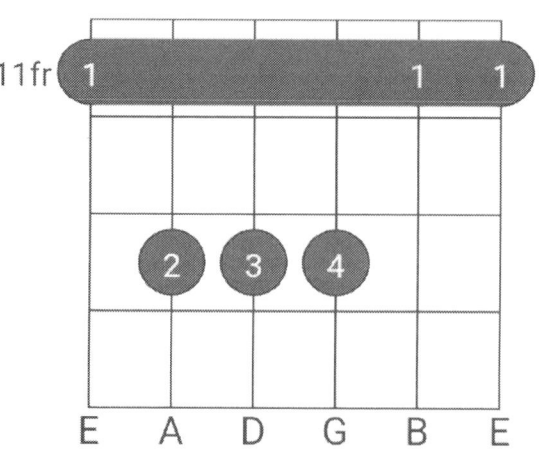

# D# / Eb aug

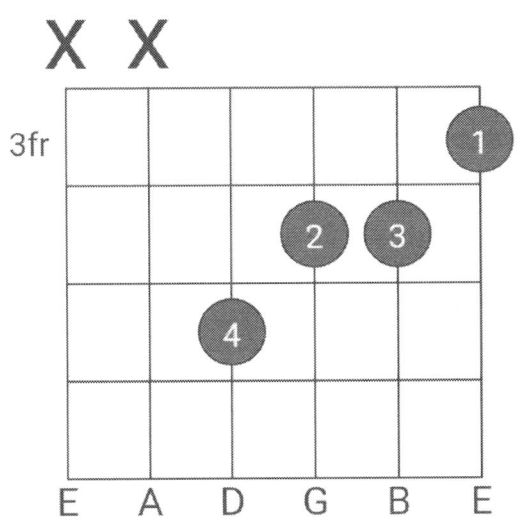
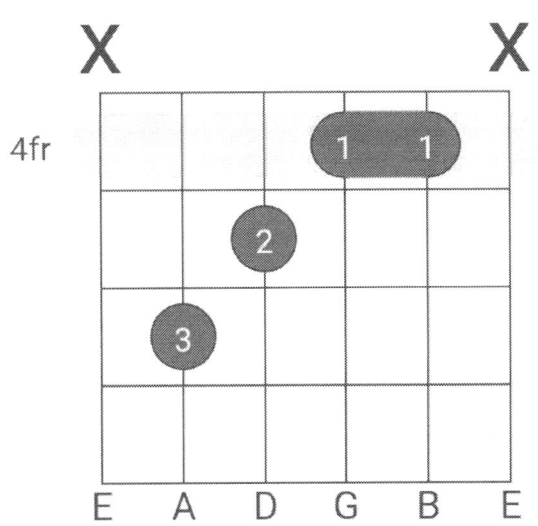
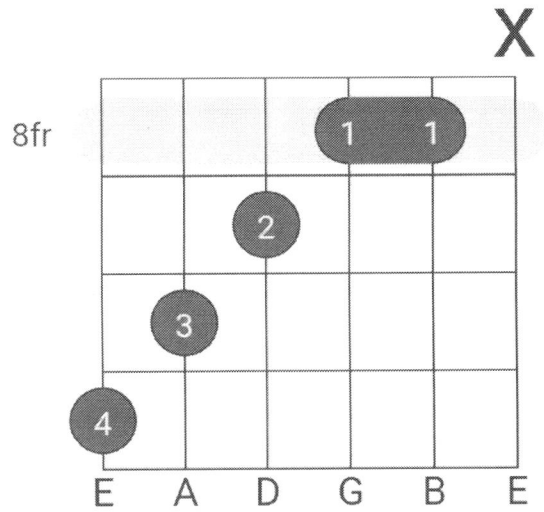
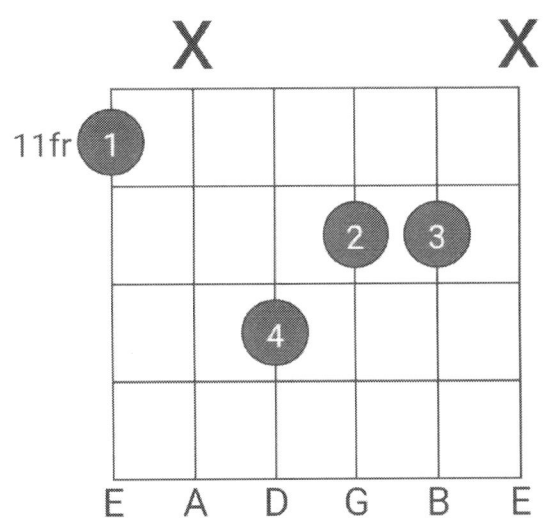

# D# / Eb7

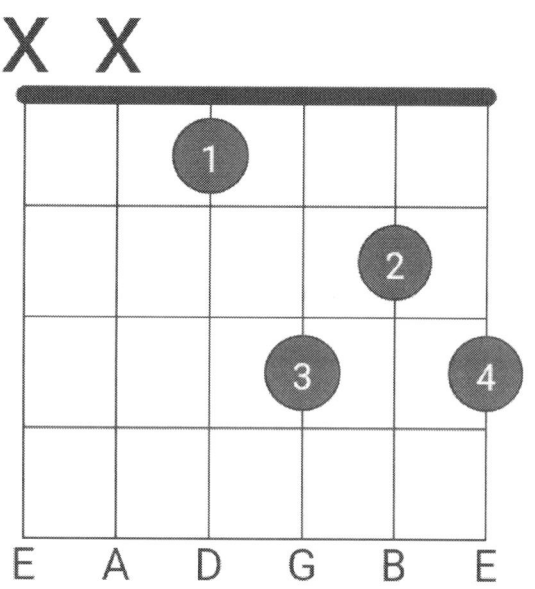
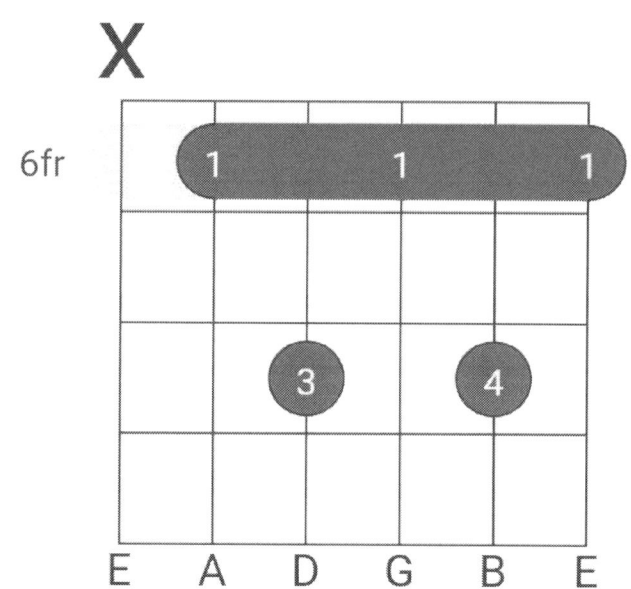
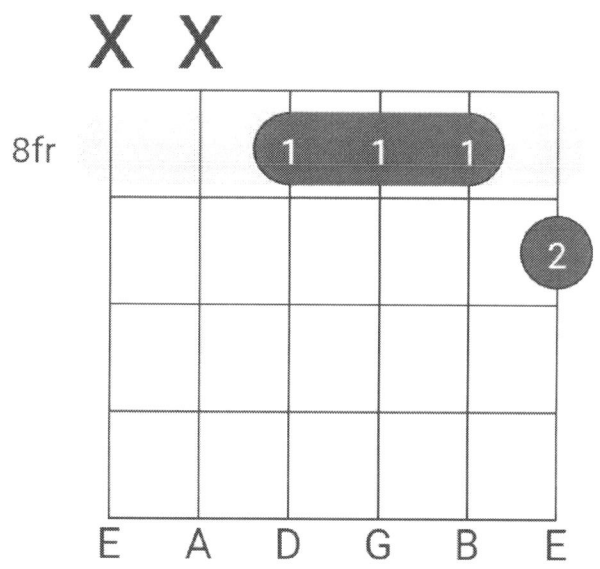
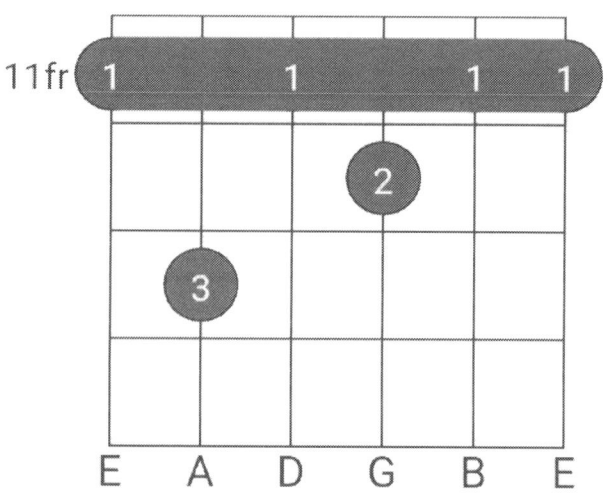

# D# / Eb maj7

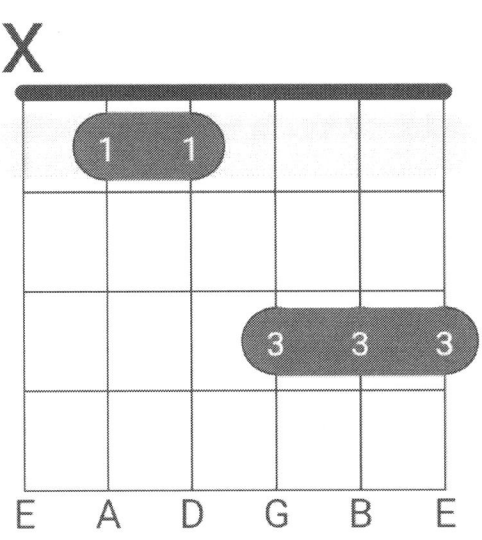
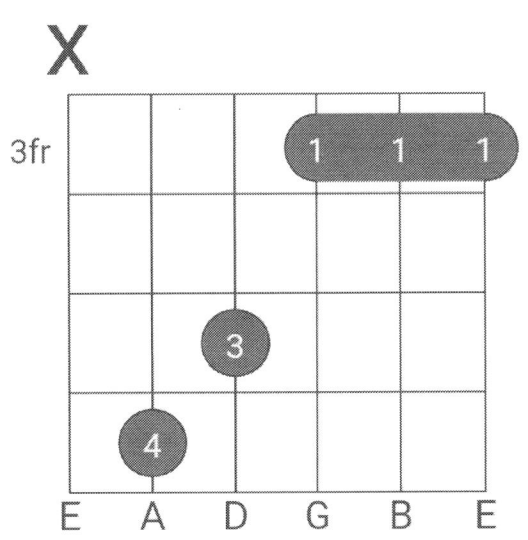
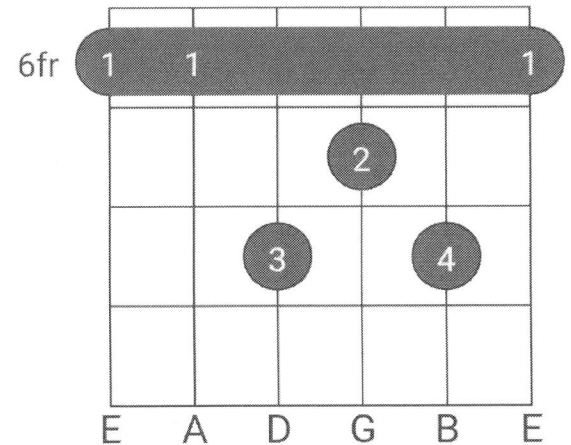
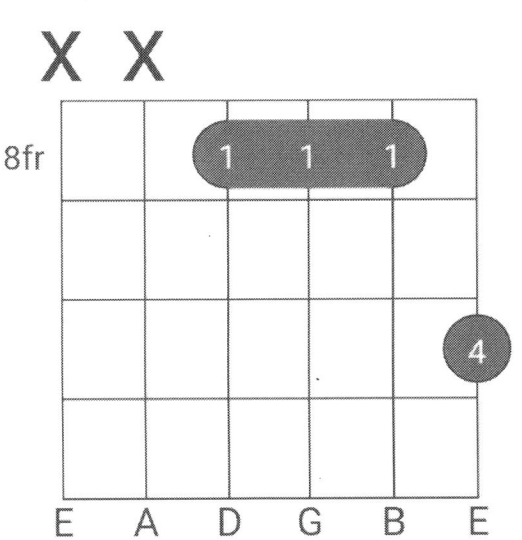

# D# / Eb m7

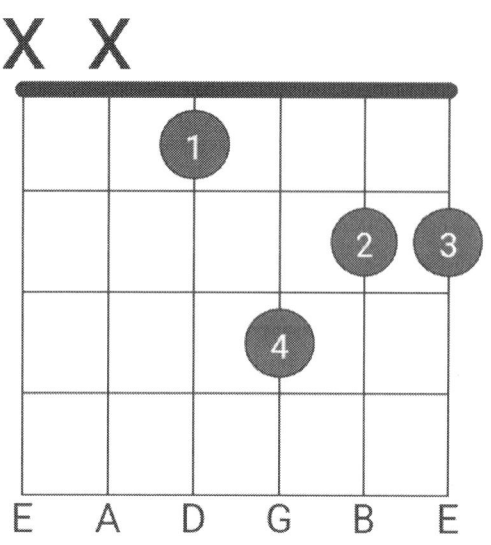
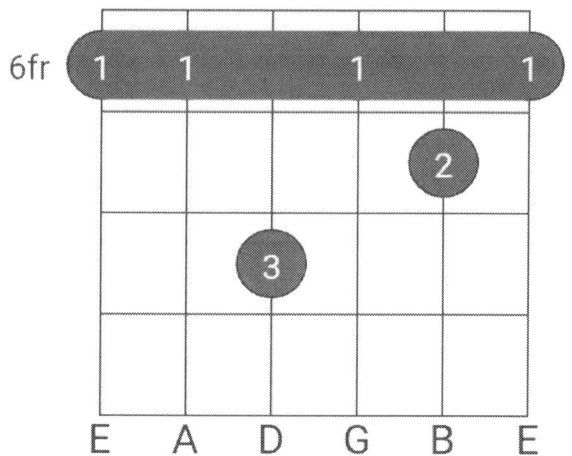
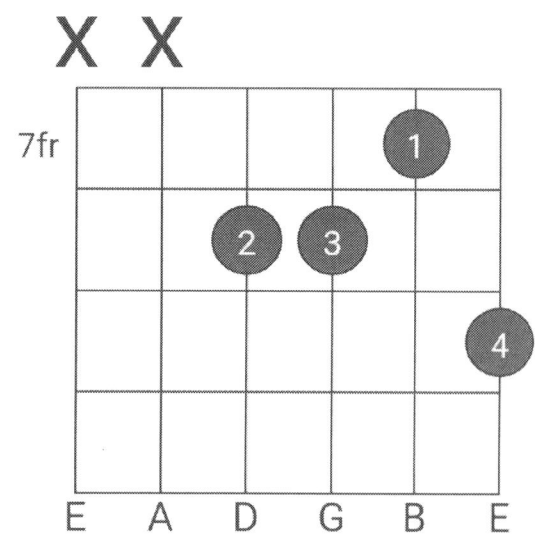
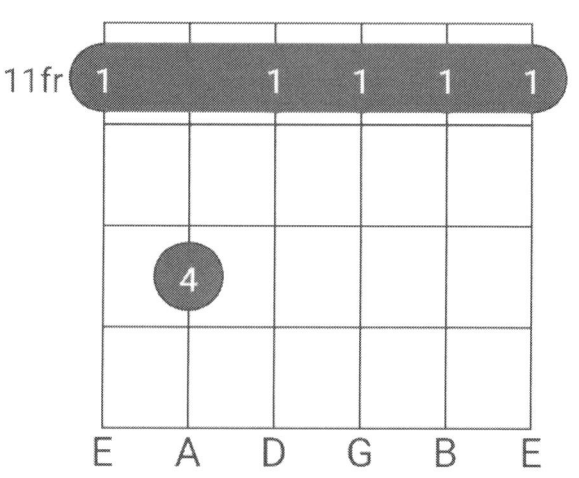

# E Major

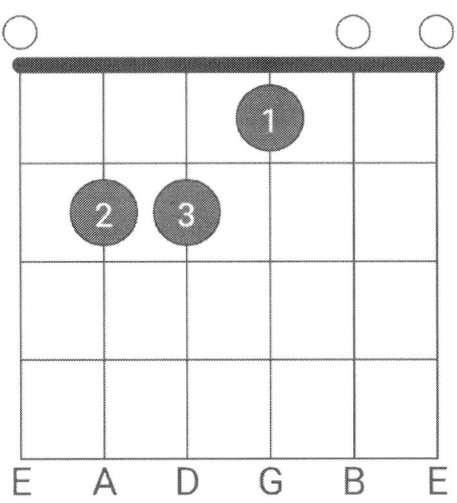
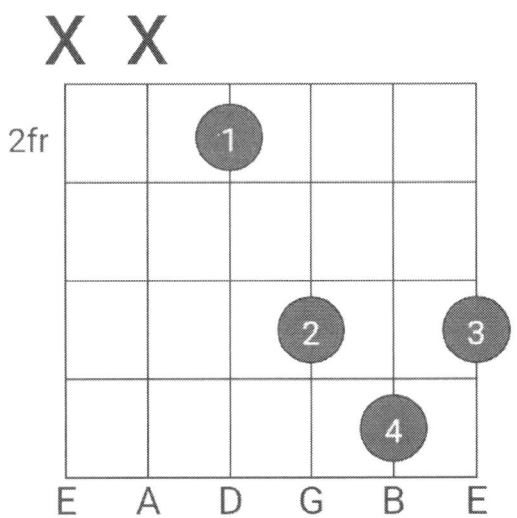
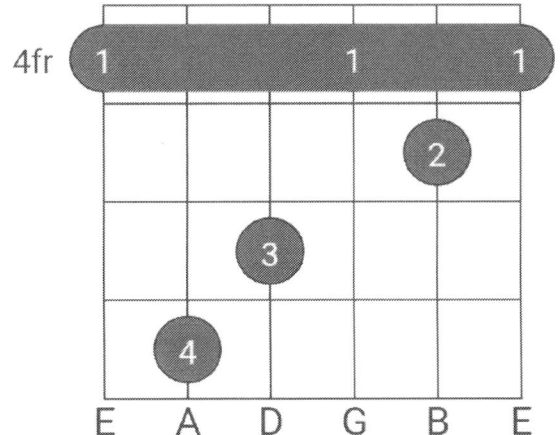
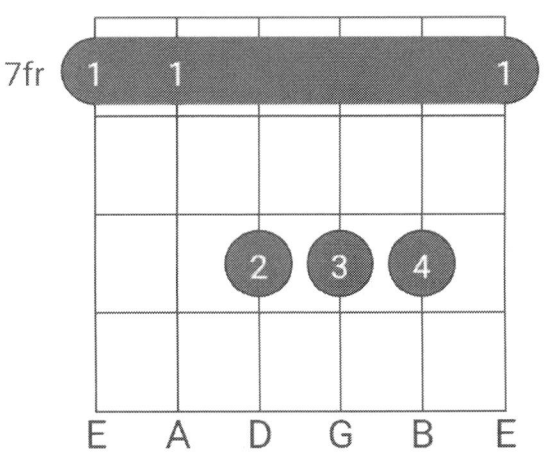

# E minor

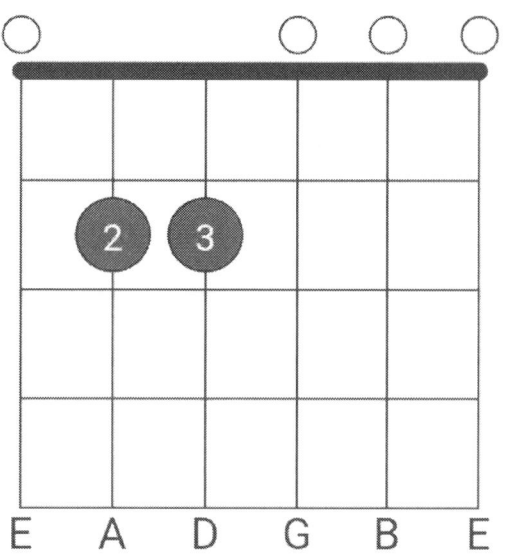
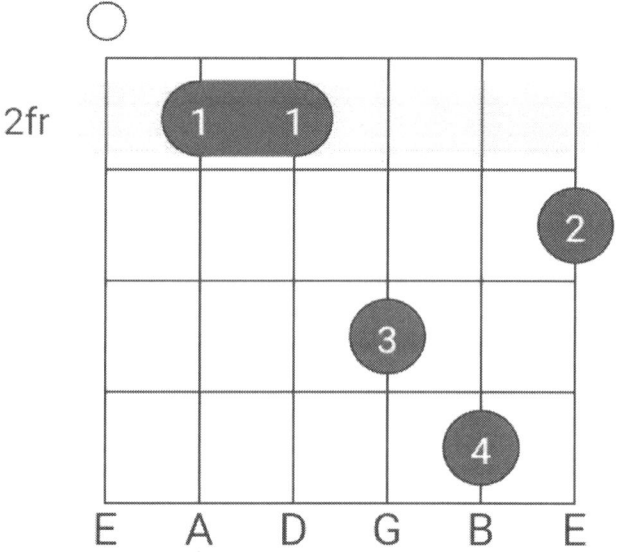
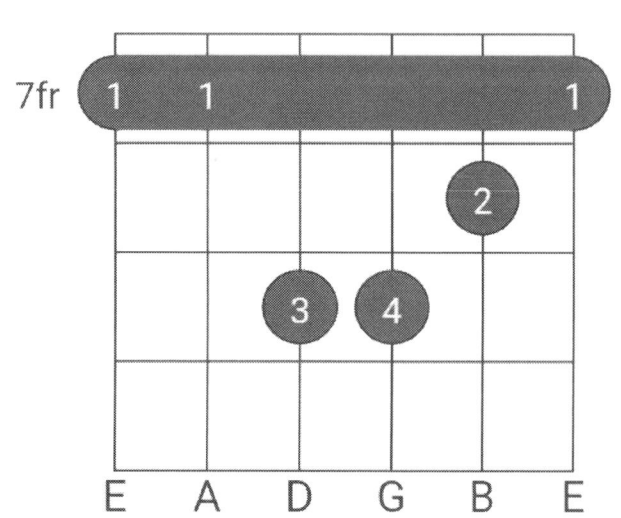
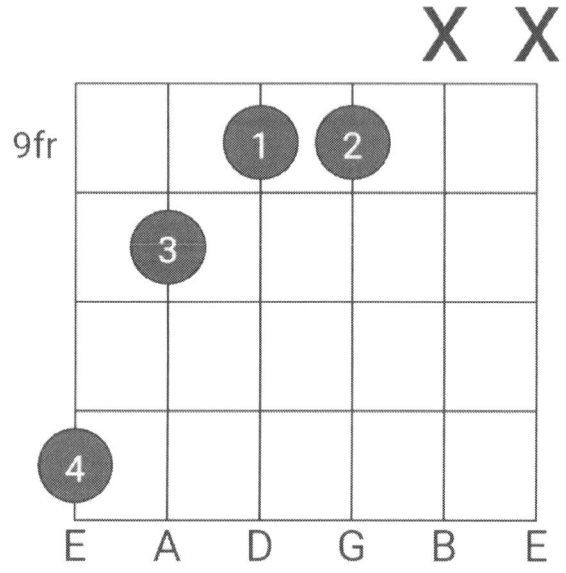

# E dim

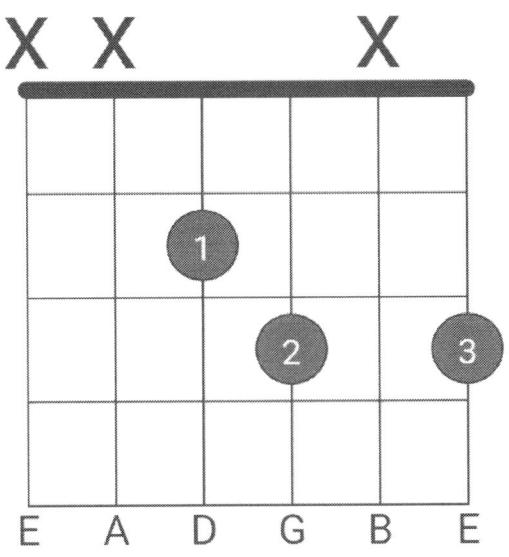 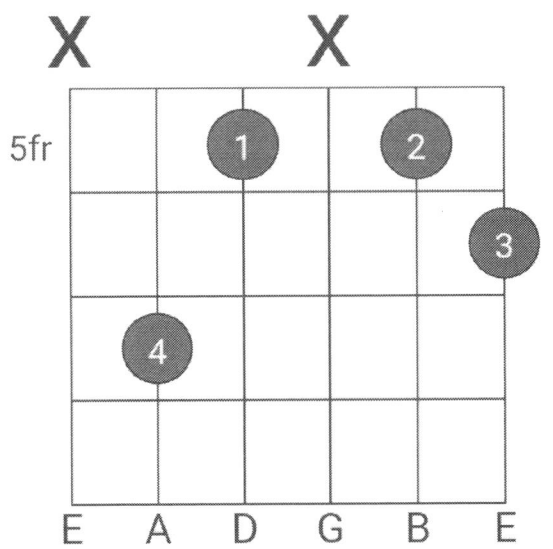
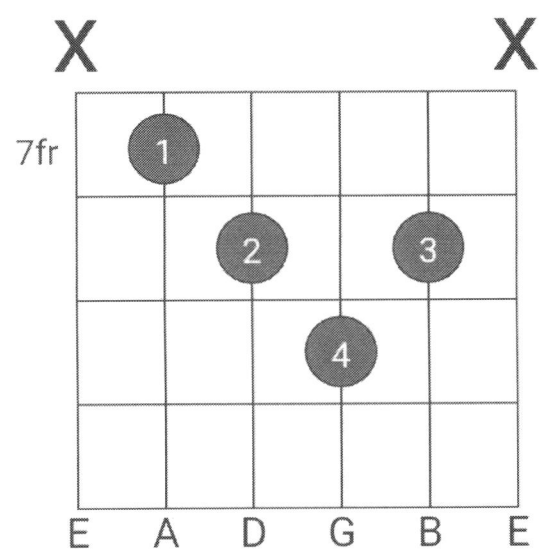 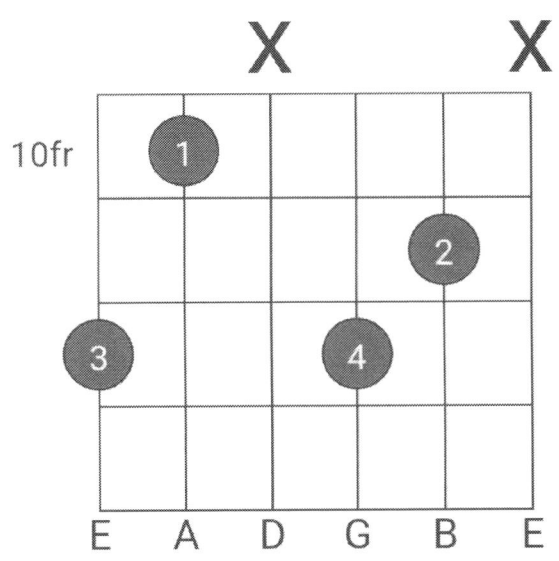

# E Sus2

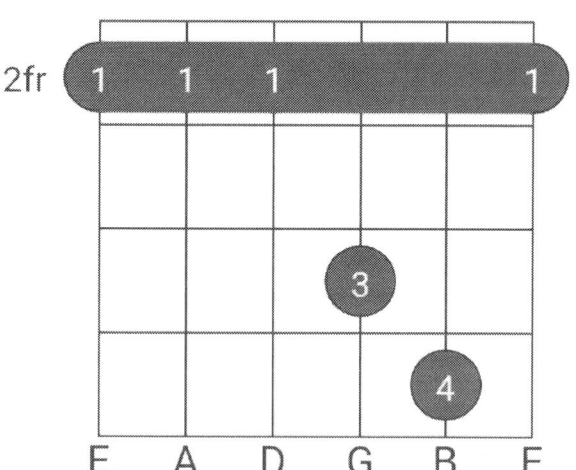
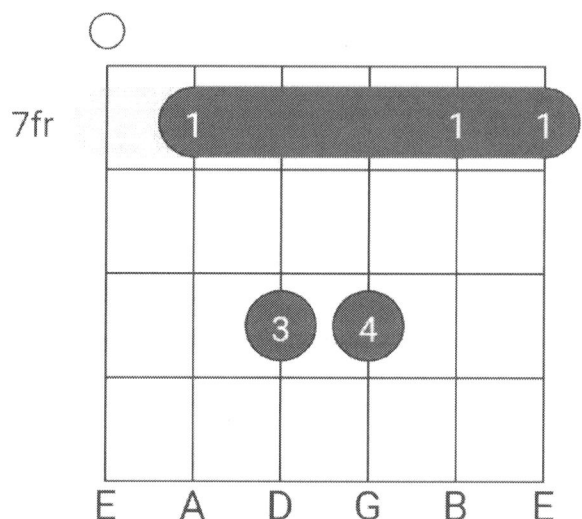
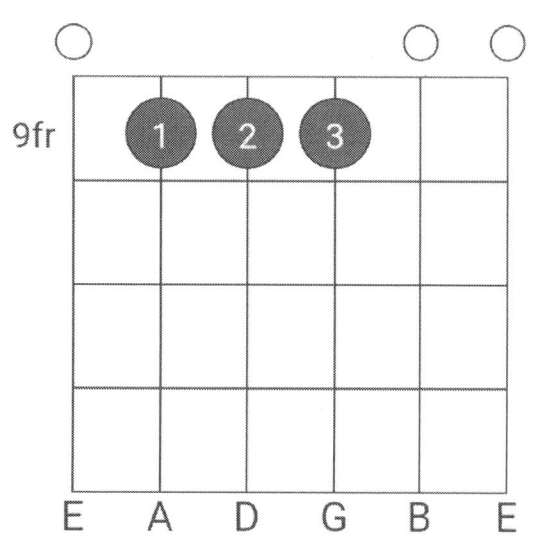
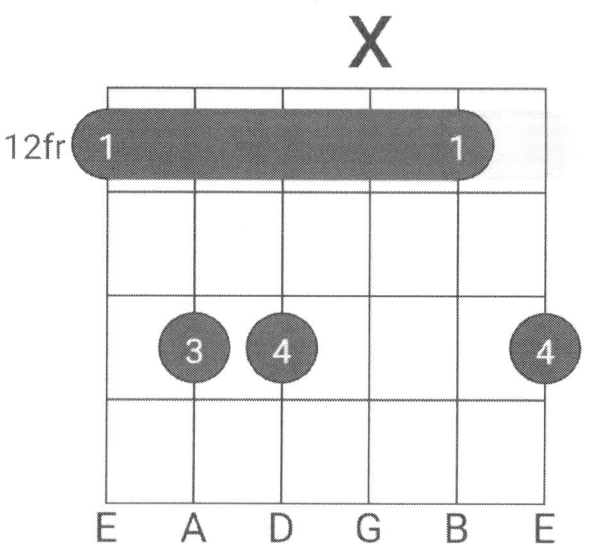

# E Sus4

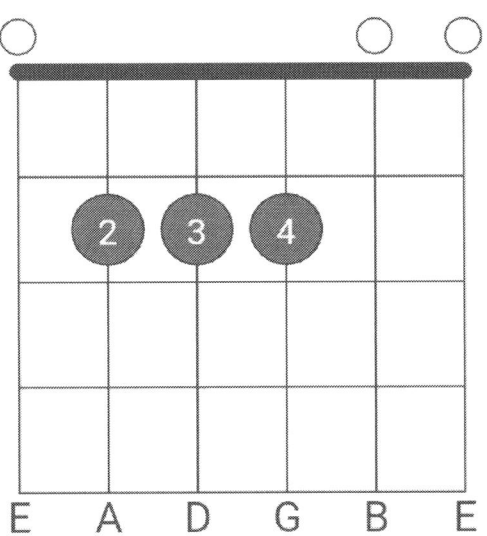
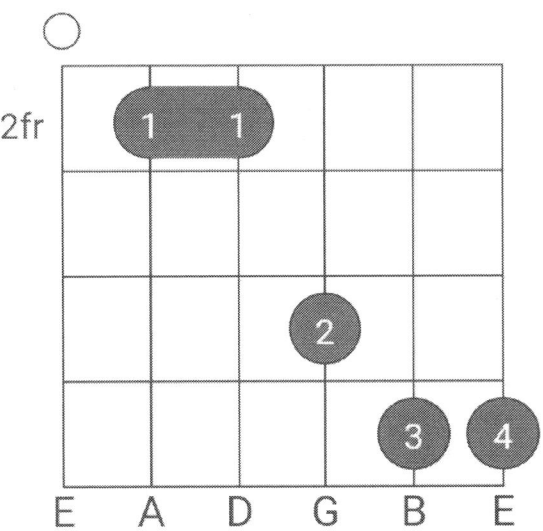
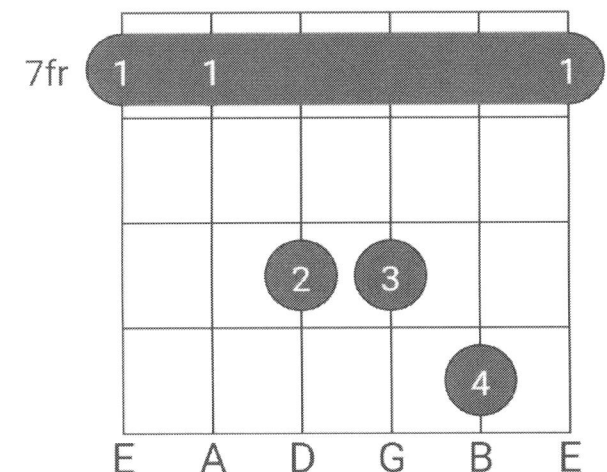
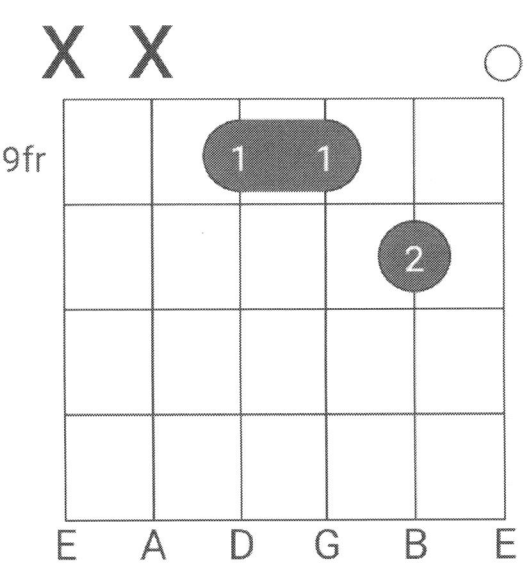

# E aug

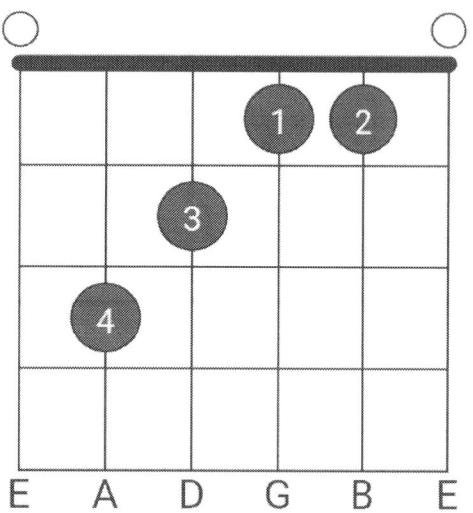
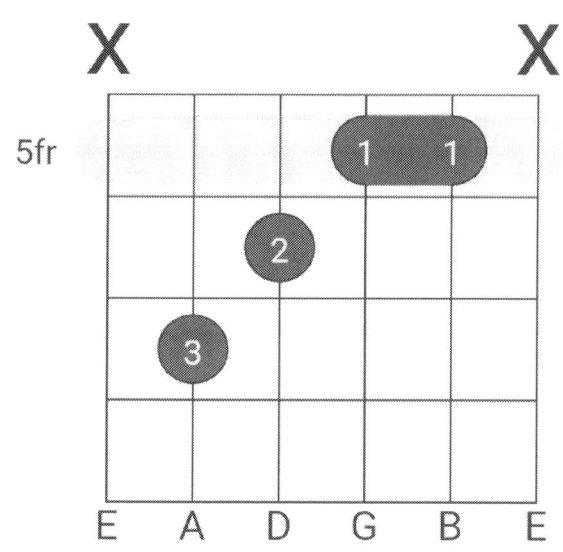
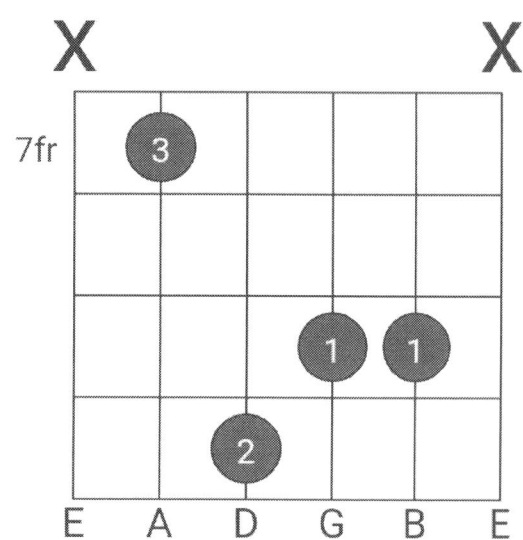
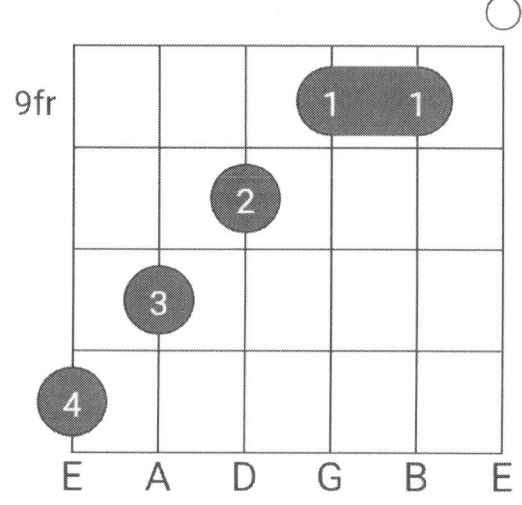

# E7

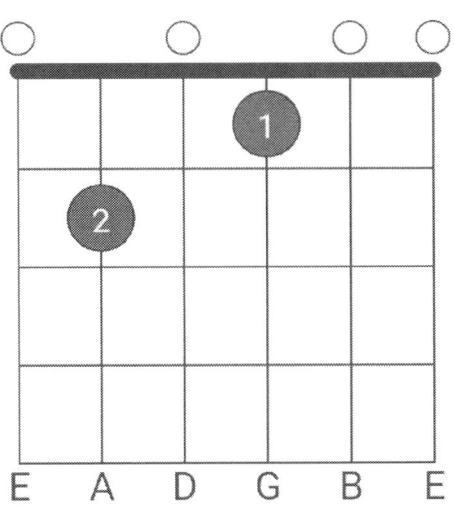
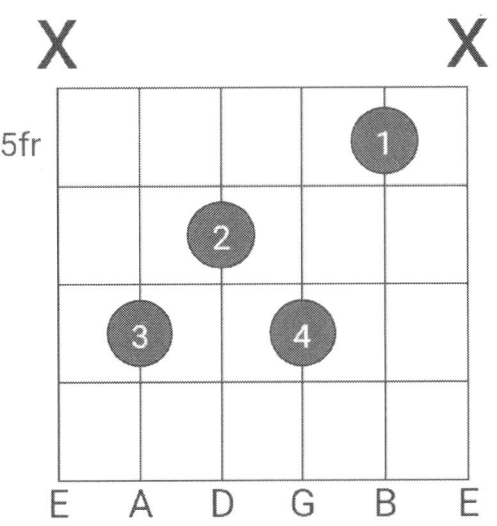
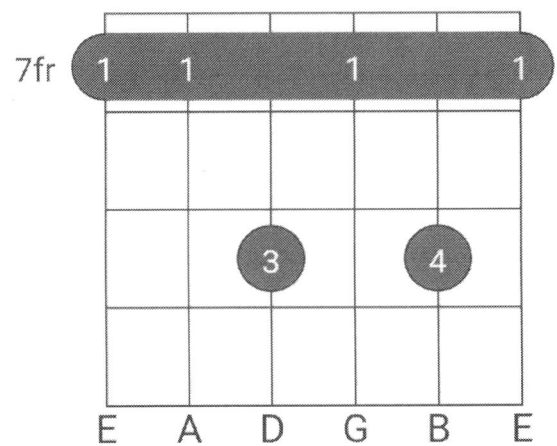
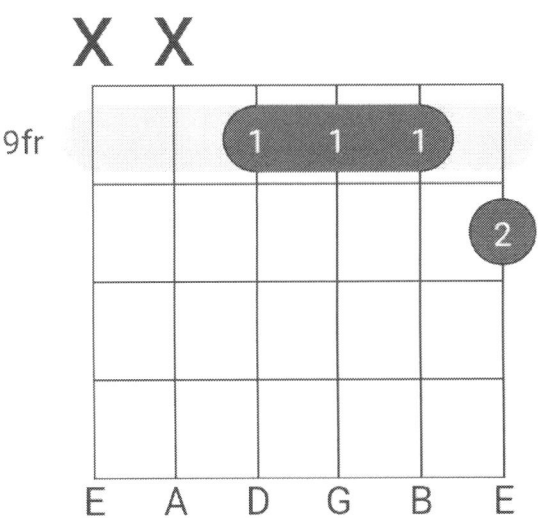

# E maj7

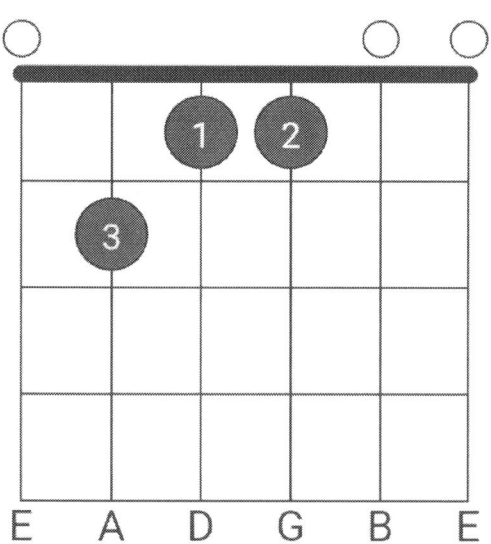
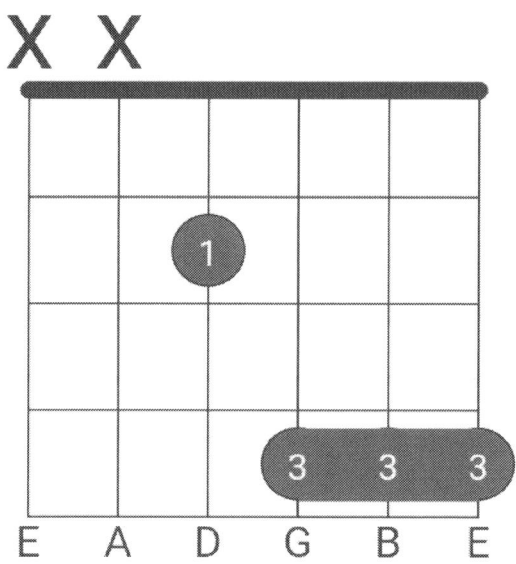
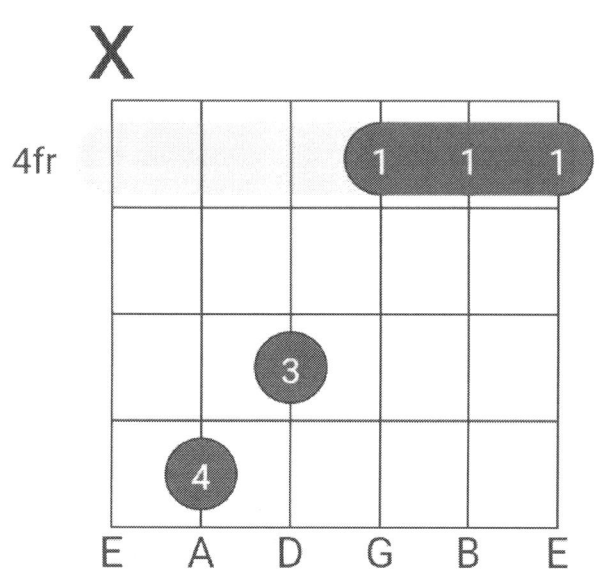
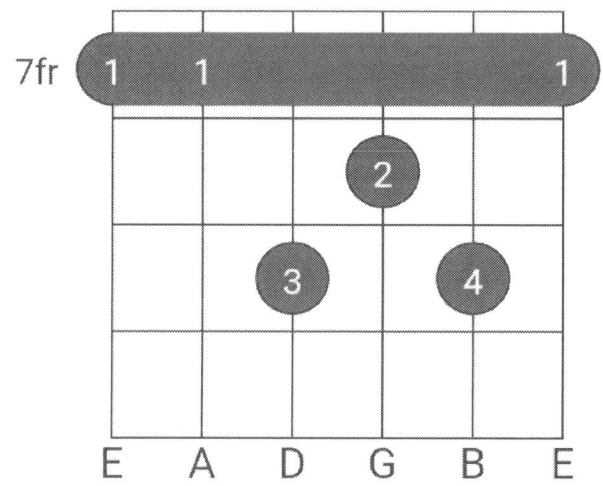

# Em7

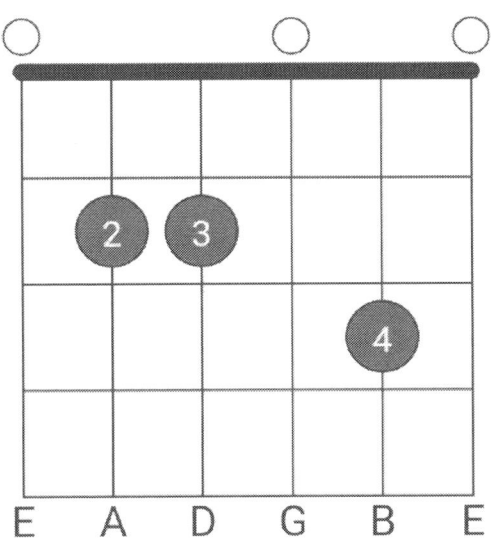
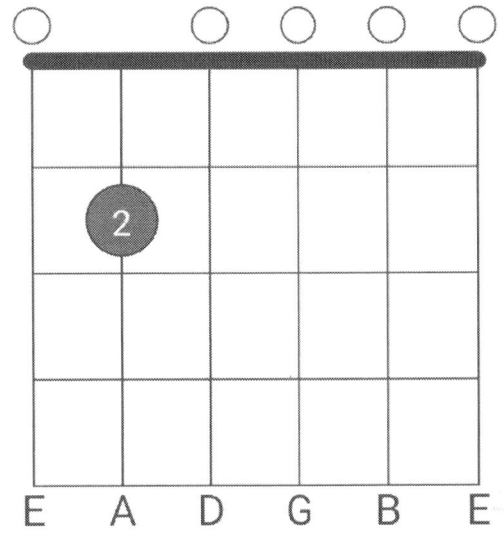
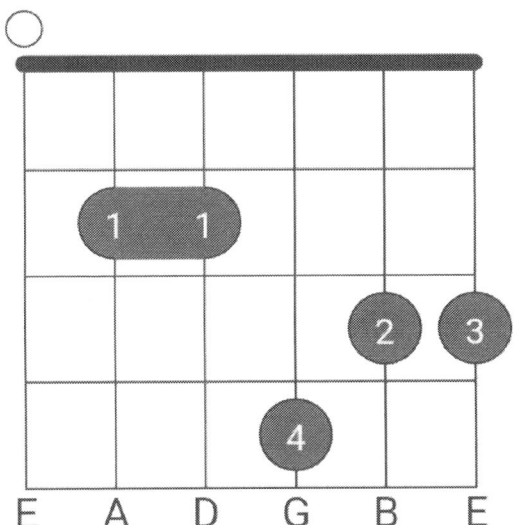
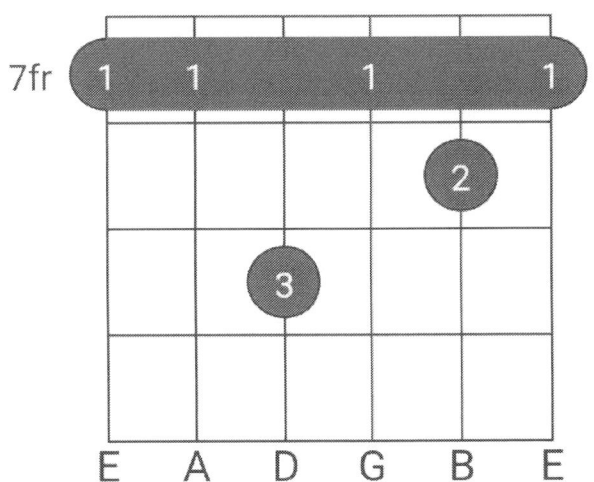

# F Major

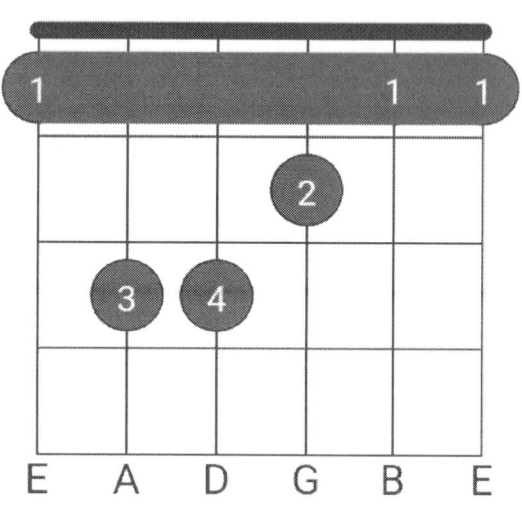
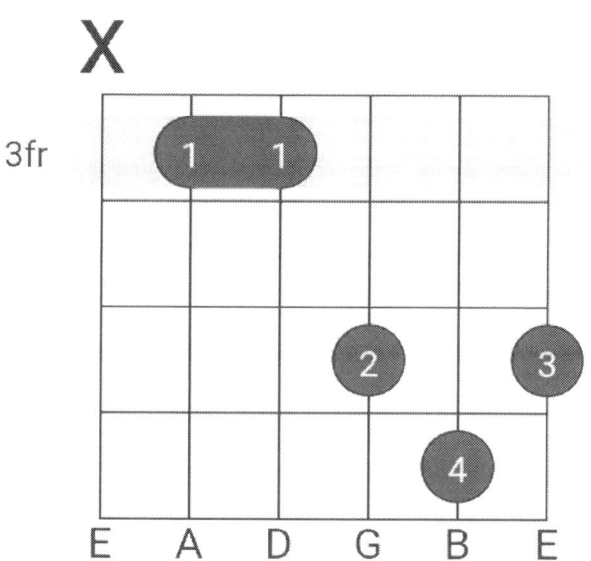
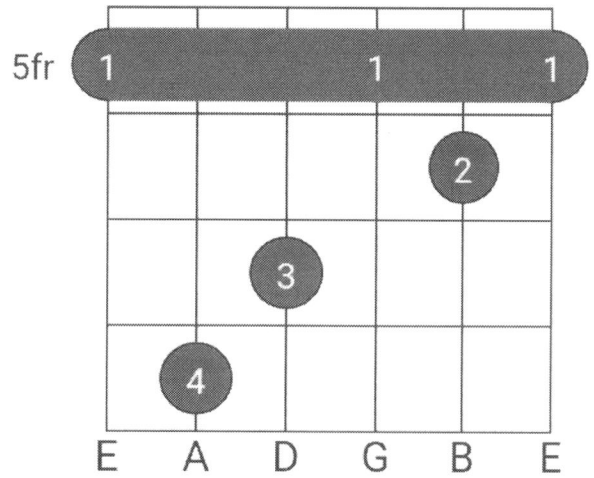
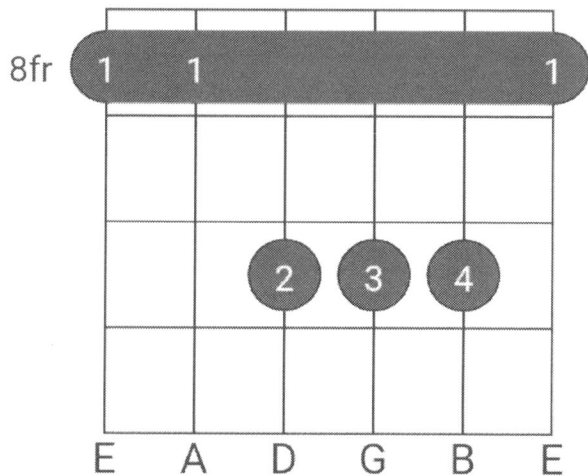

# F minor

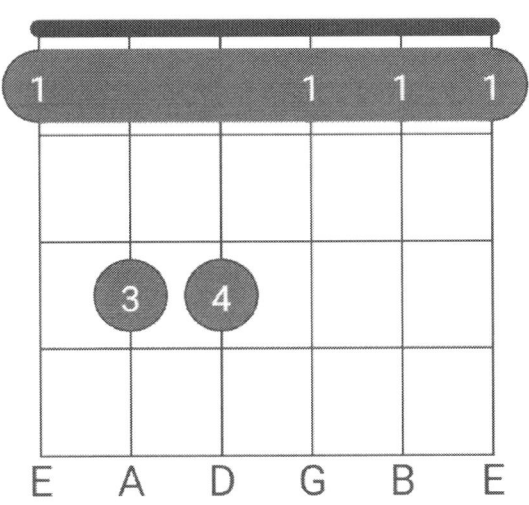
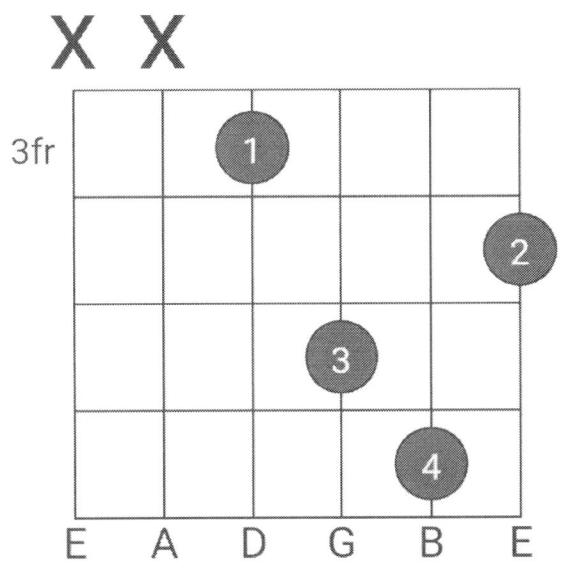
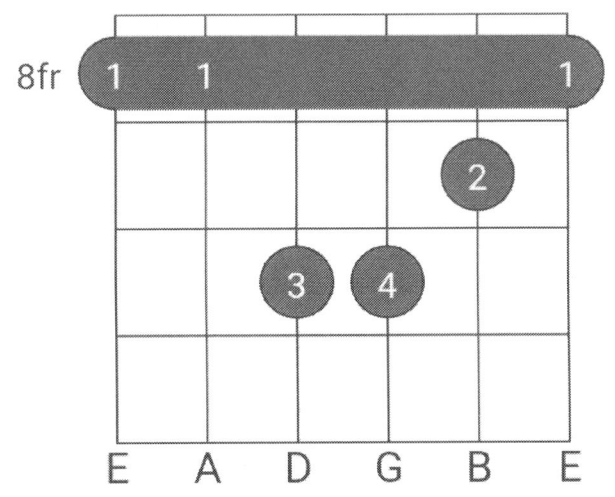
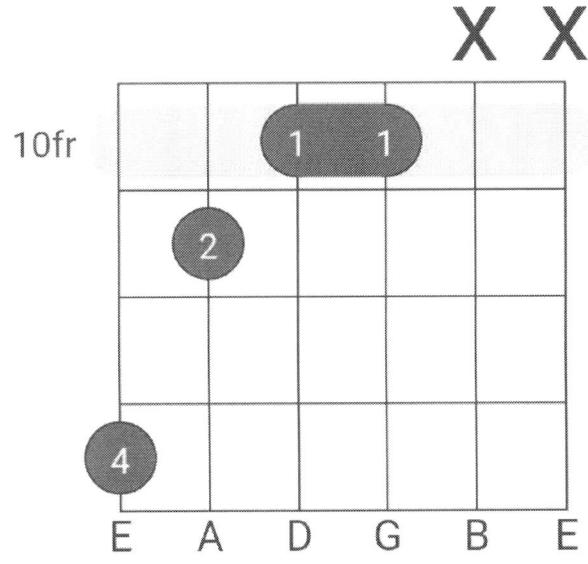

# F dim

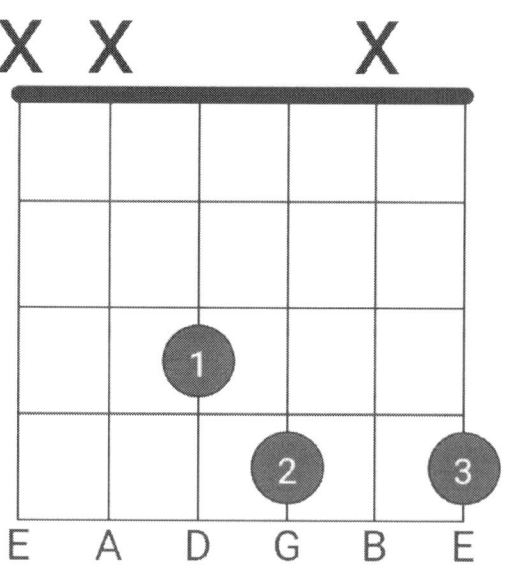
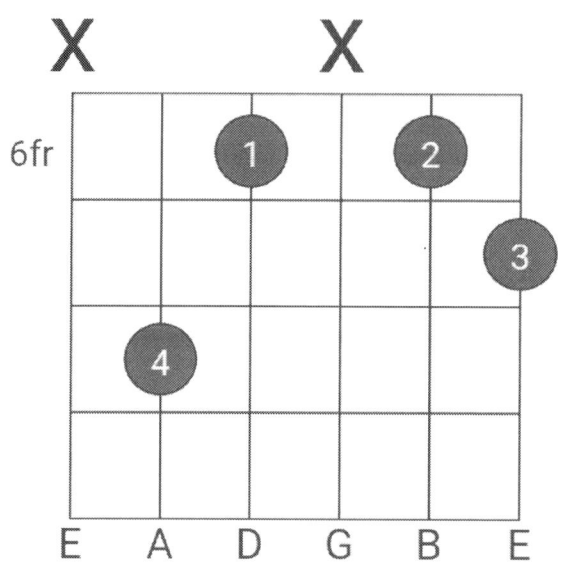
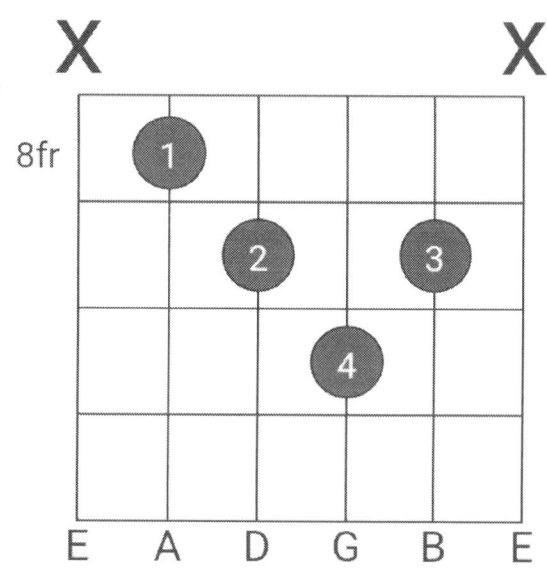
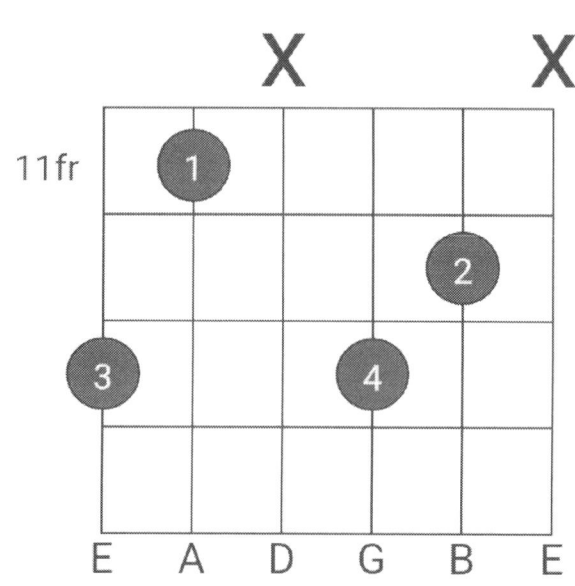

# F Sus2

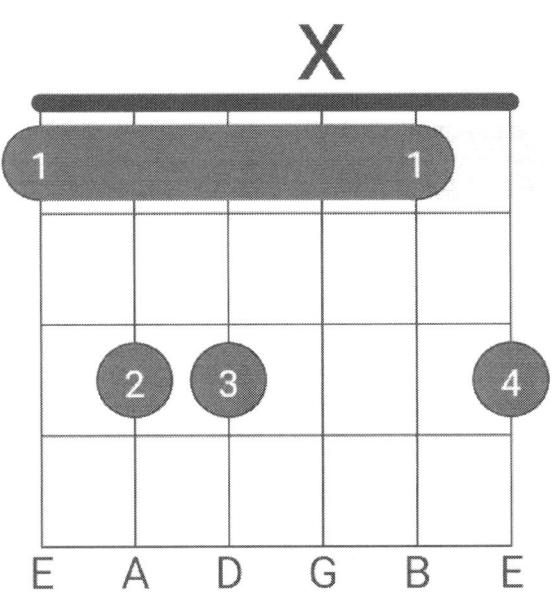
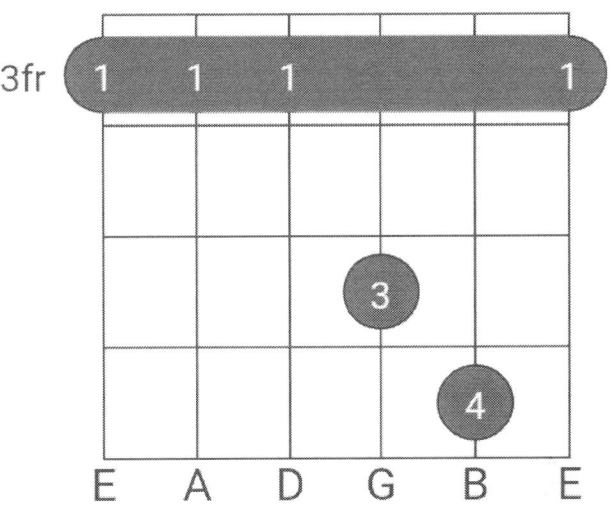
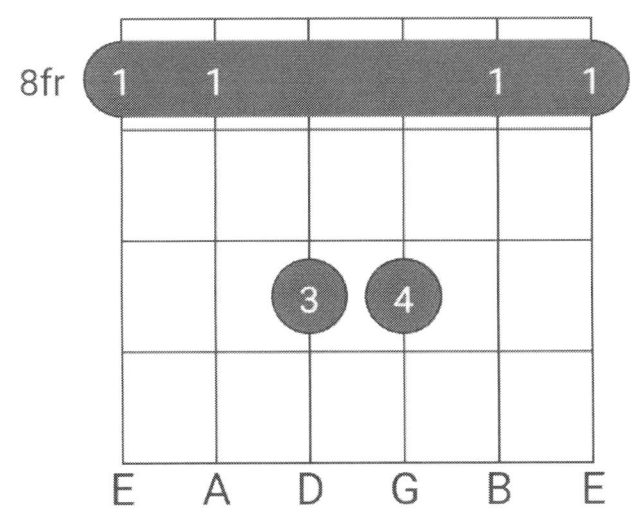
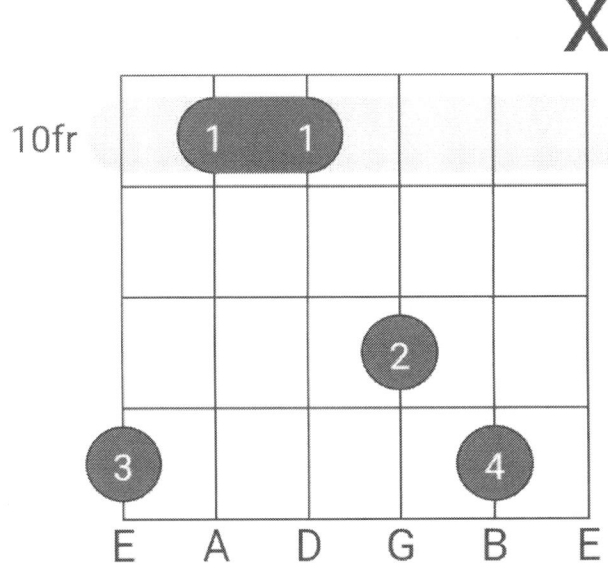

# F Sus4

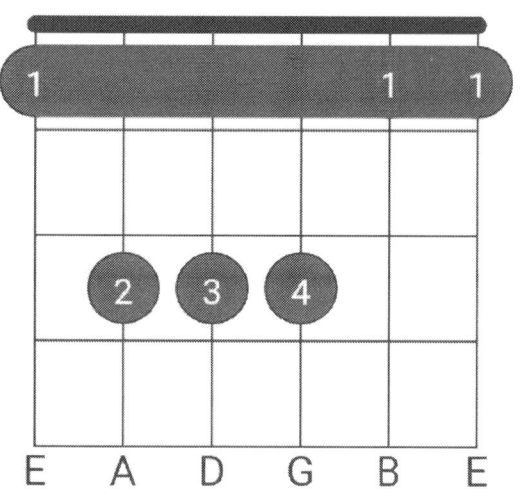
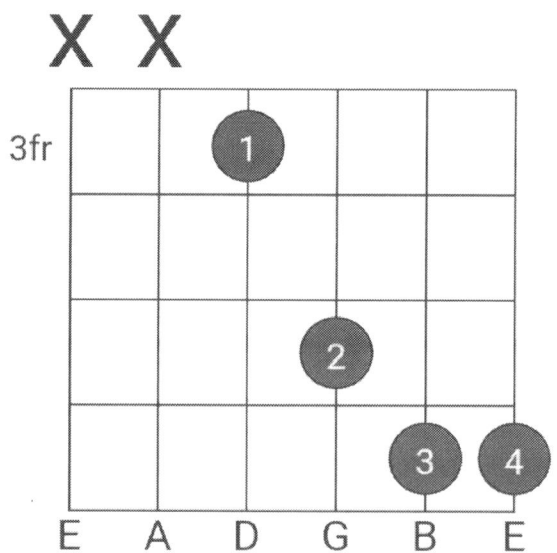
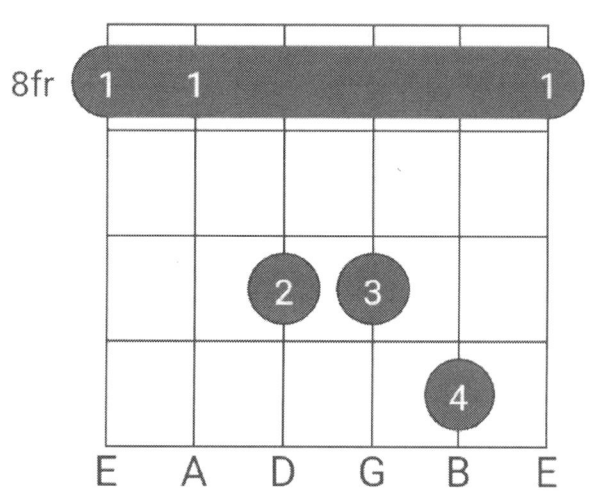
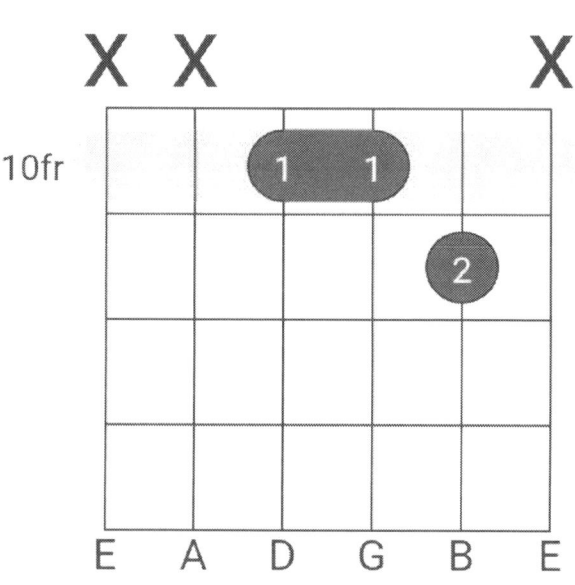

# F aug

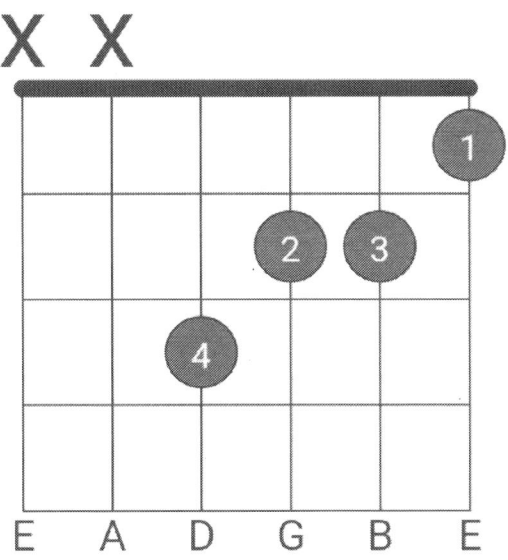
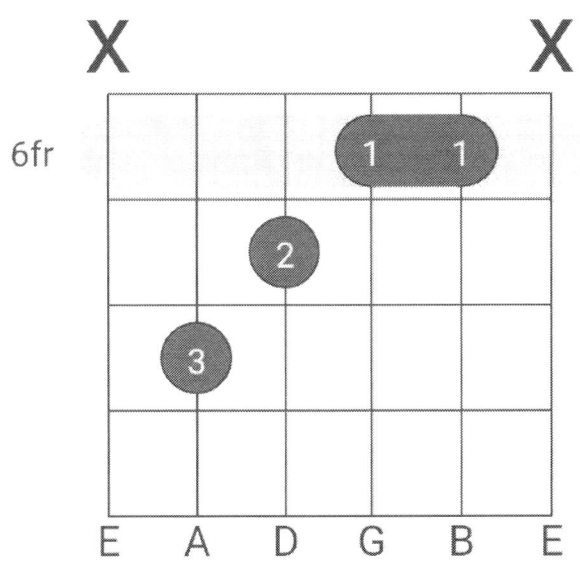
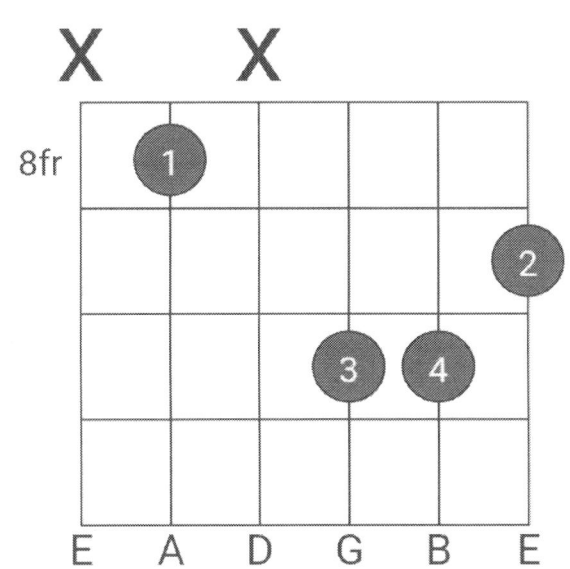
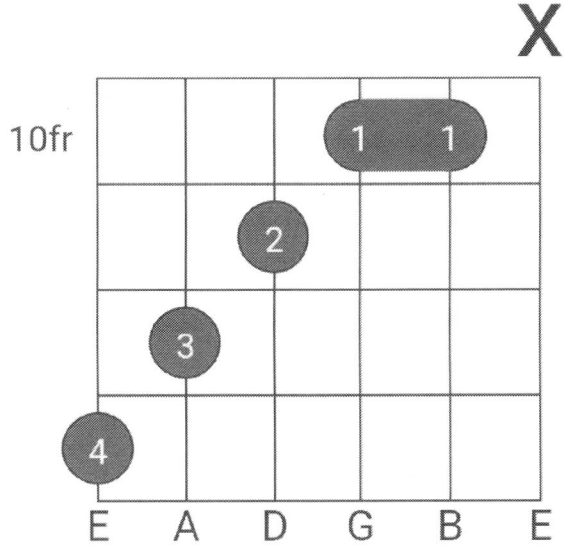

# F7

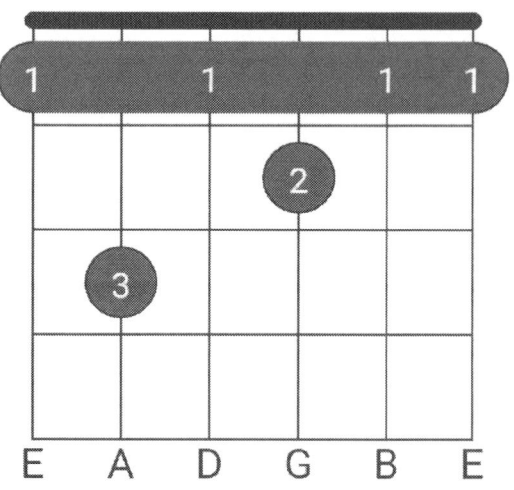
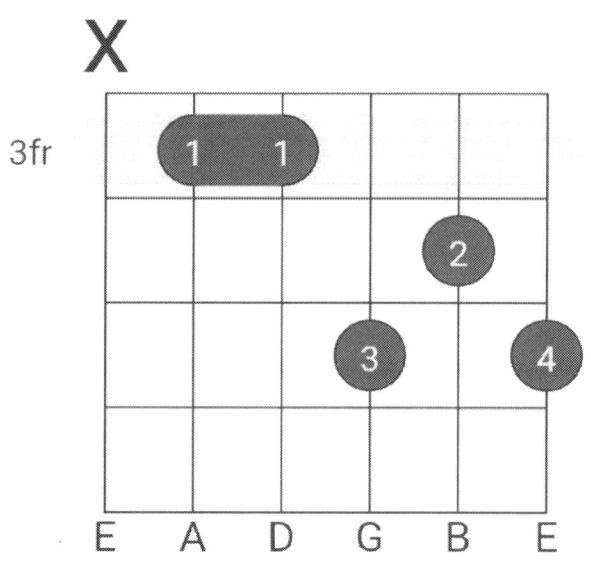
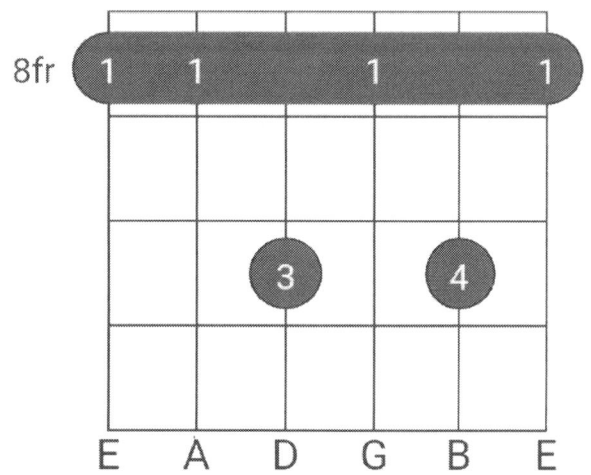
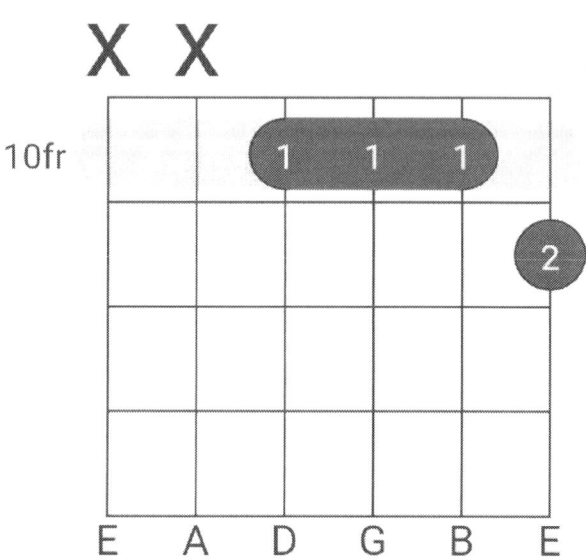

# F maj7

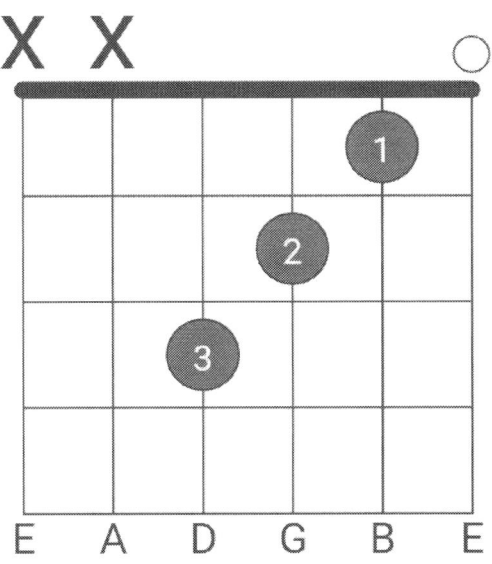 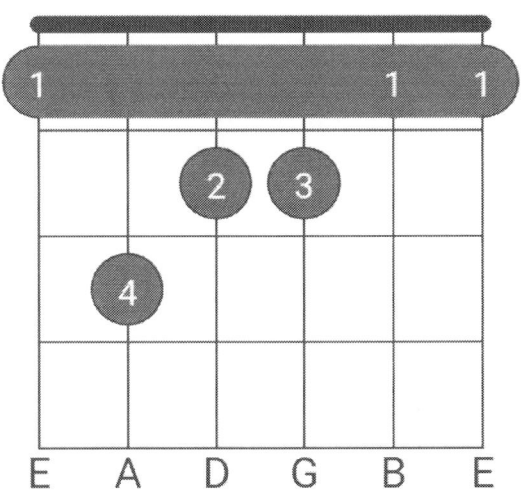

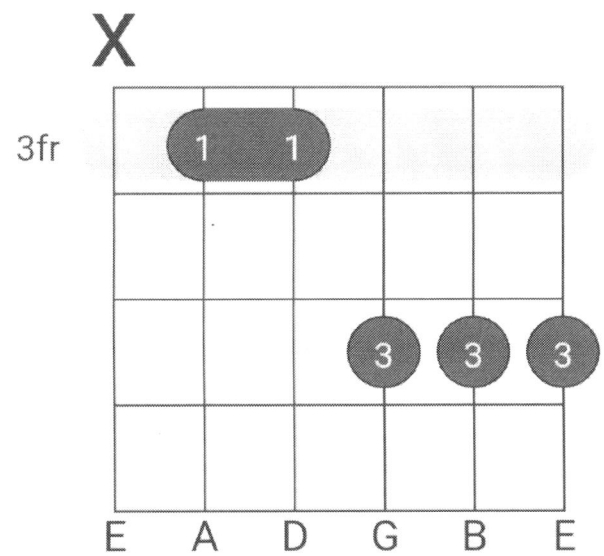 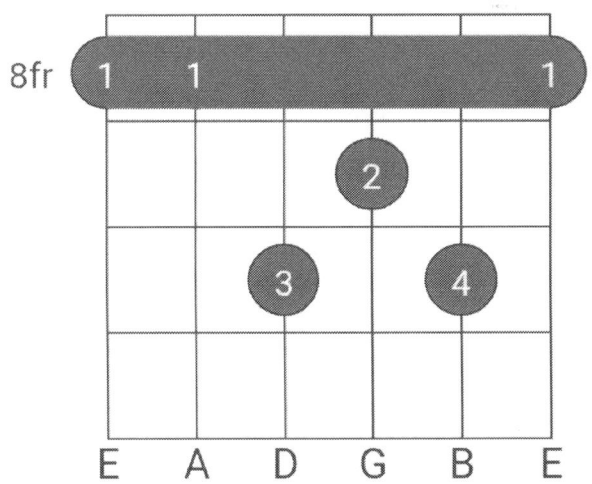

# Fm7

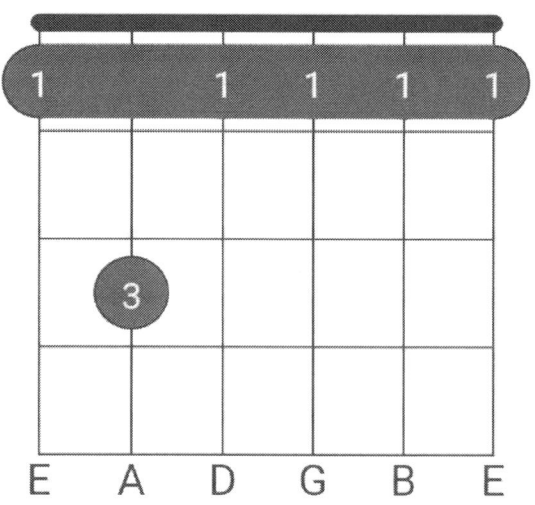
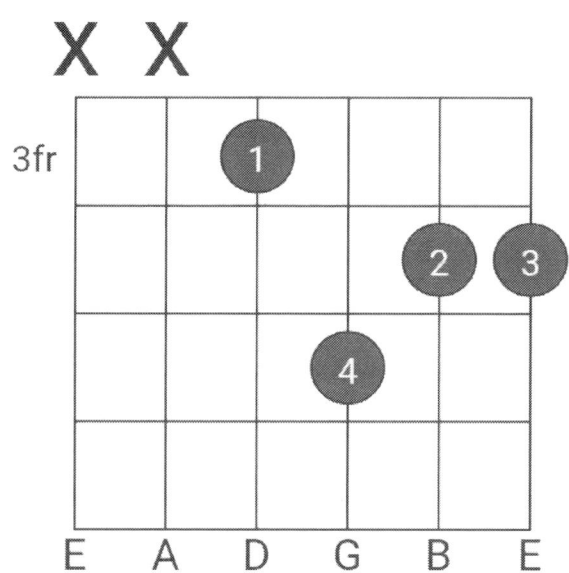
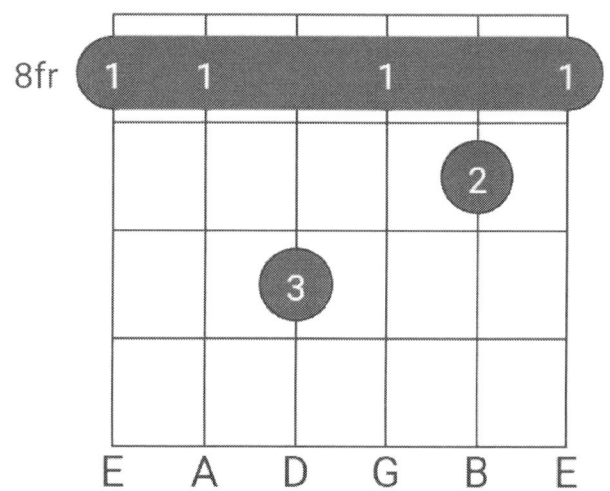
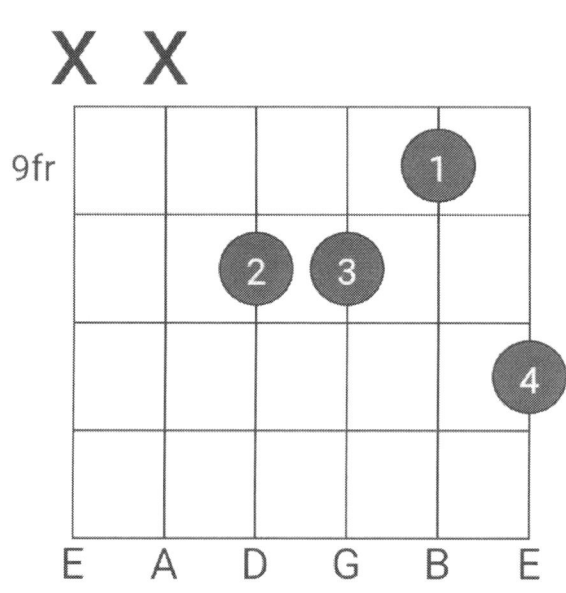

# F# / Gb Major

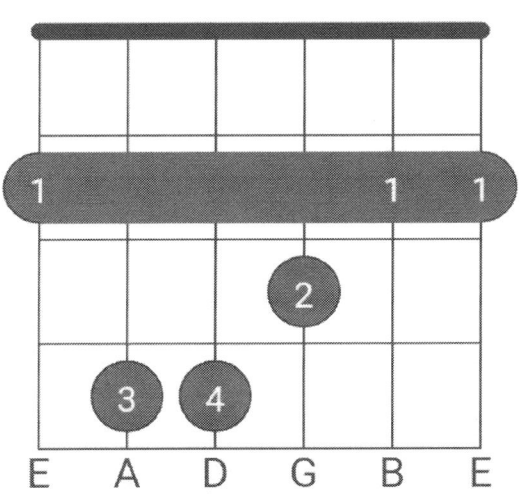
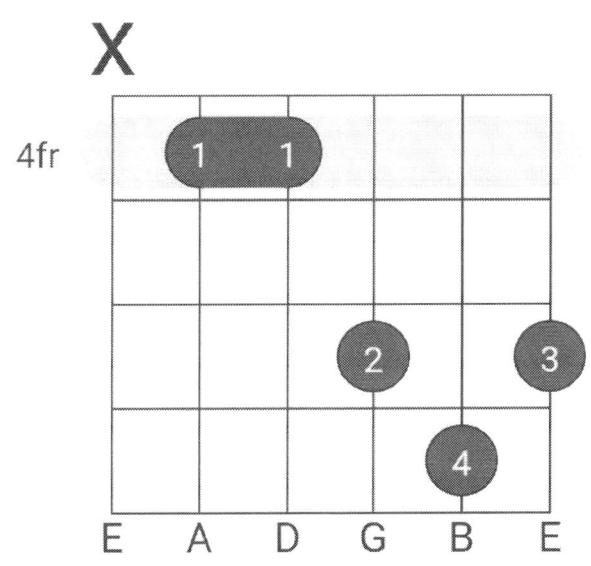
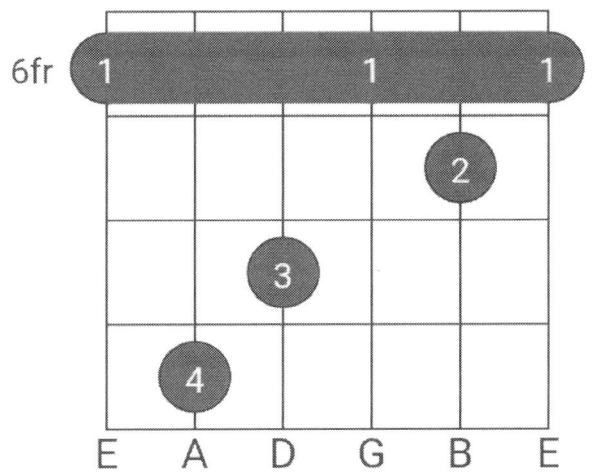
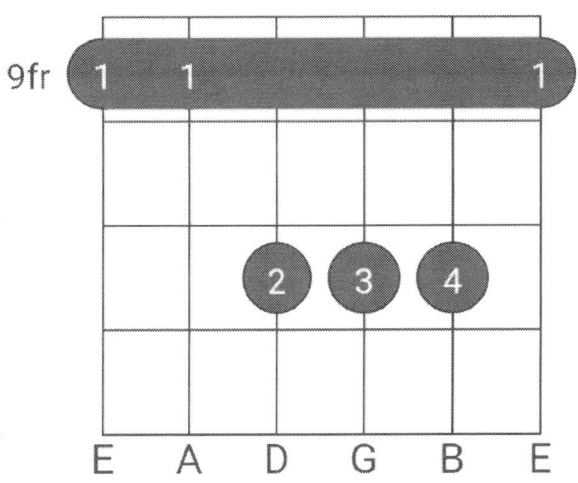

# F# / Gb minor

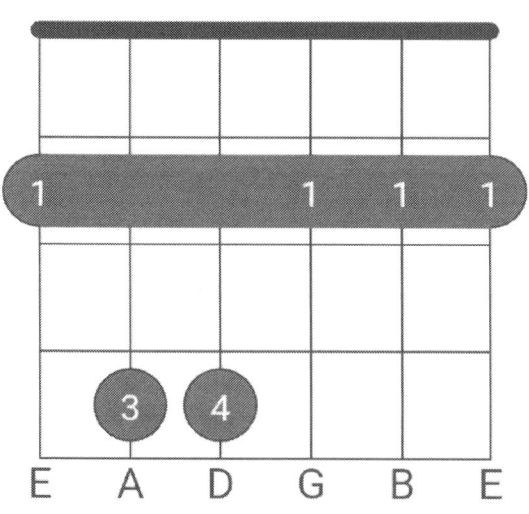
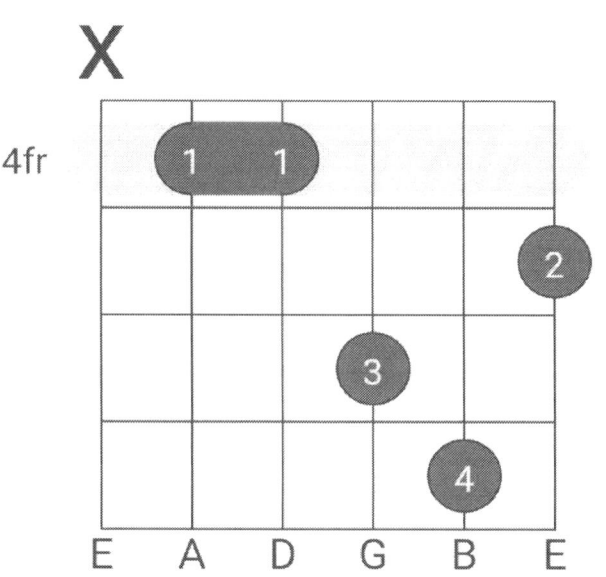
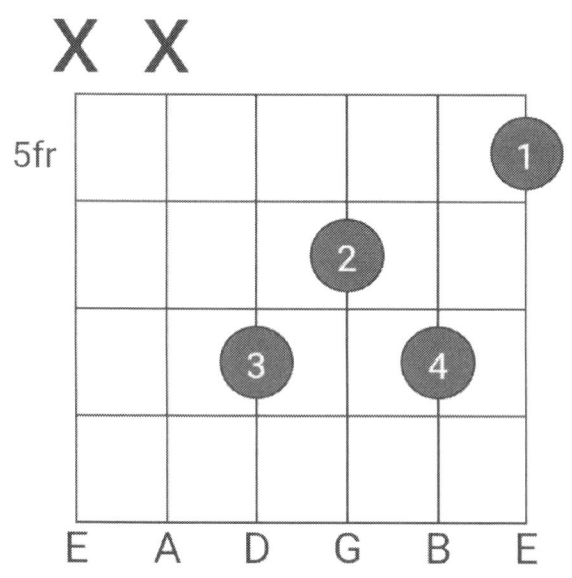
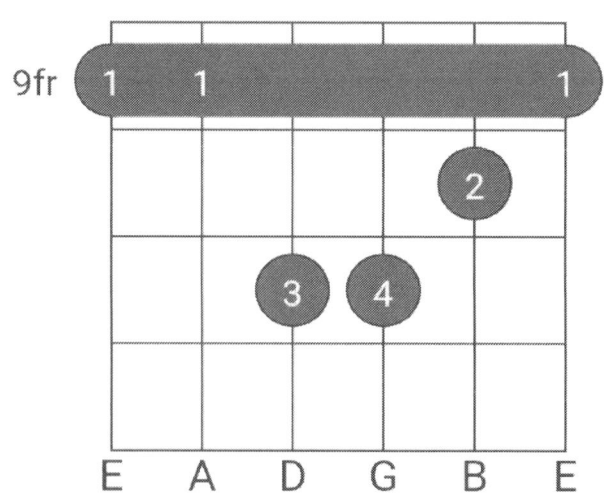

# F# / Gb dim

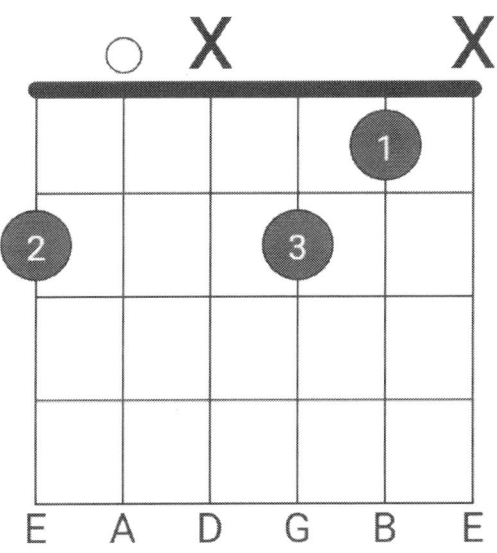
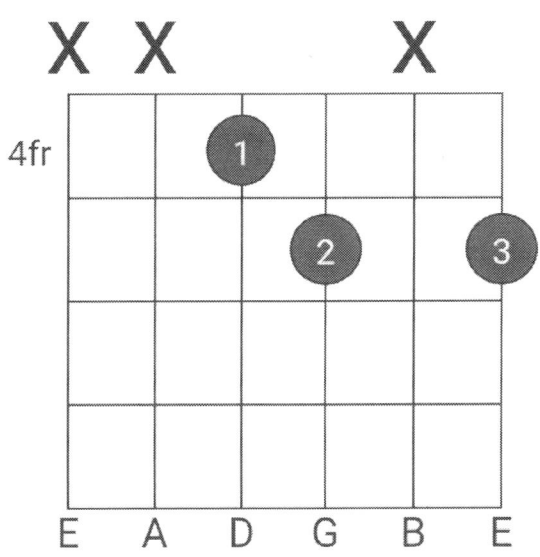
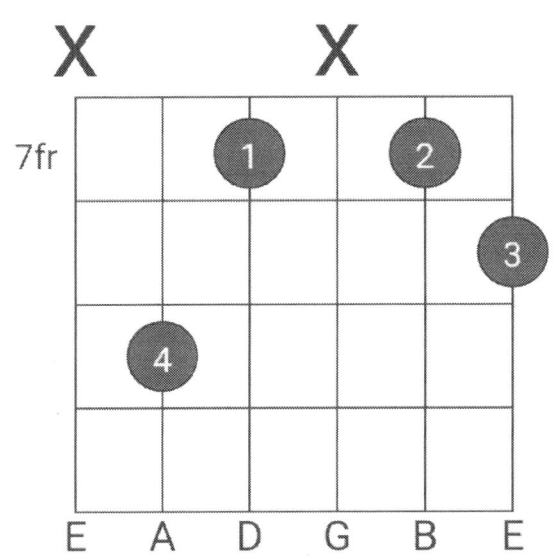
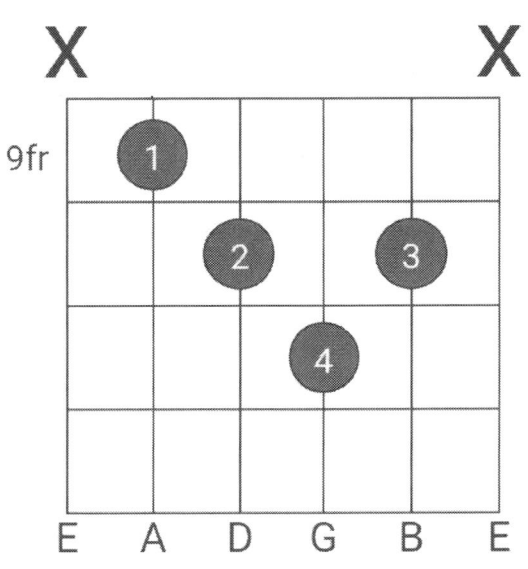

# F# / Gb Sus2

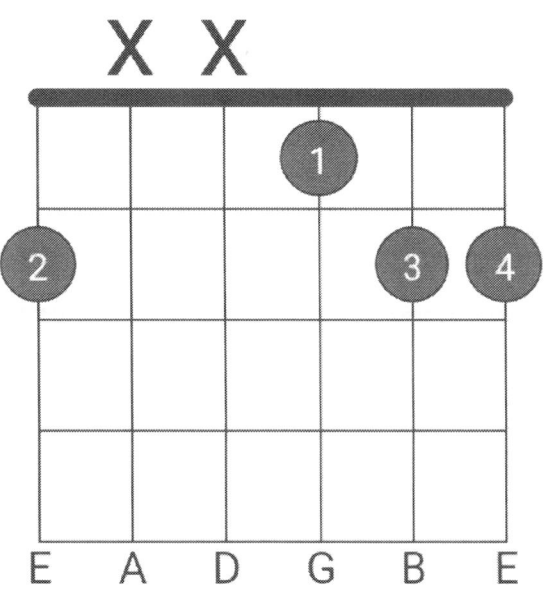
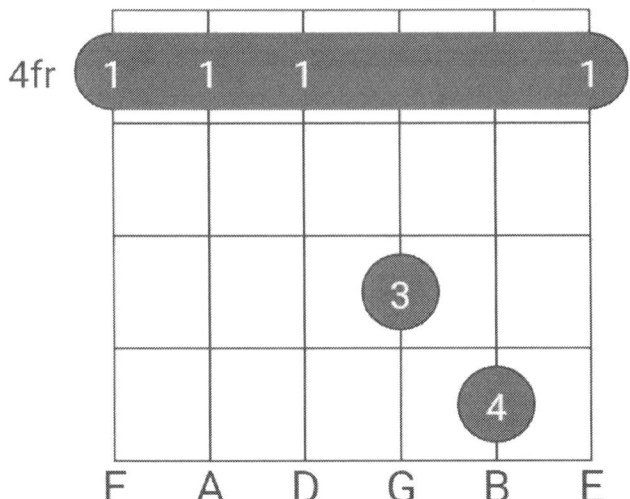
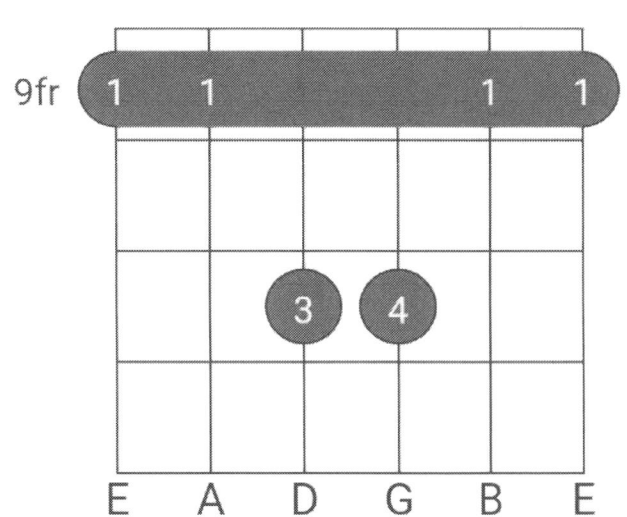
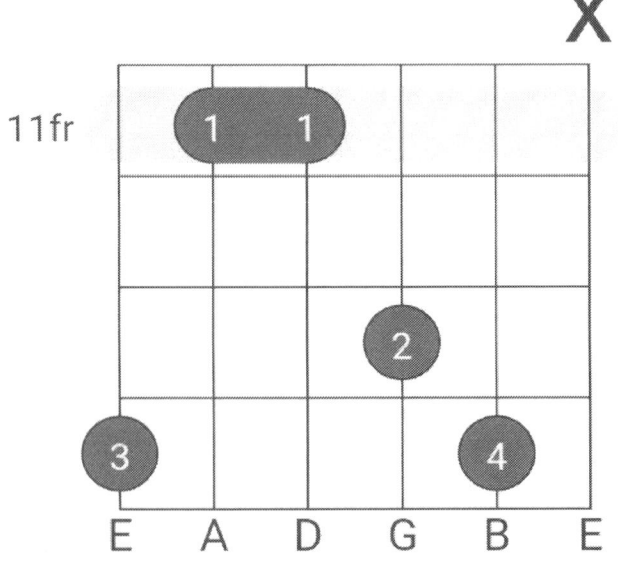

# F# / Gb Sus4

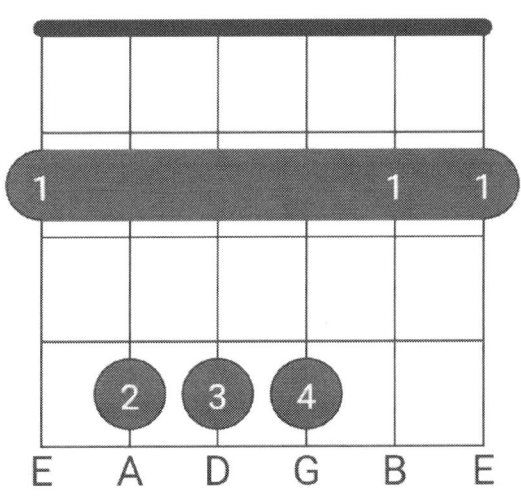
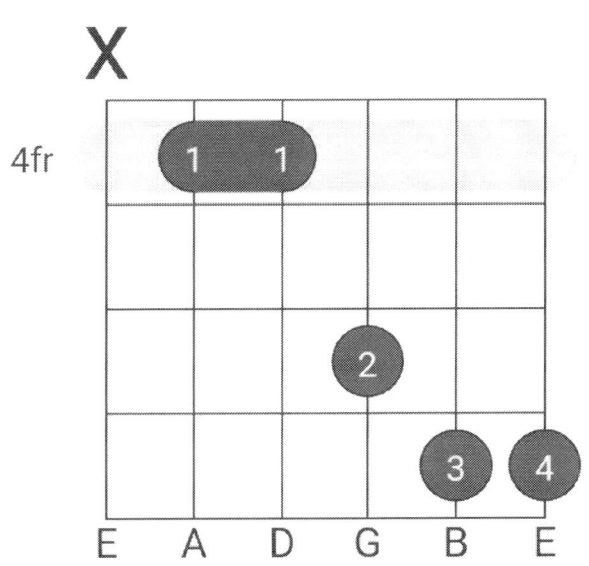
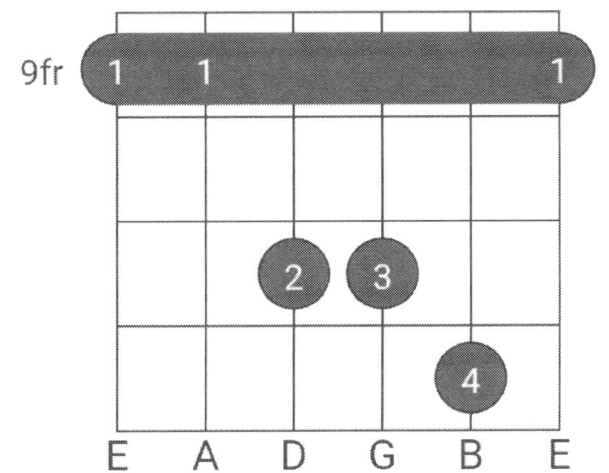
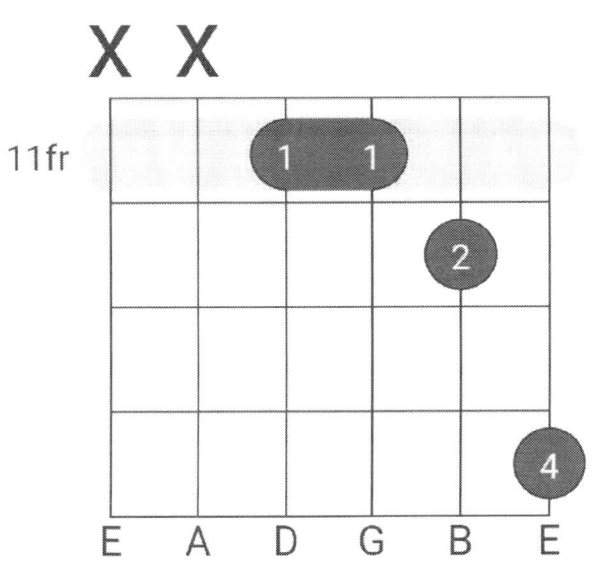

# F# / Gb aug

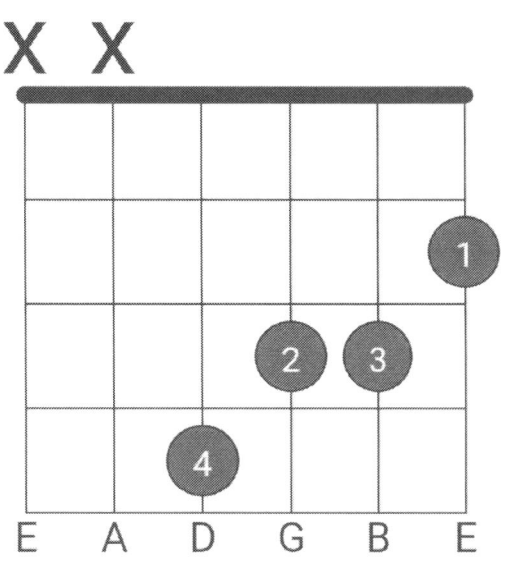
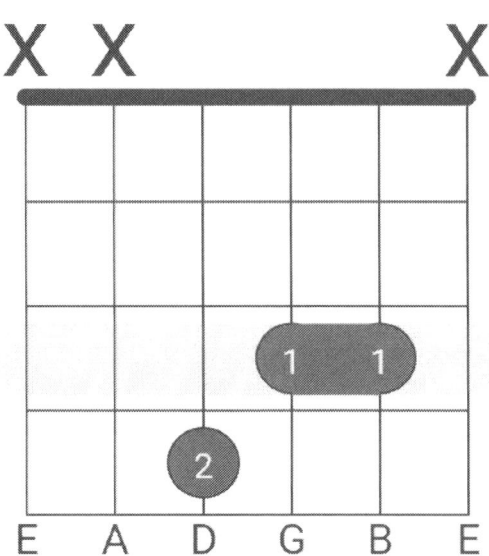
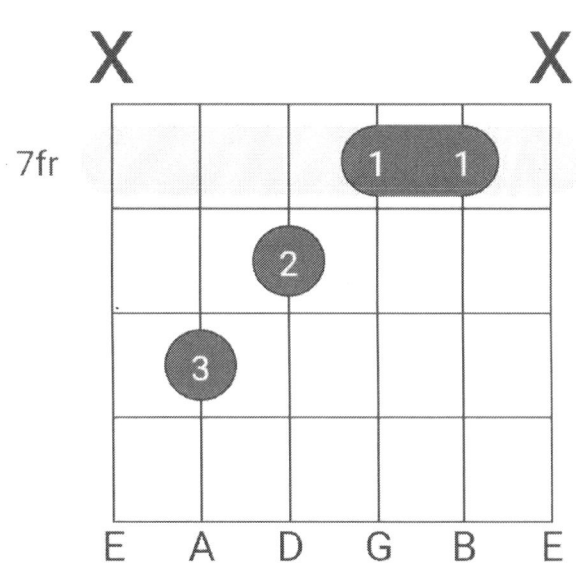
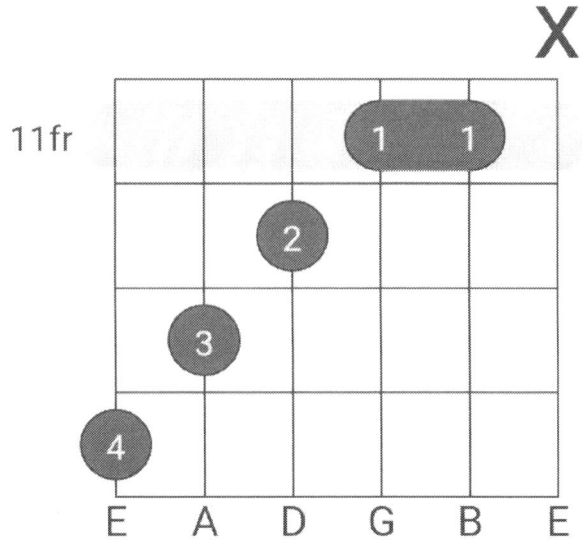

# F# / Gb7

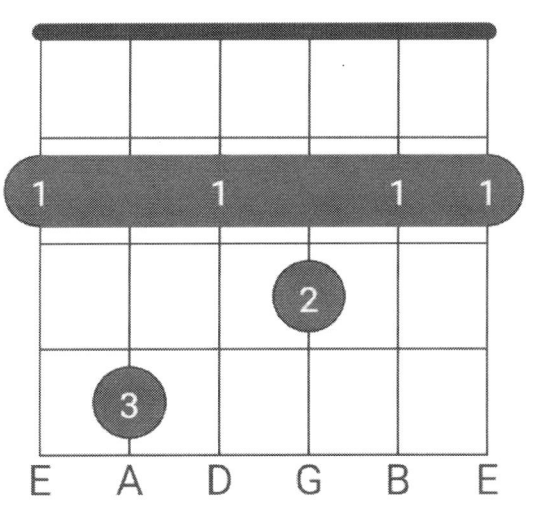
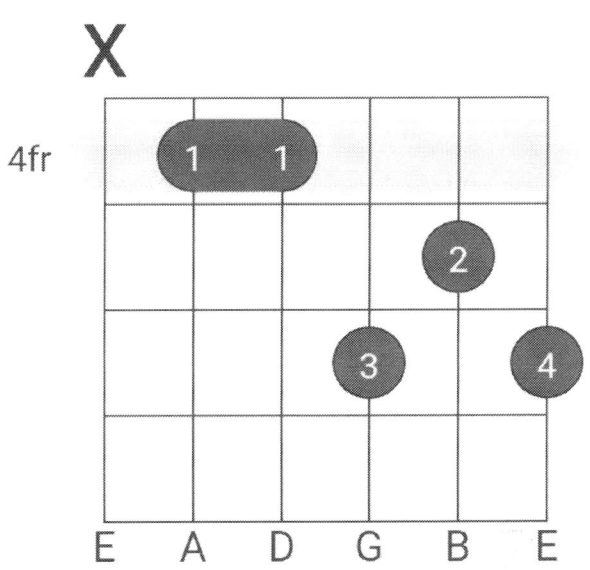
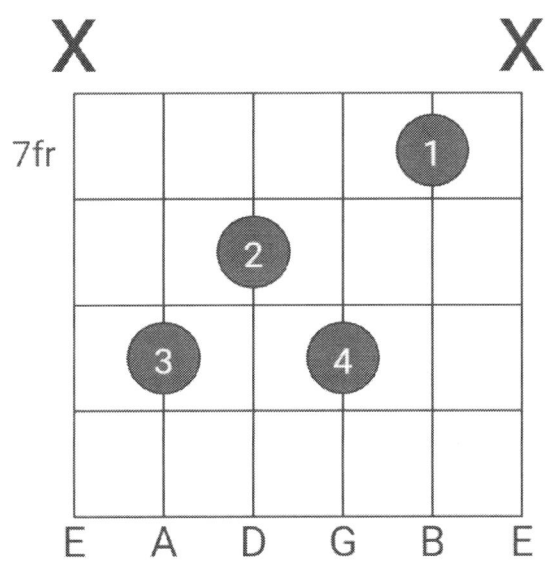
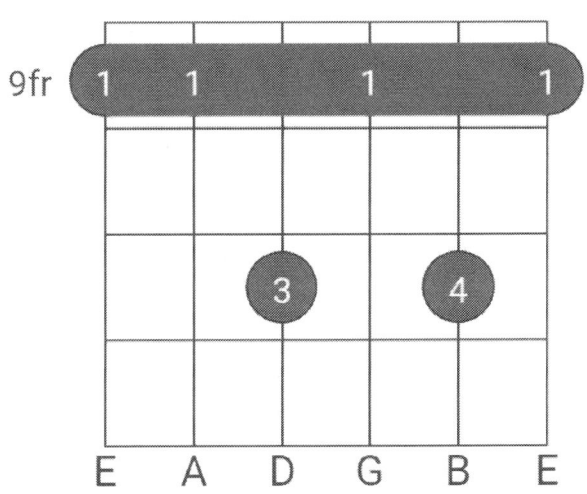

# F# / Gb maj7

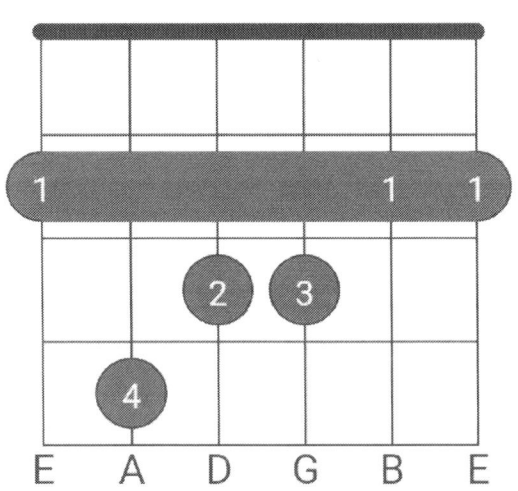
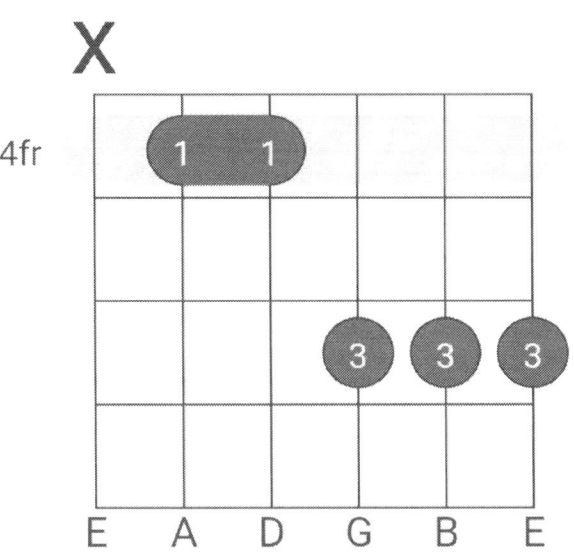
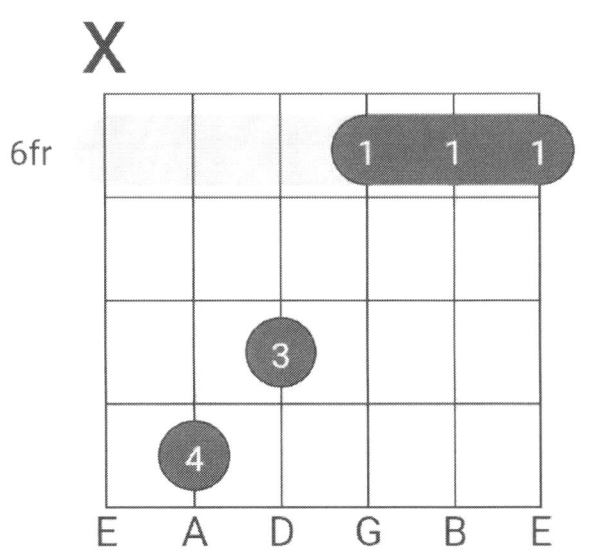
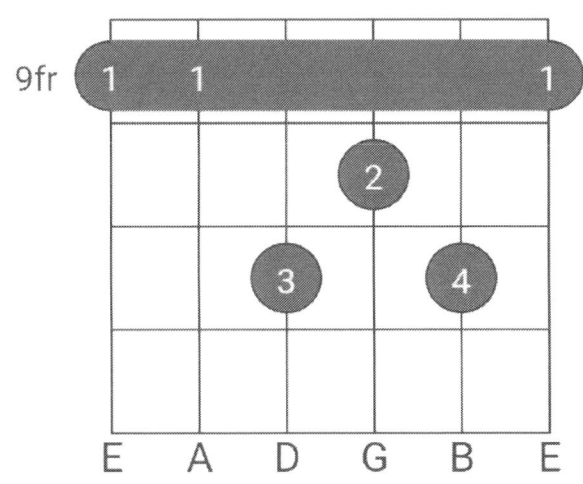

# F# / Gb m7

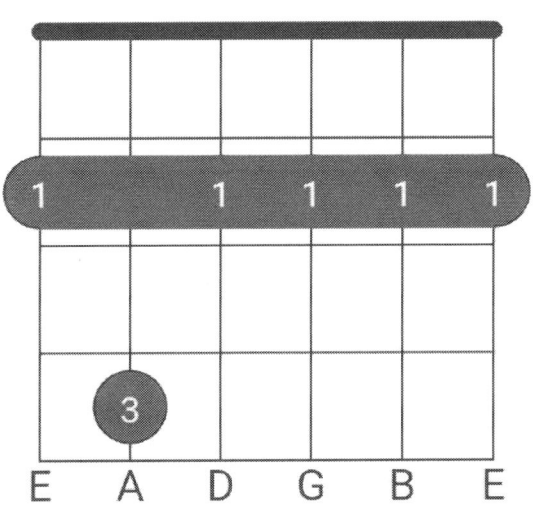
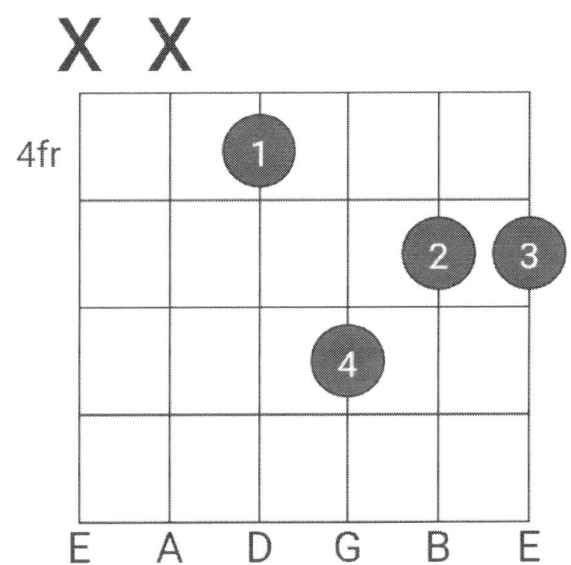
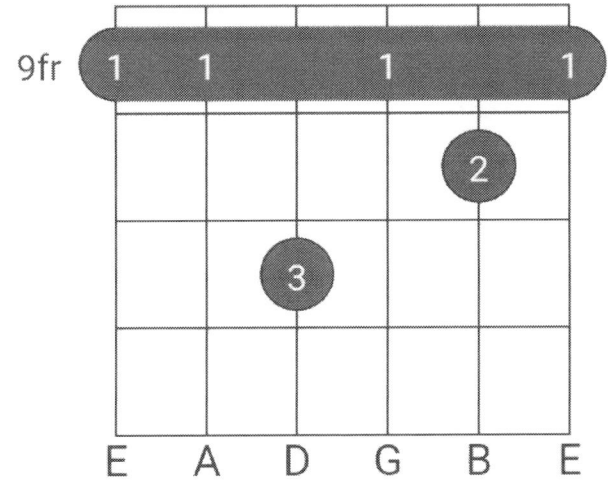
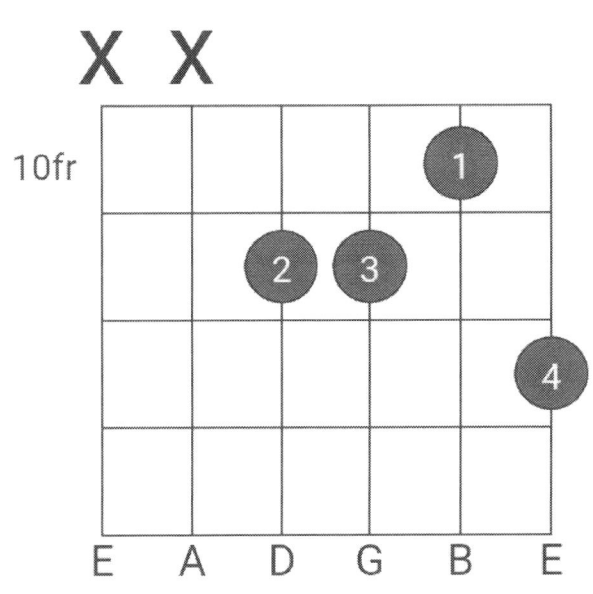

# G Major

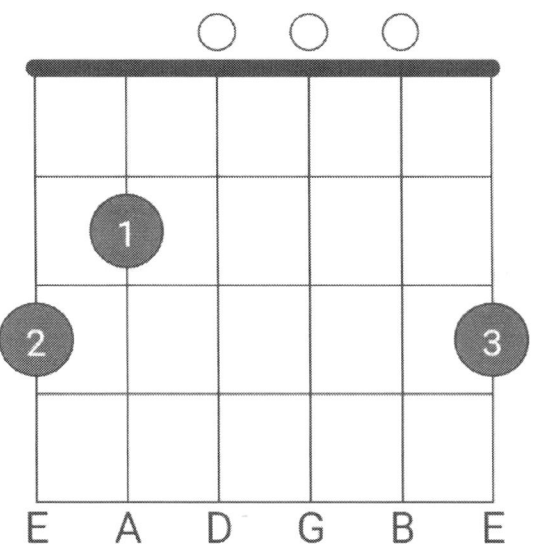
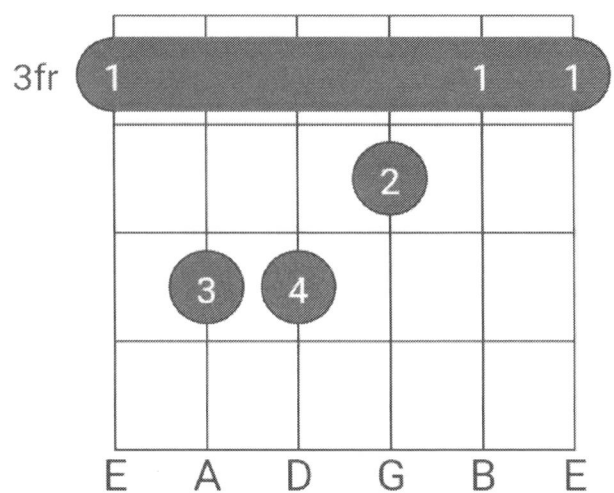
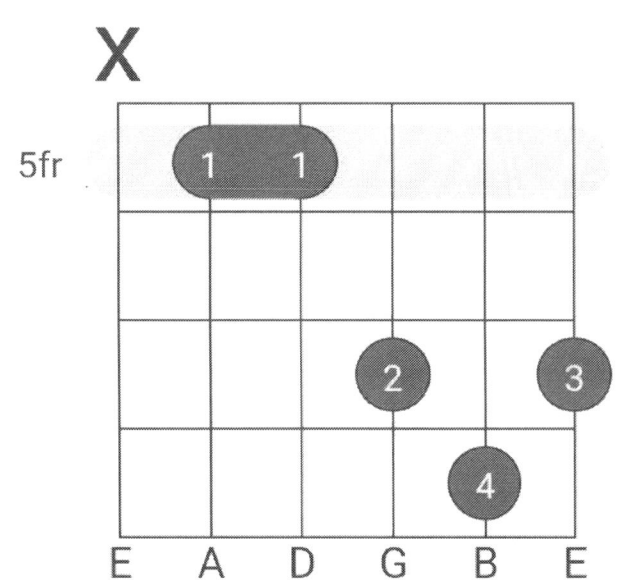
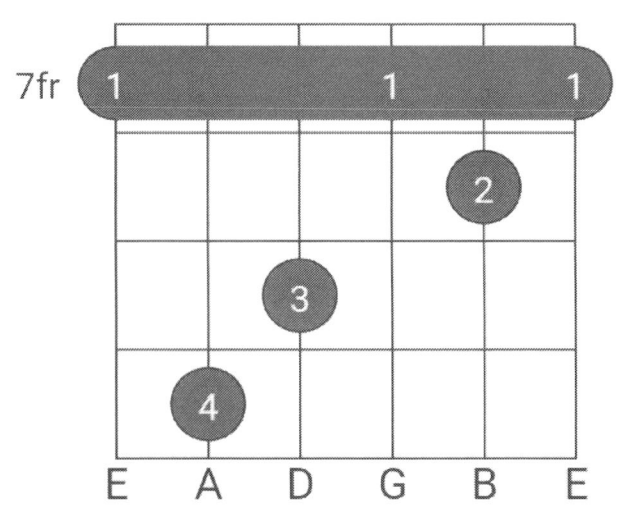

# G minor

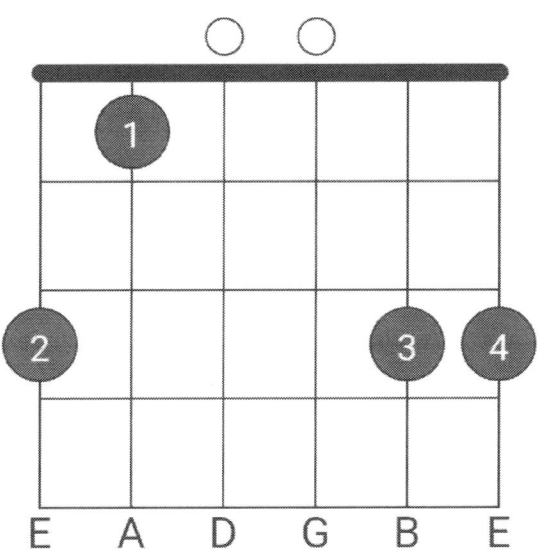
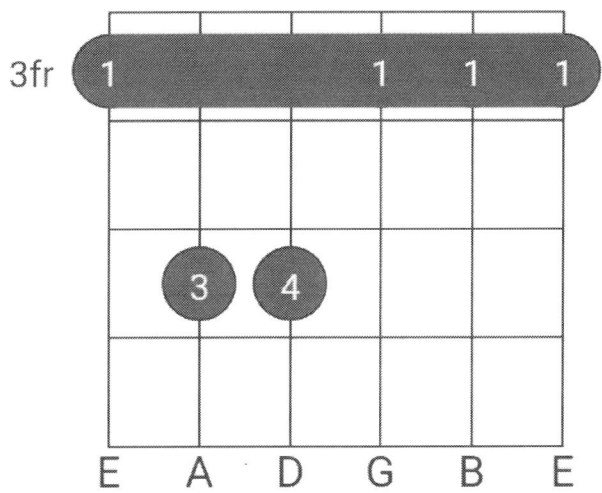
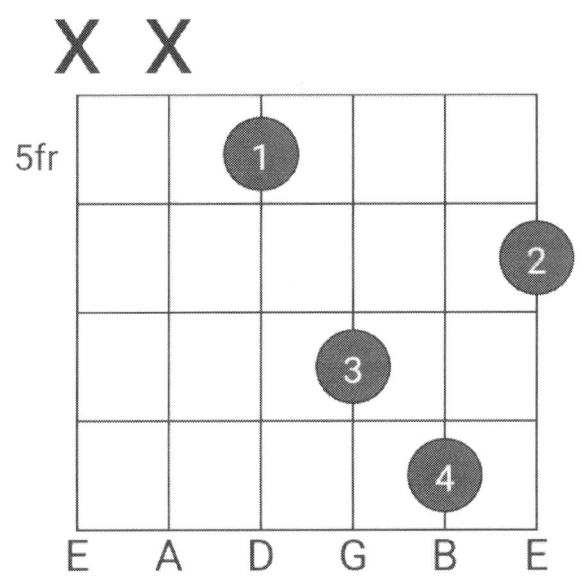
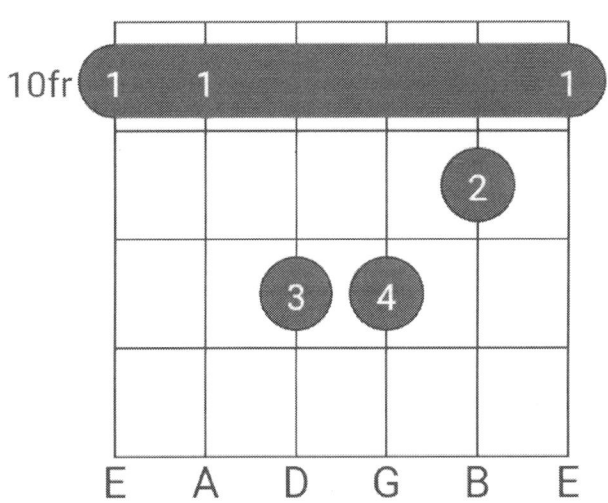

# G dim

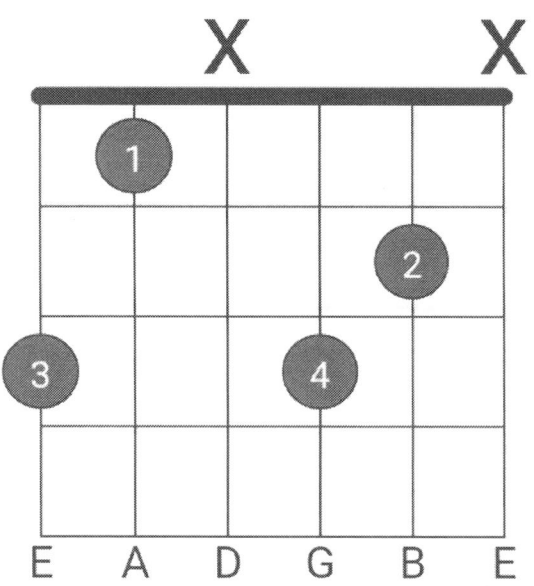
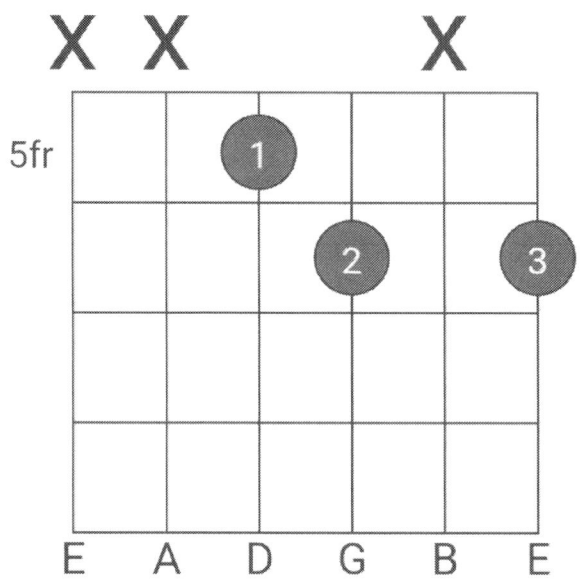
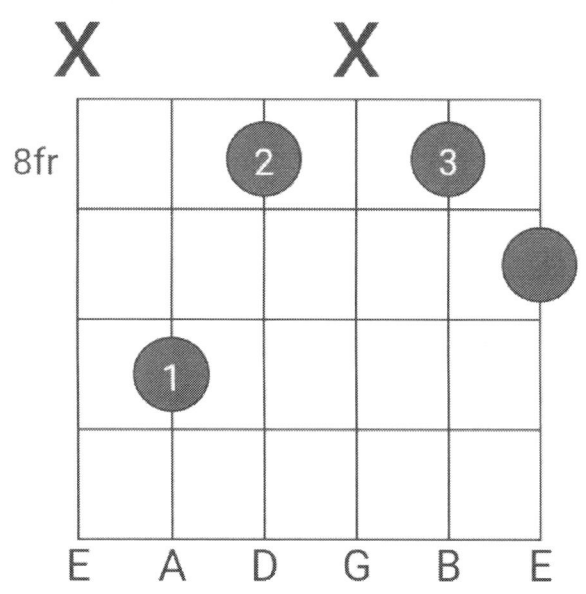
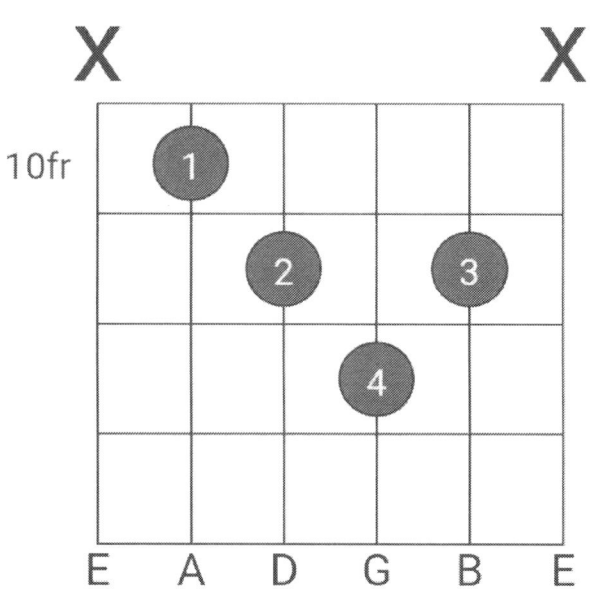

# G Sus2

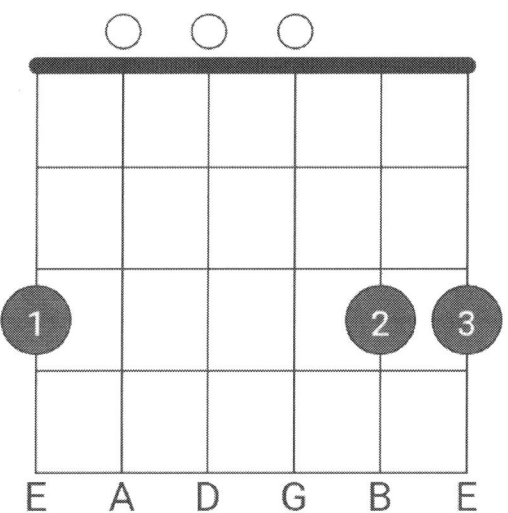
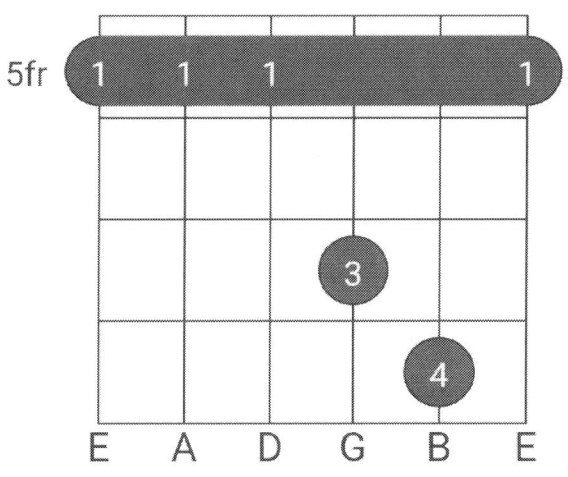
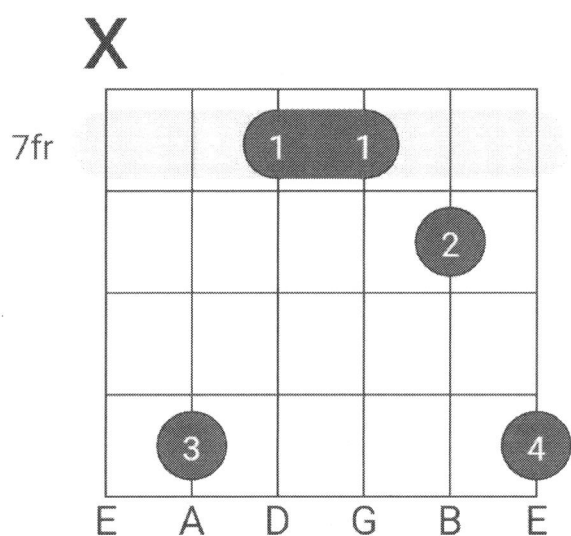
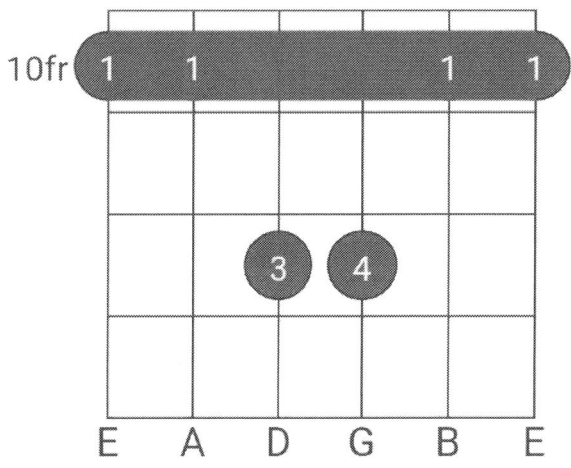

# G Sus4

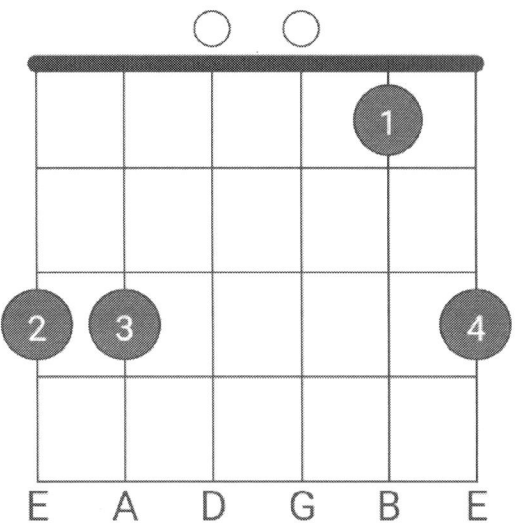
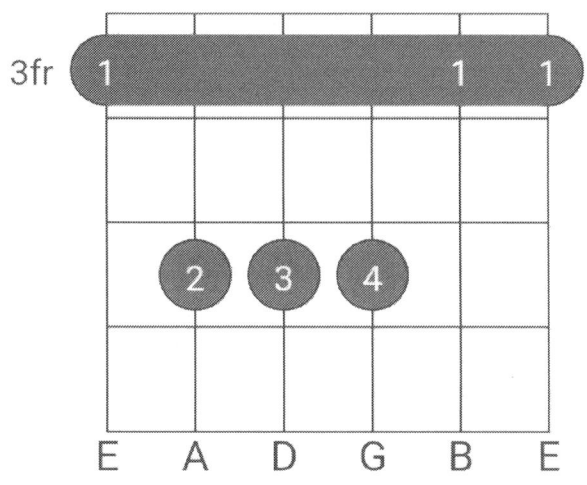
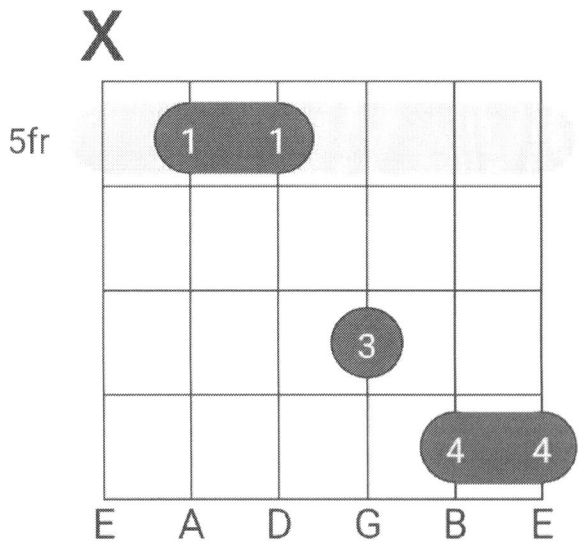
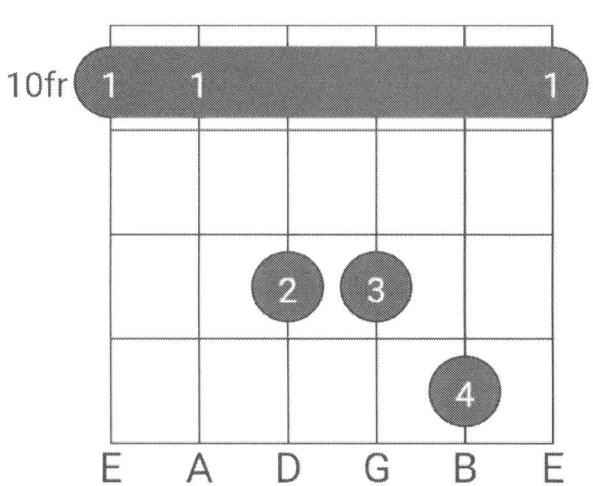

# G aug

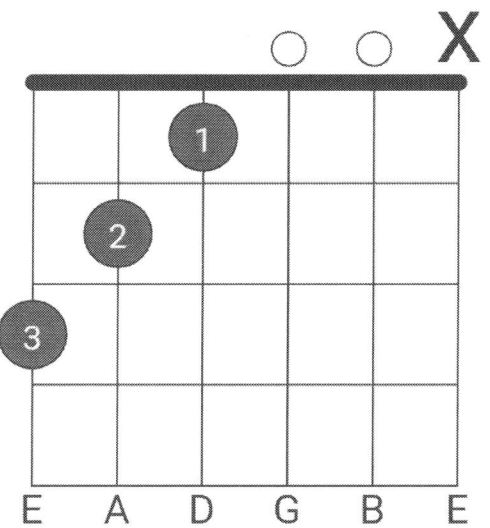
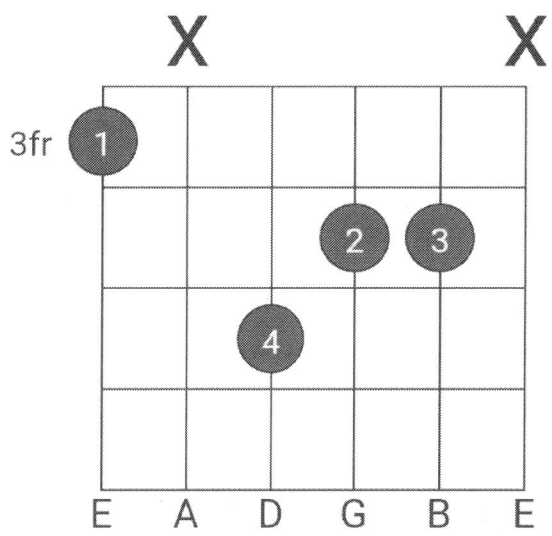
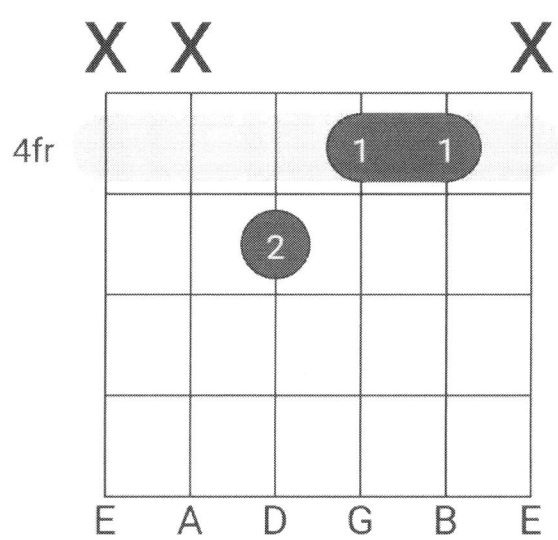
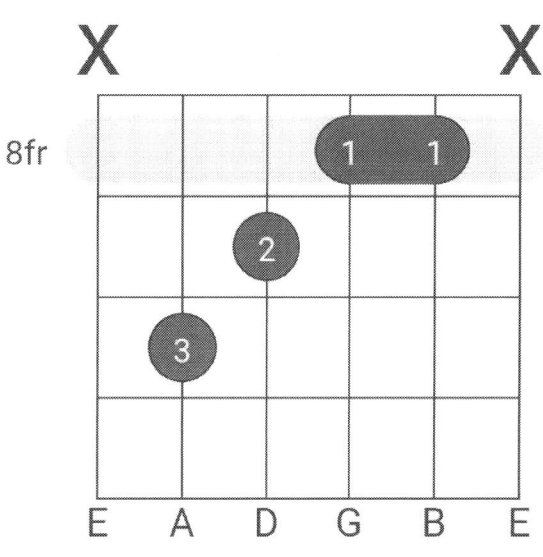

# G7

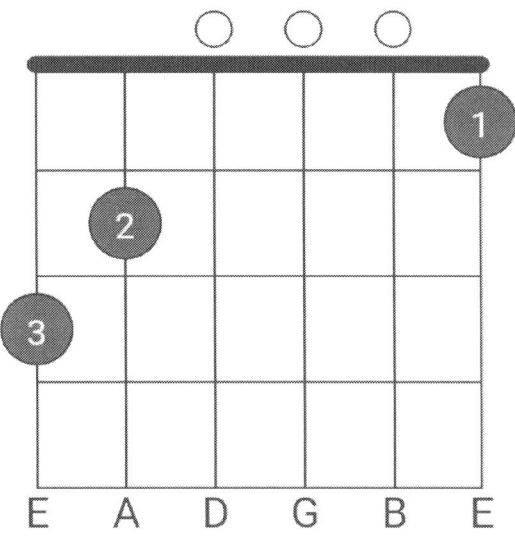
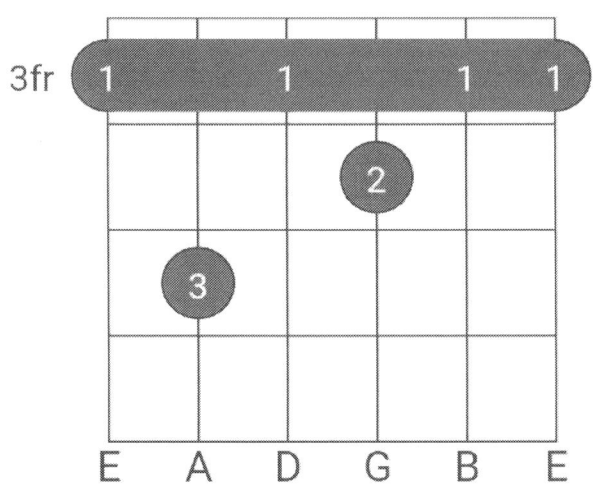
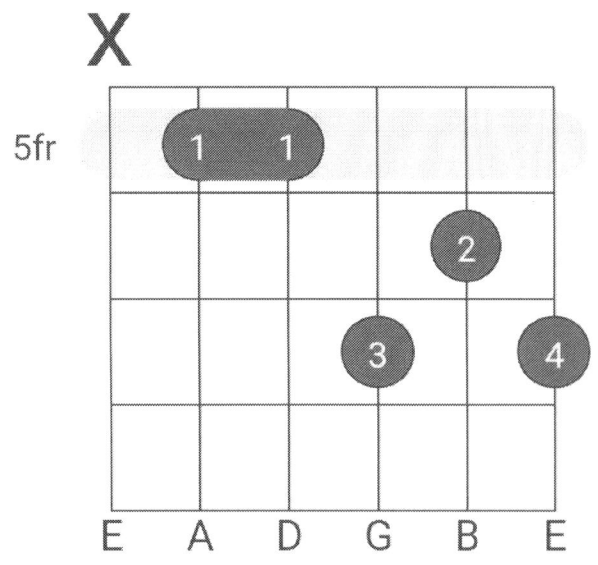
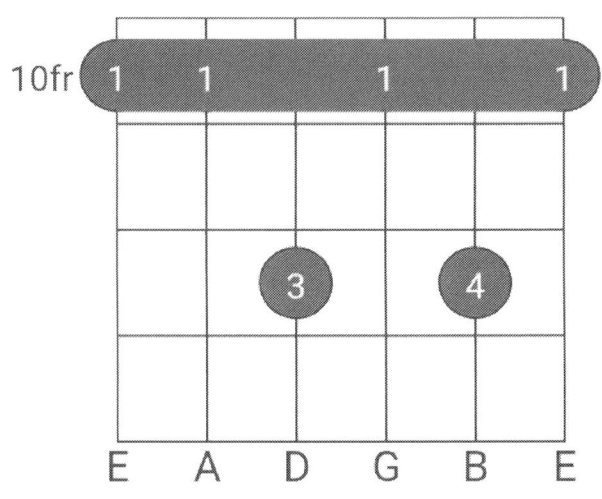

# G maj7

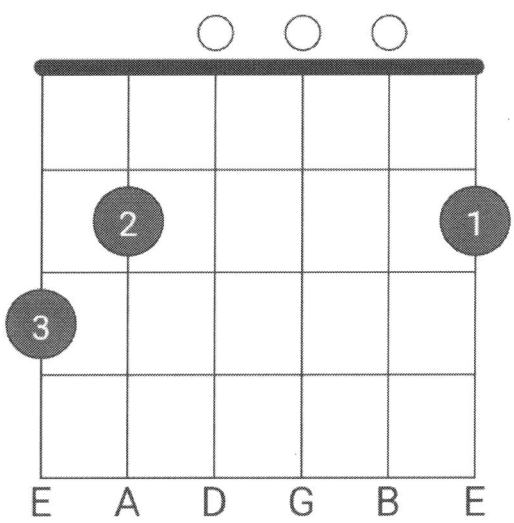
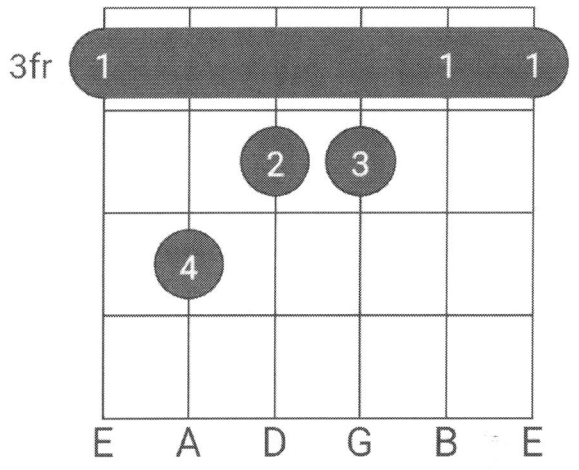
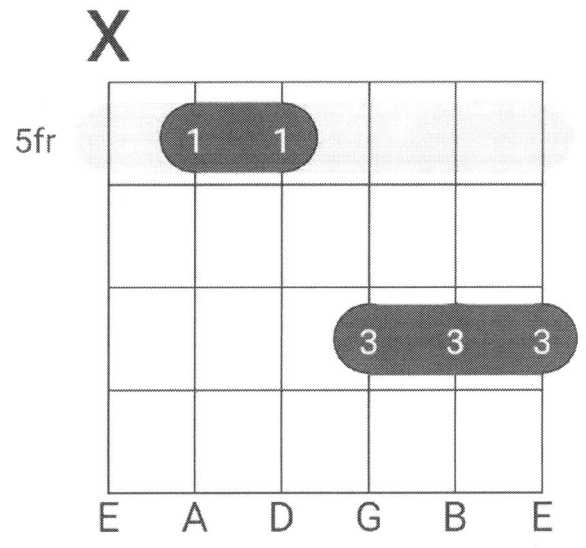
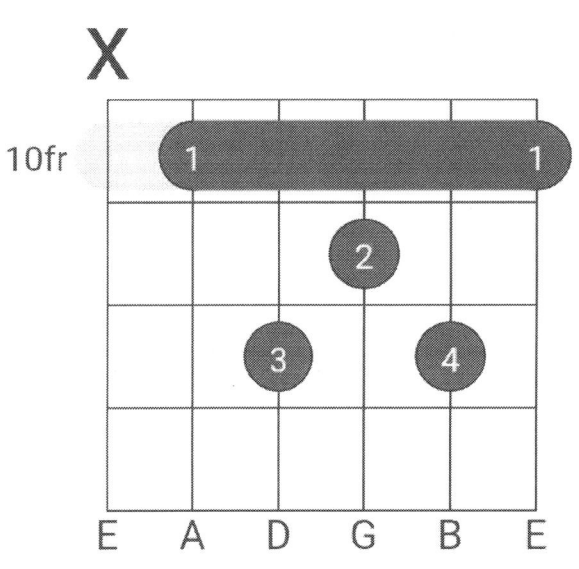

# Gm7

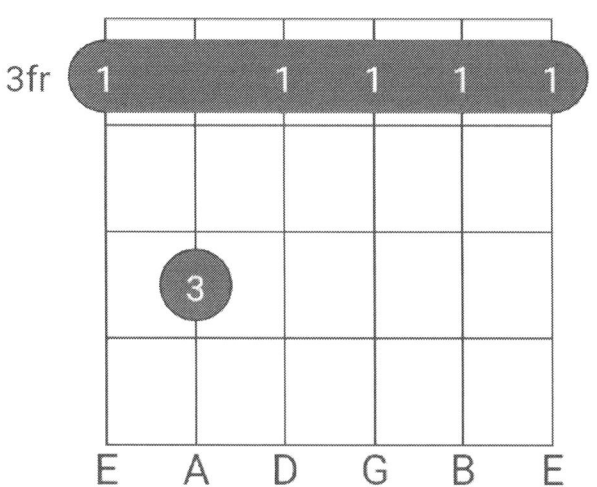
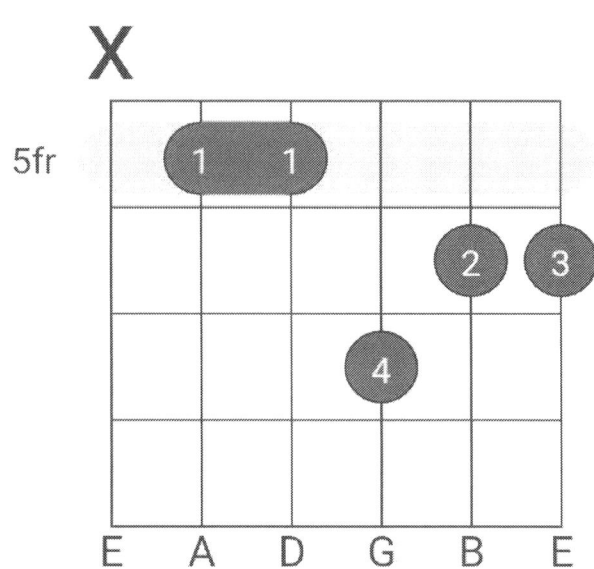
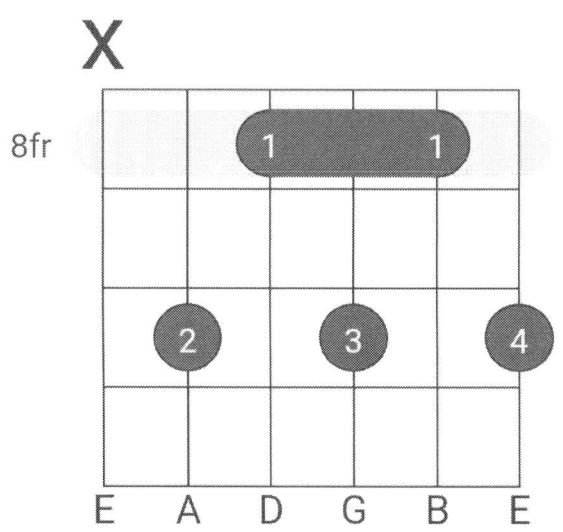
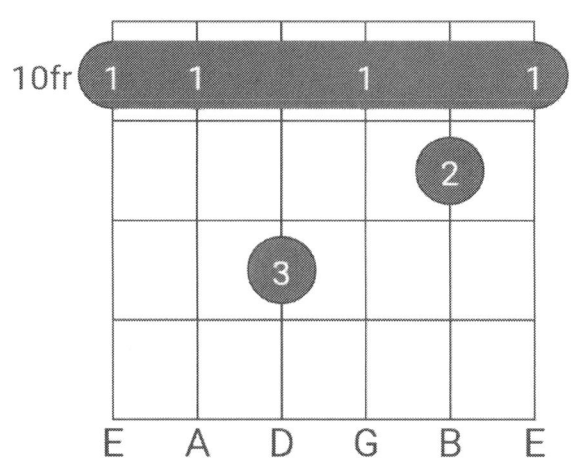

# G# / Ab Major

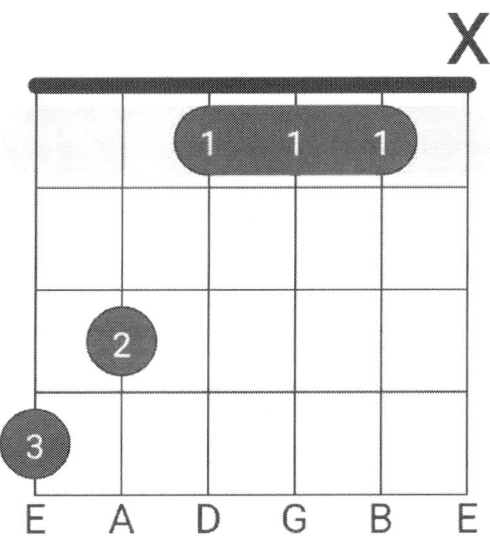
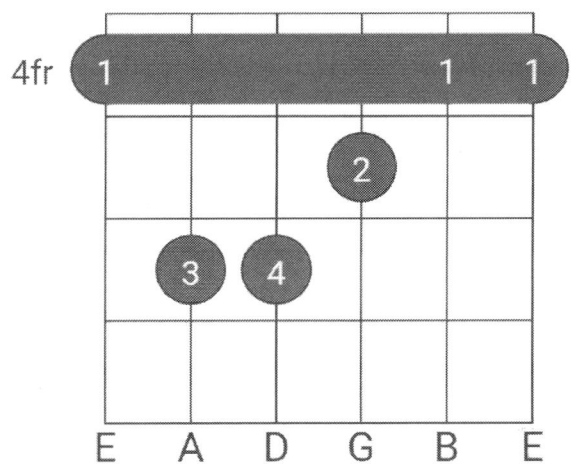
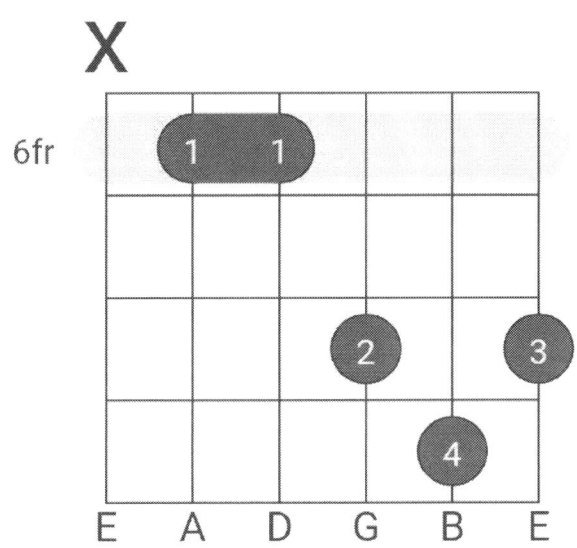
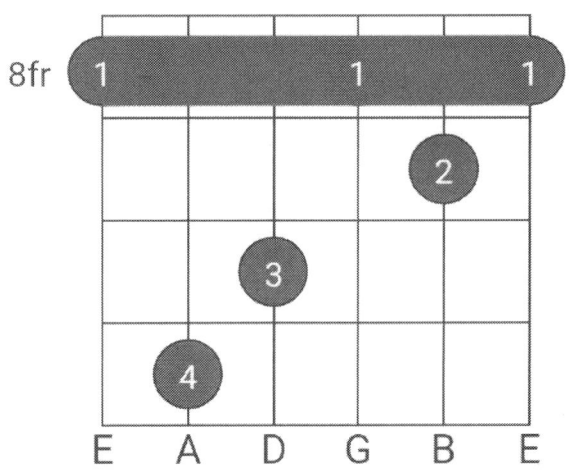

# G# / Ab minor

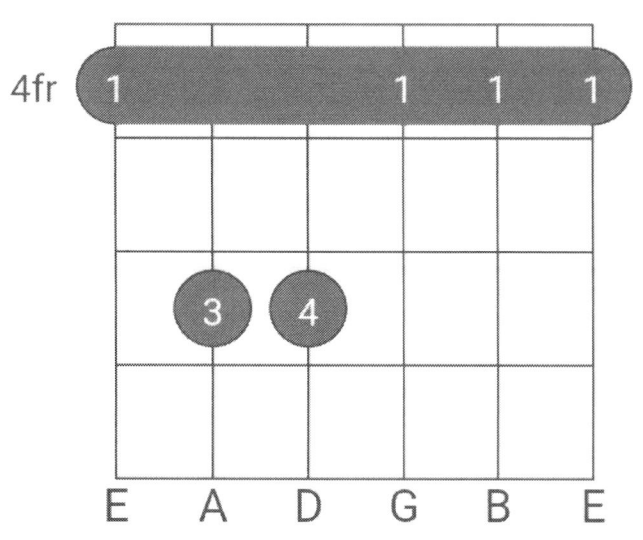
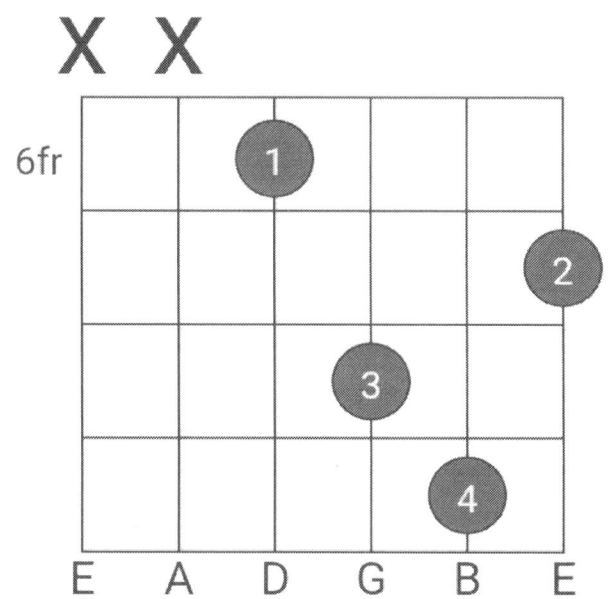
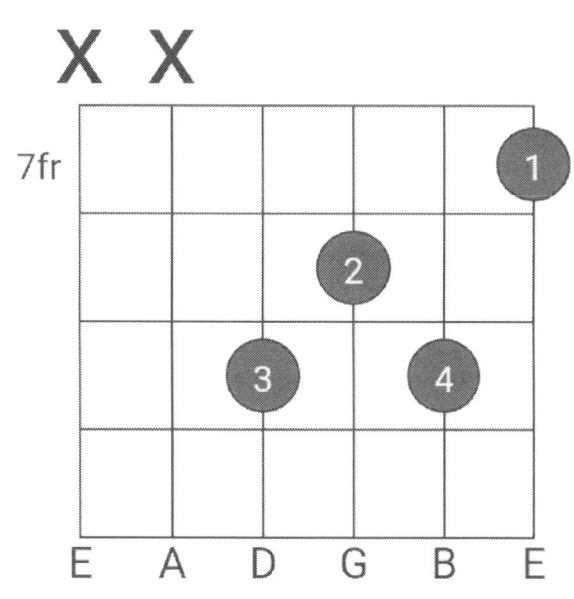
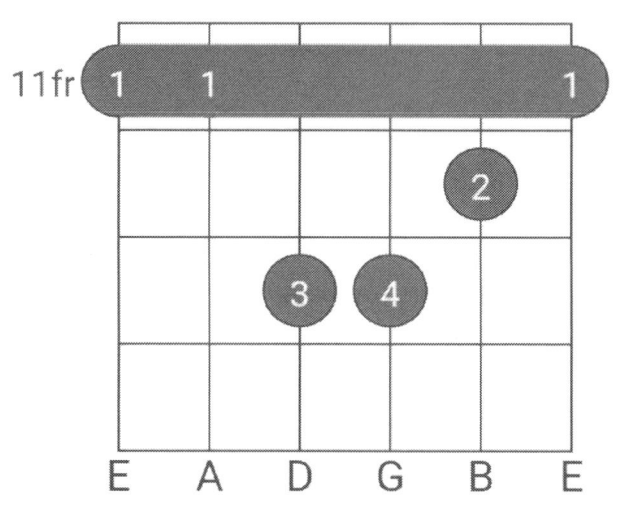

# G# / Ab dim

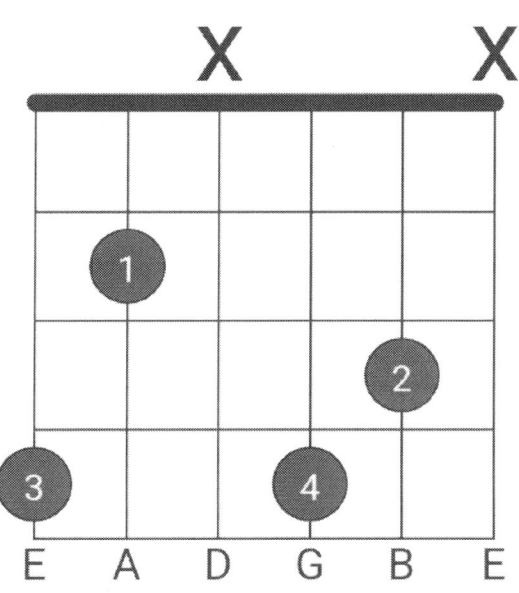
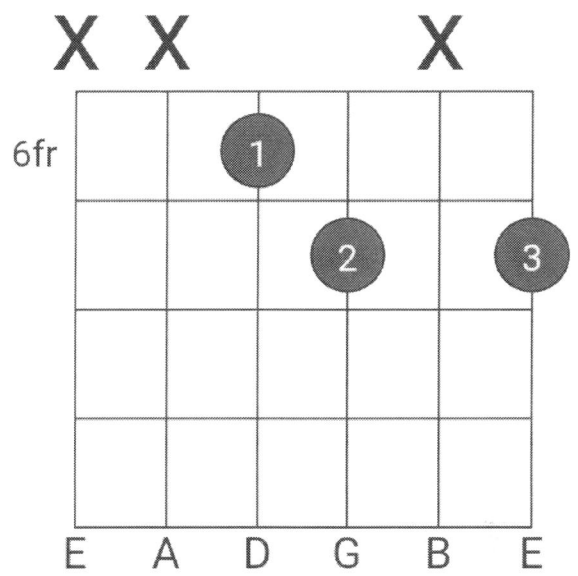
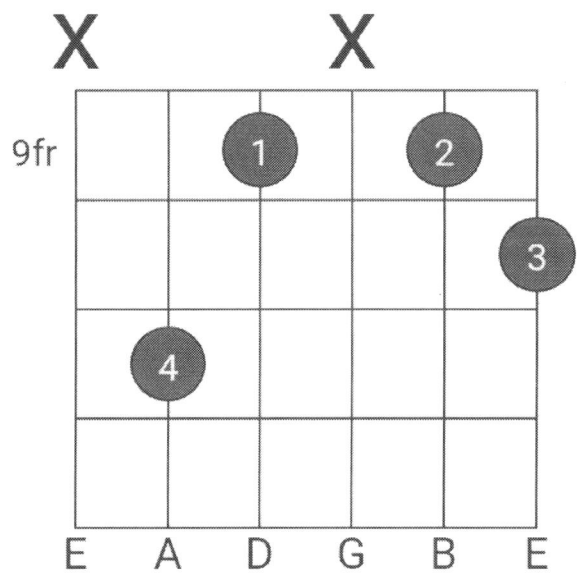
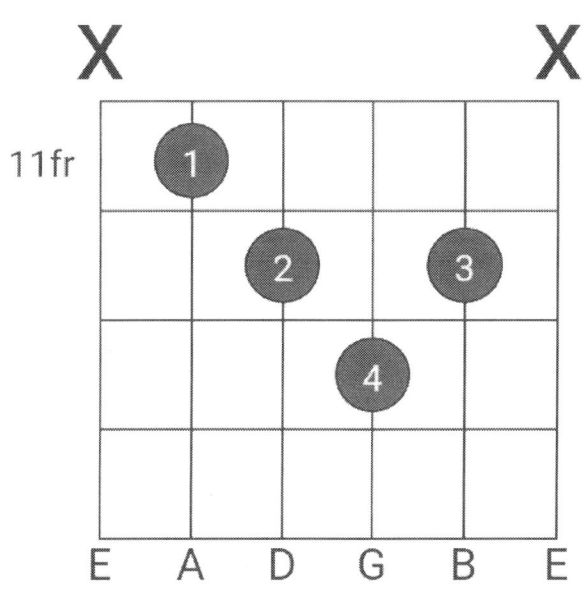

# G# / Ab Sus2

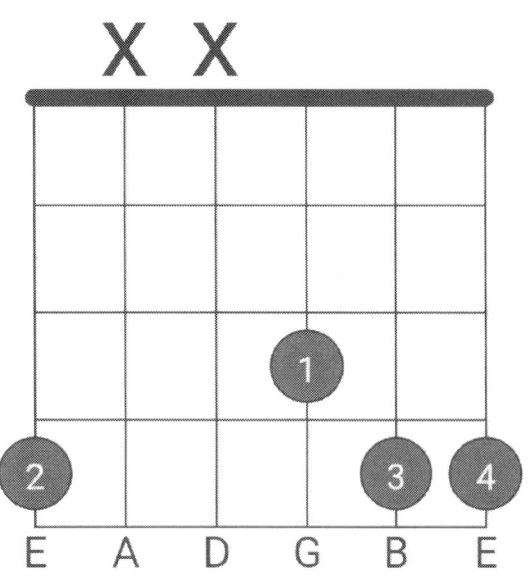
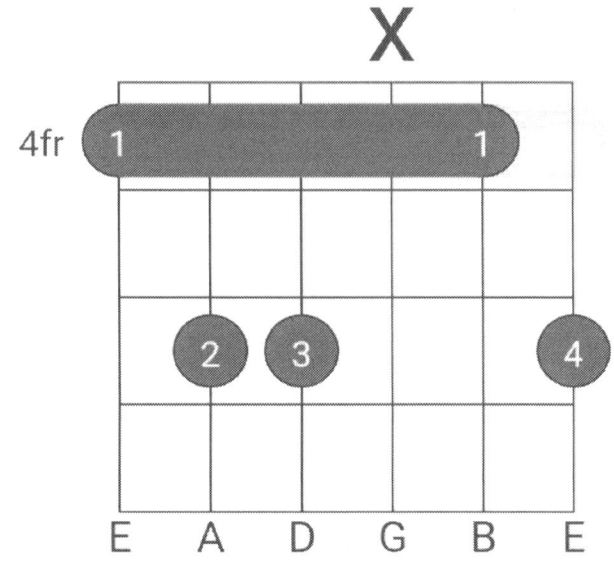
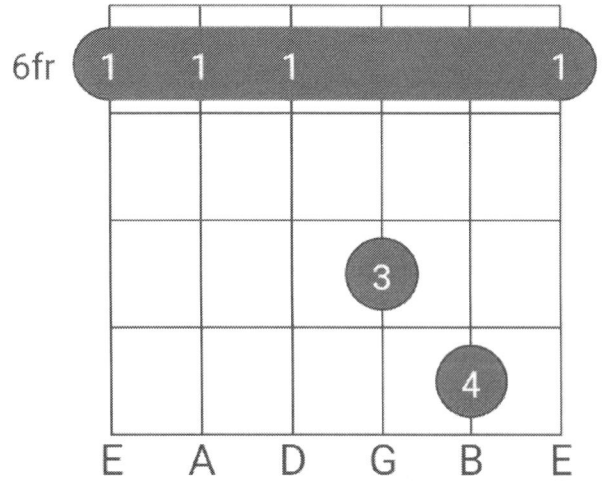
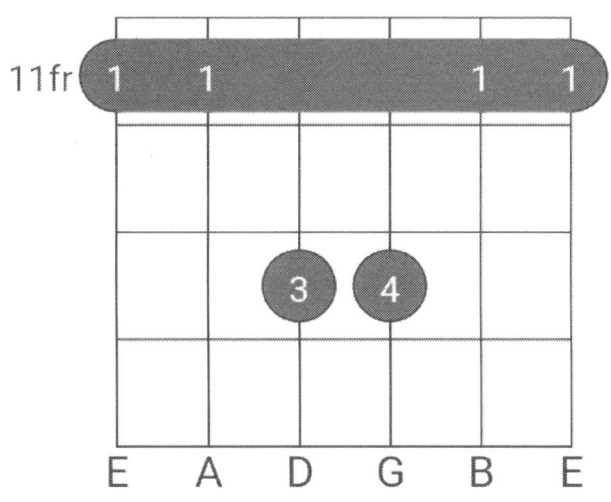

# G# / Ab Sus4

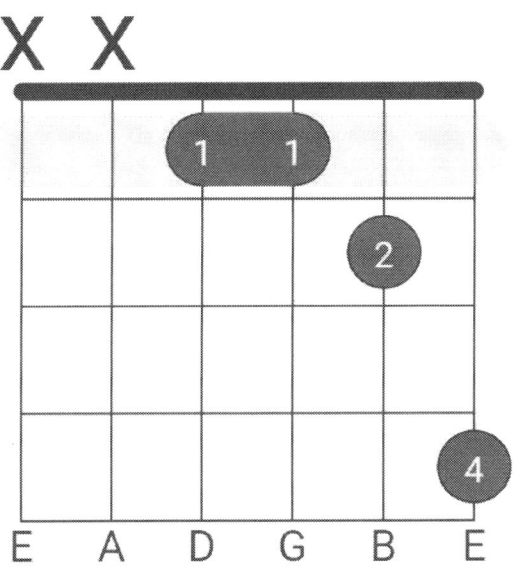
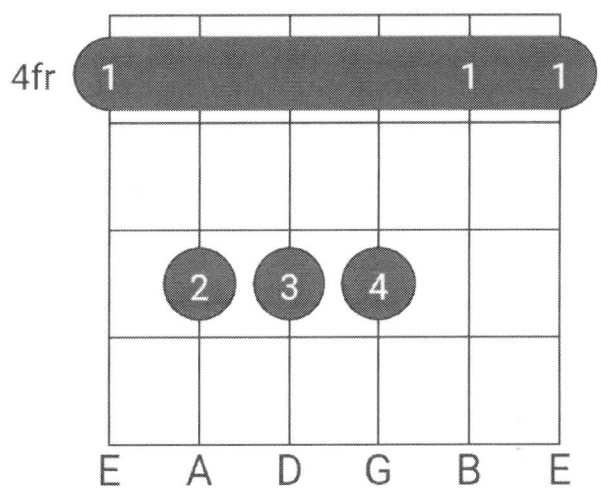
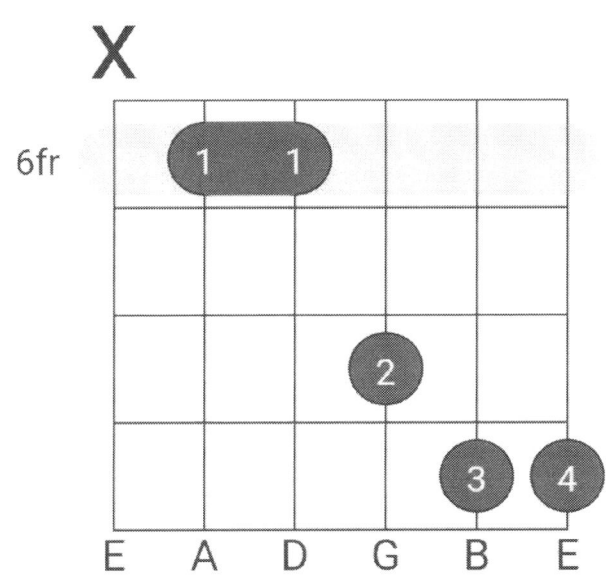
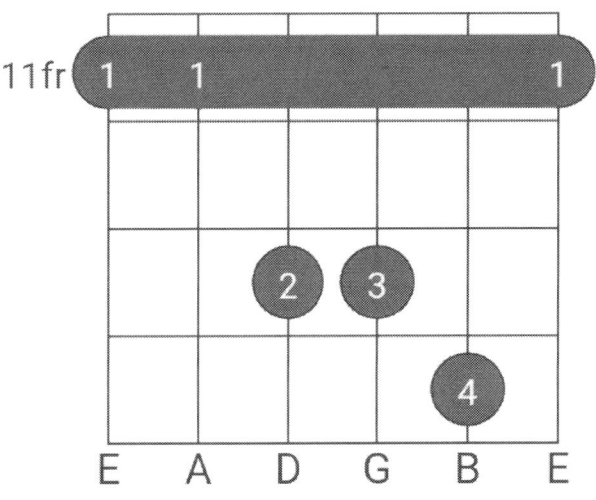

# G# / Ab aug

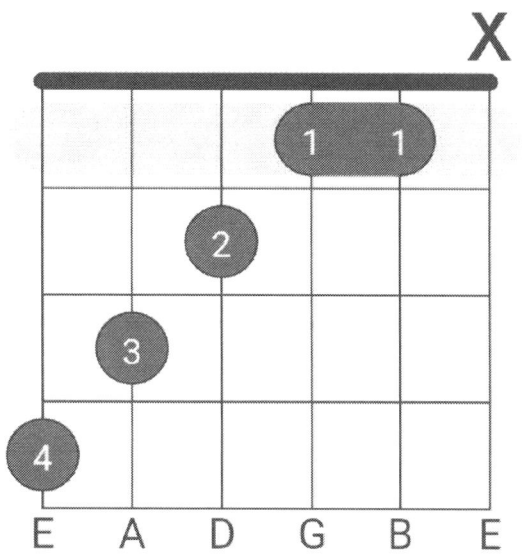
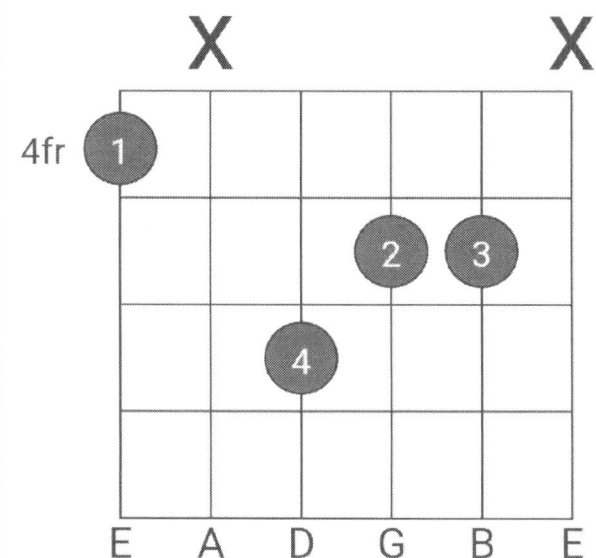
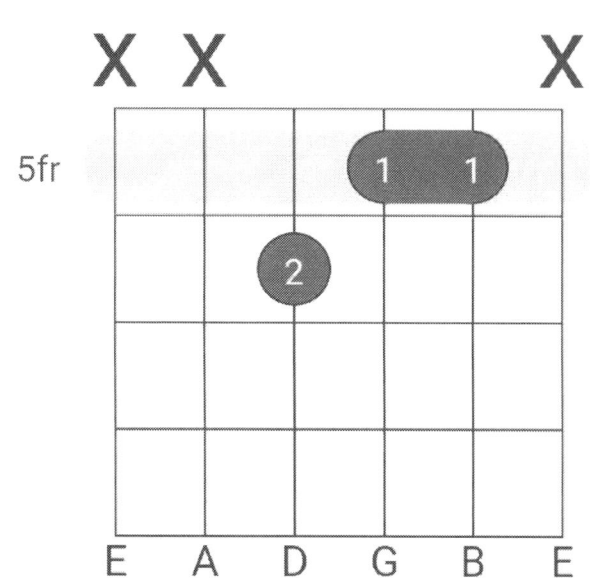
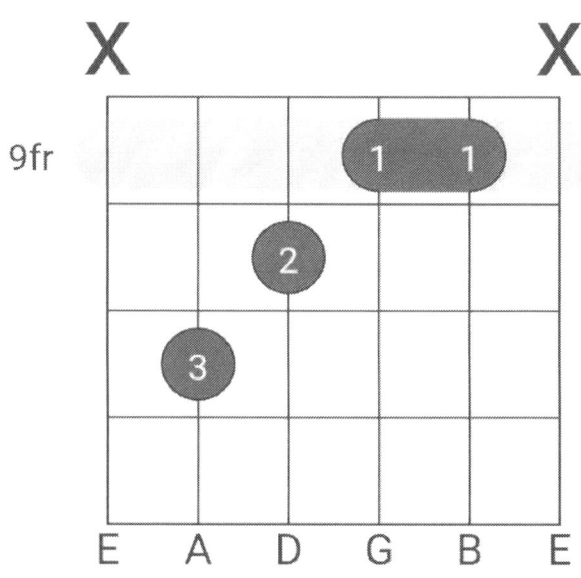

# G# / Ab7

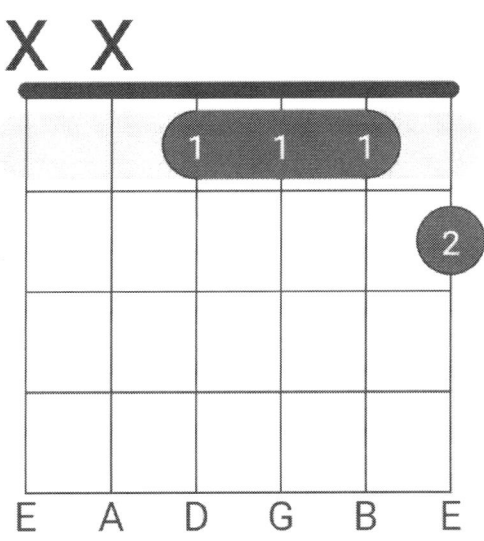
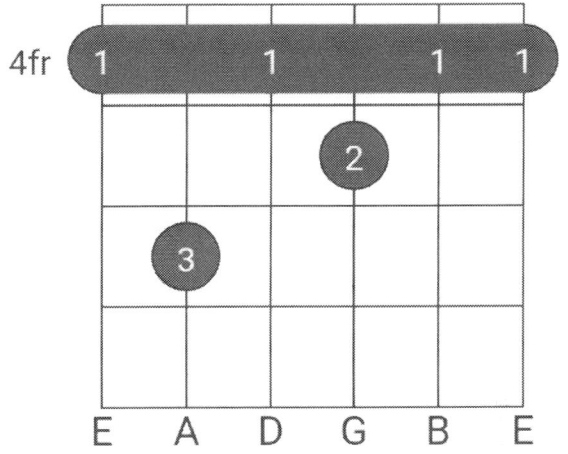
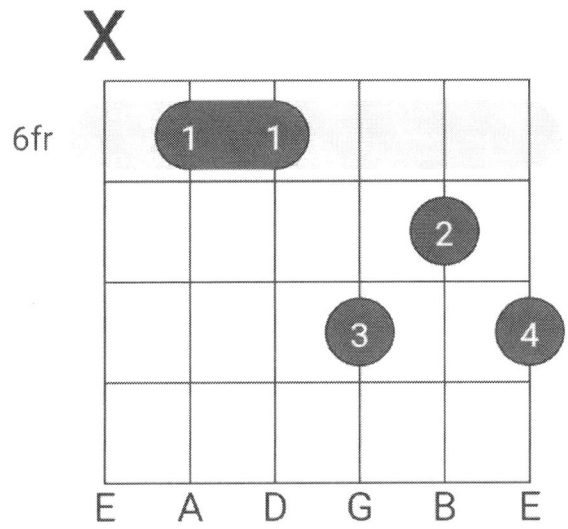
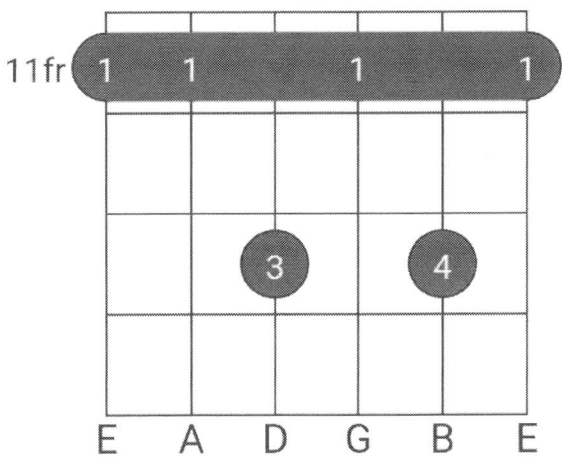

# G# / Ab maj7

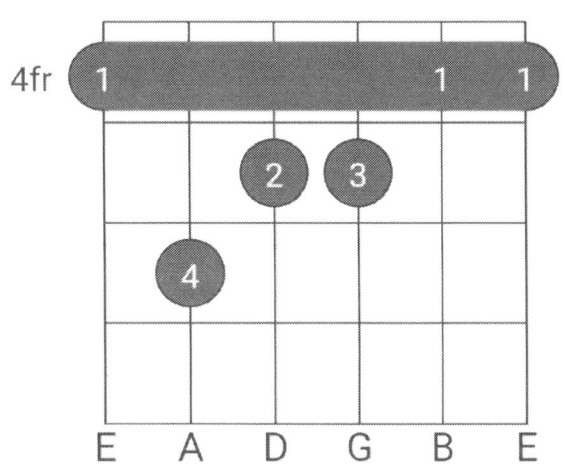
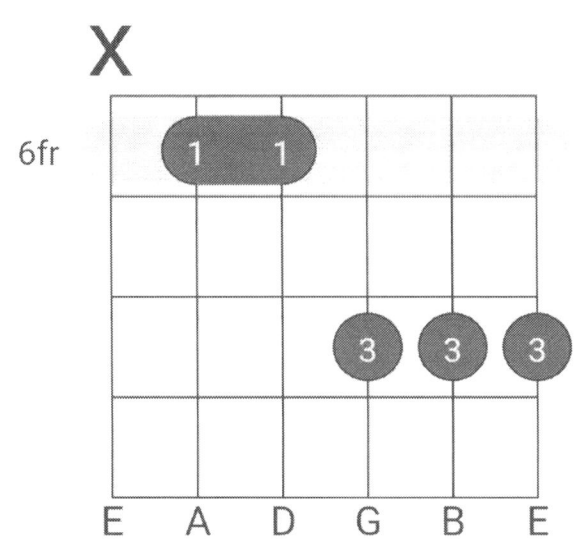
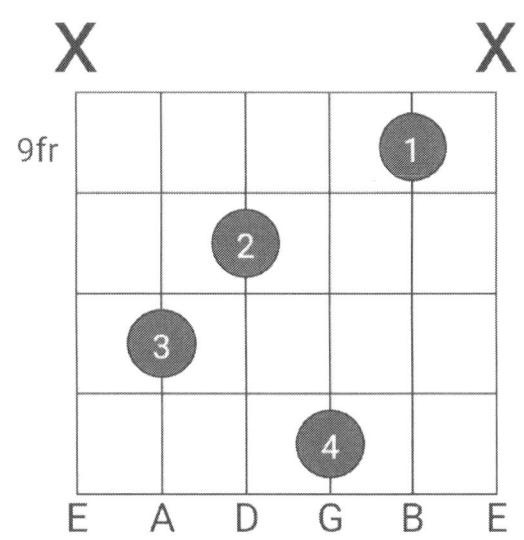
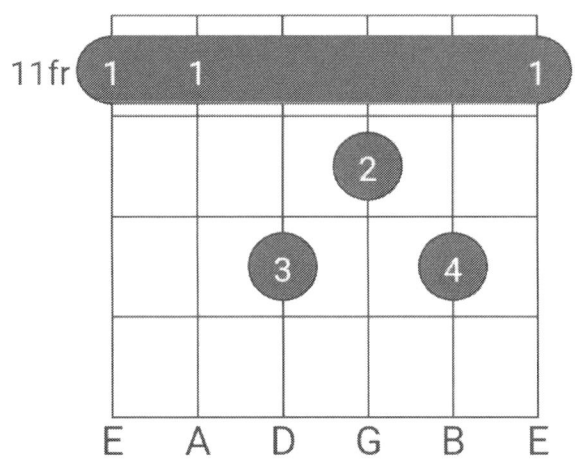

# G# / Ab m7

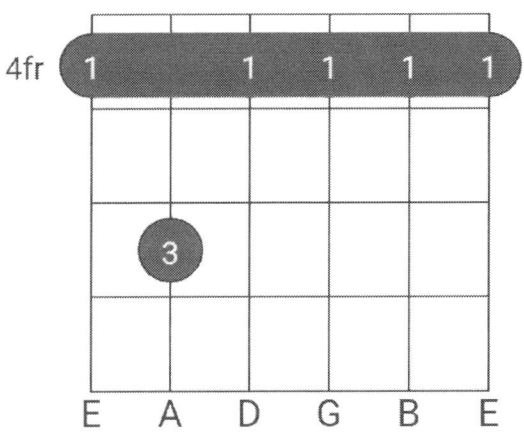
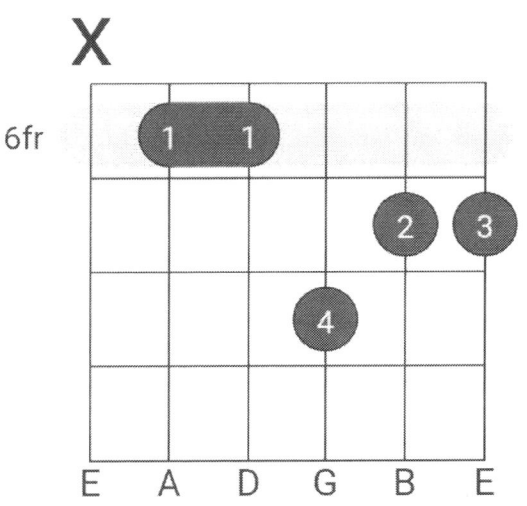
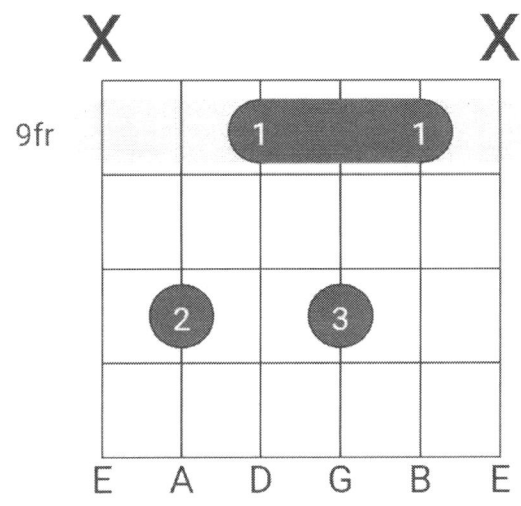
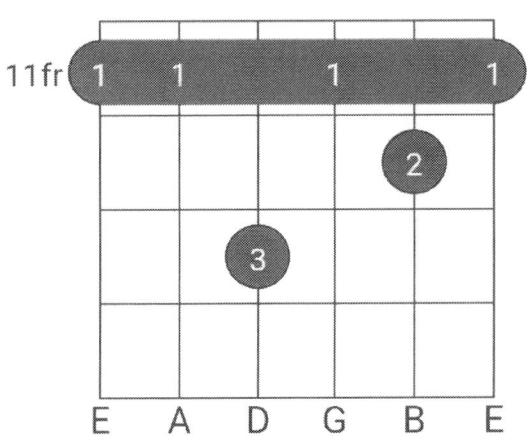

# A Major

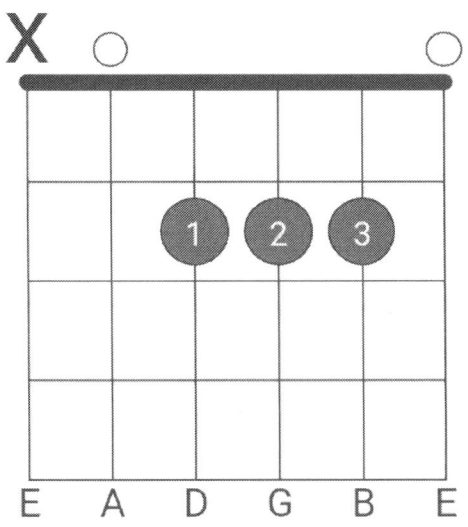
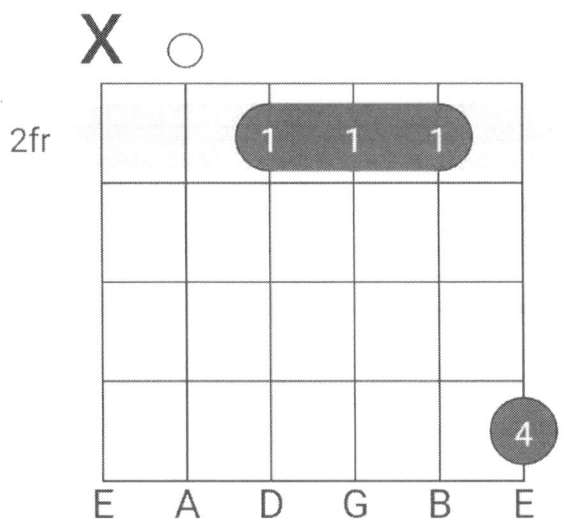
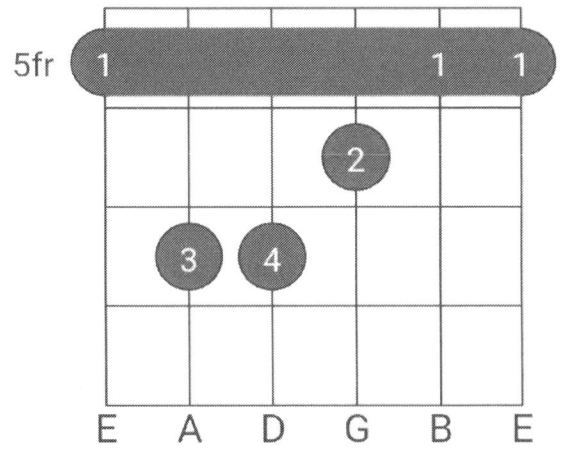
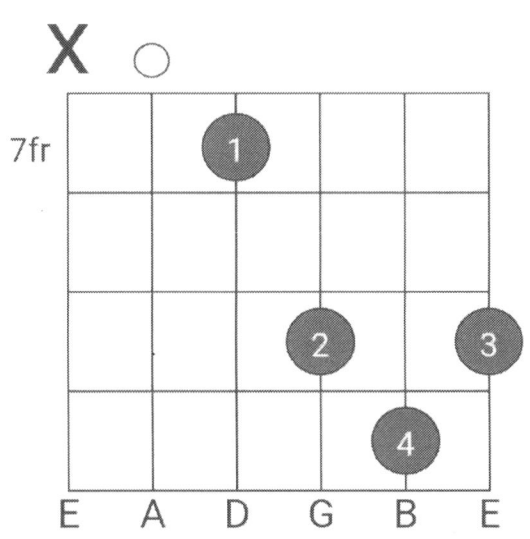

# A minor

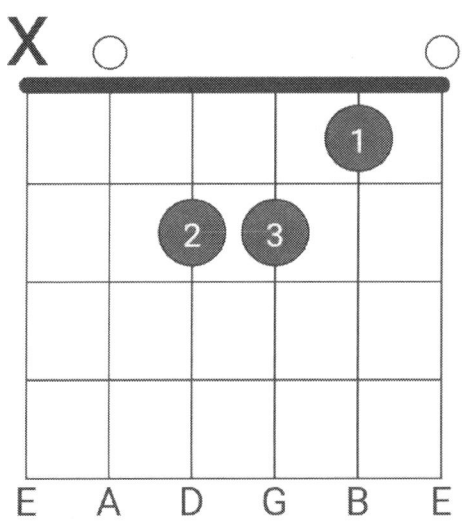
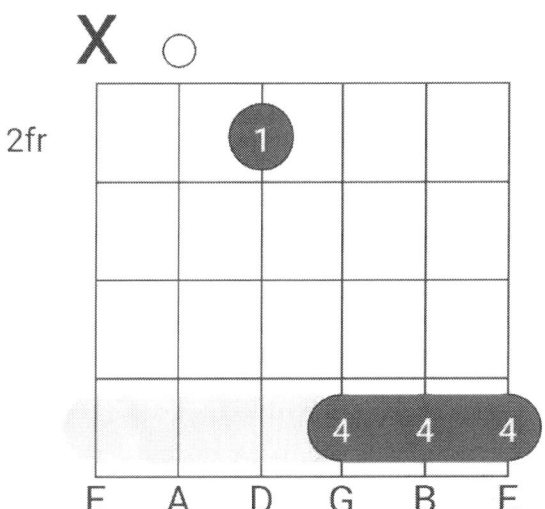
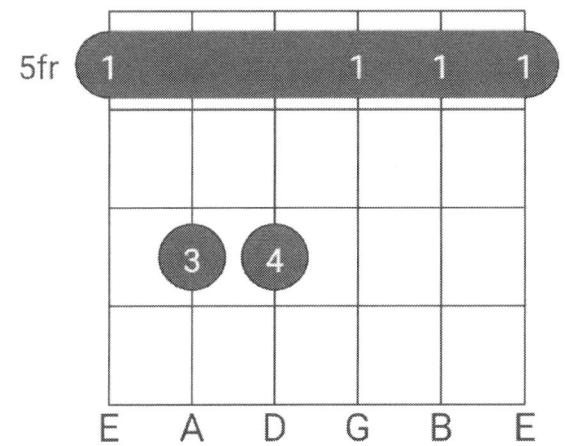
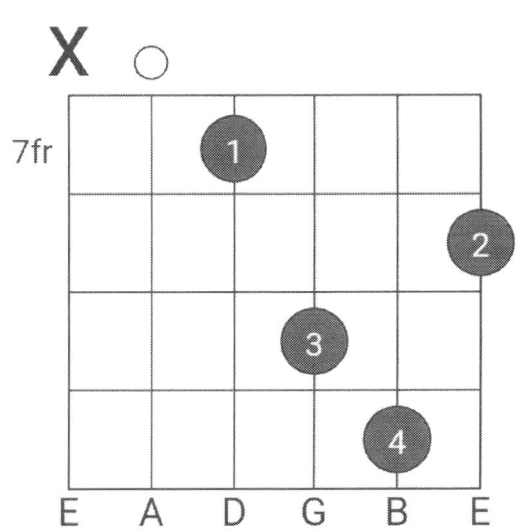

# A dim

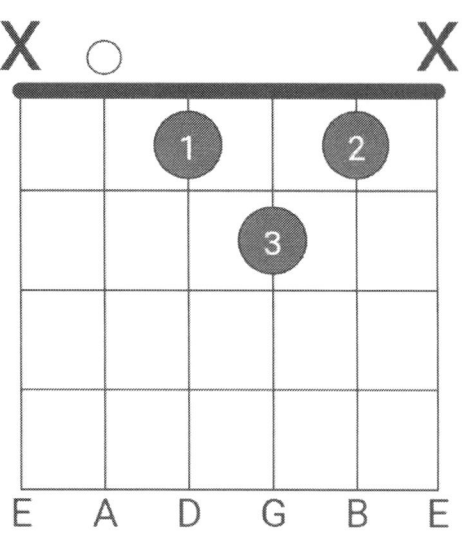
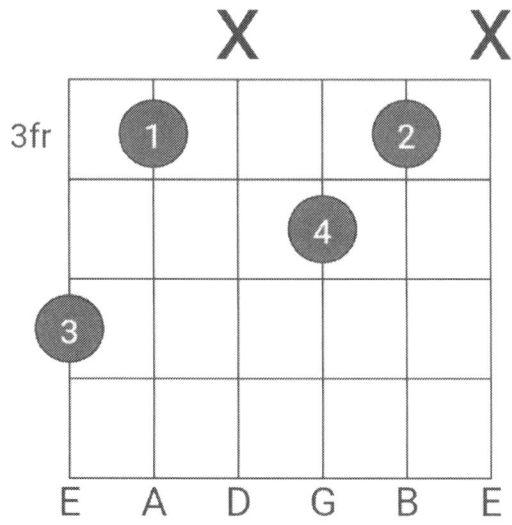
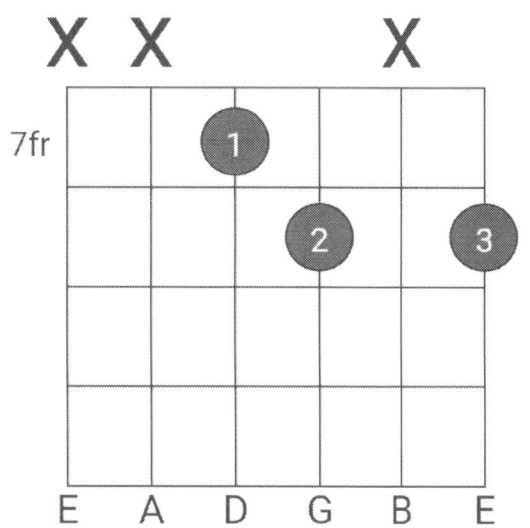
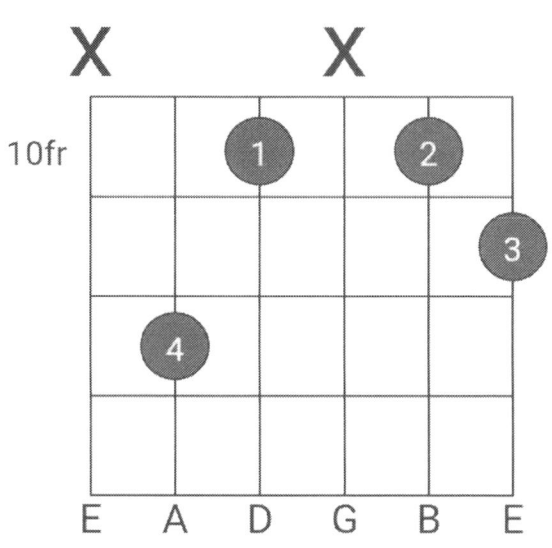

# A Sus2

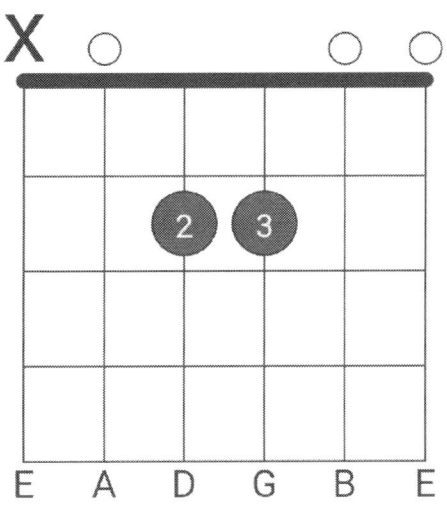
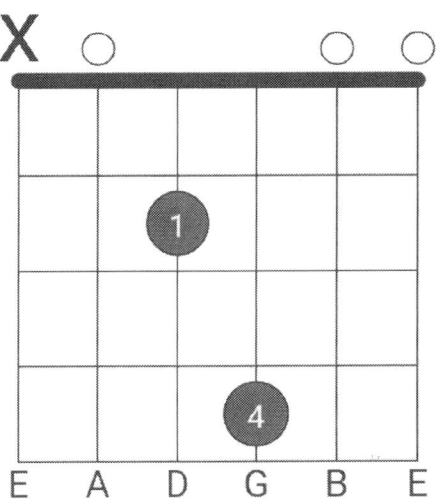
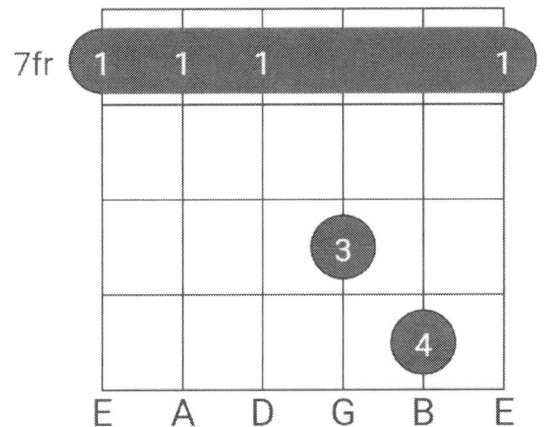
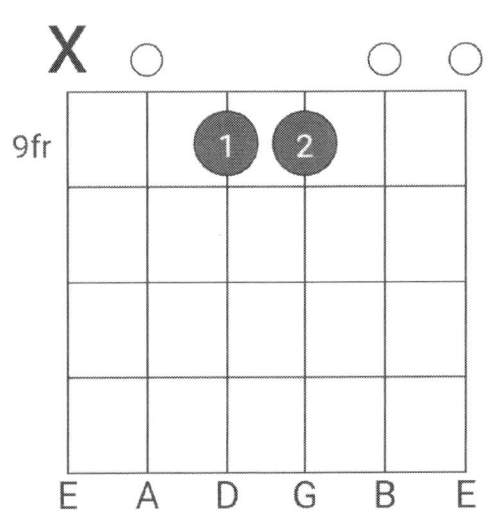

# A Sus4

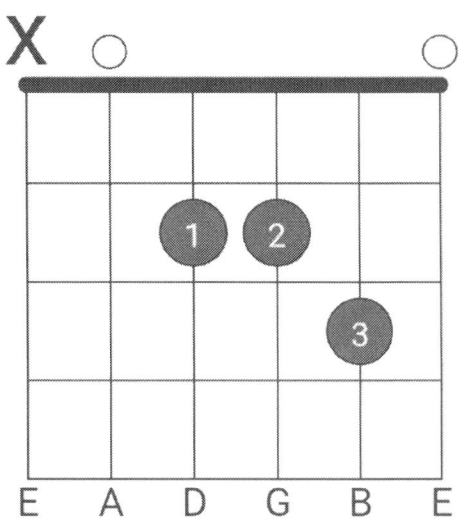
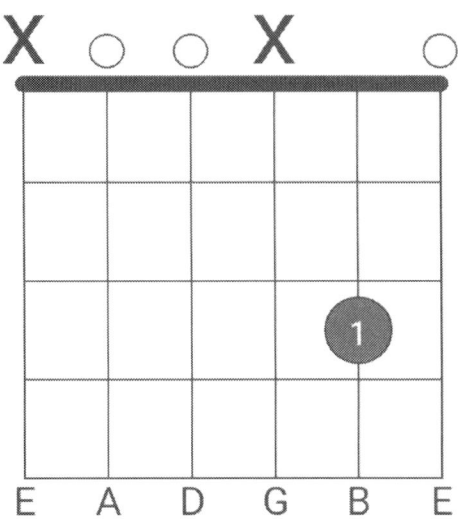
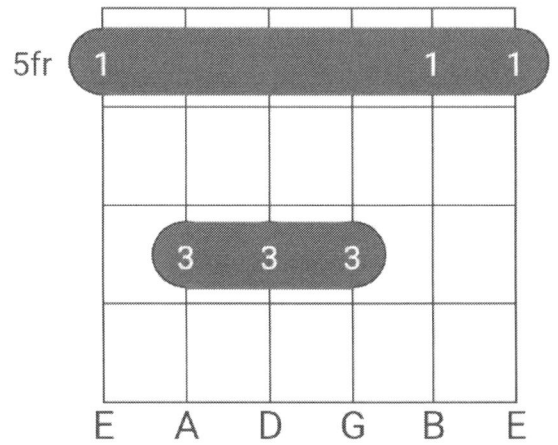
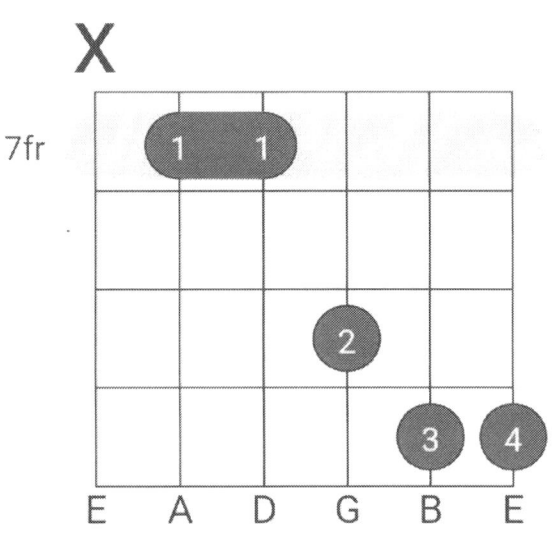

# A aug

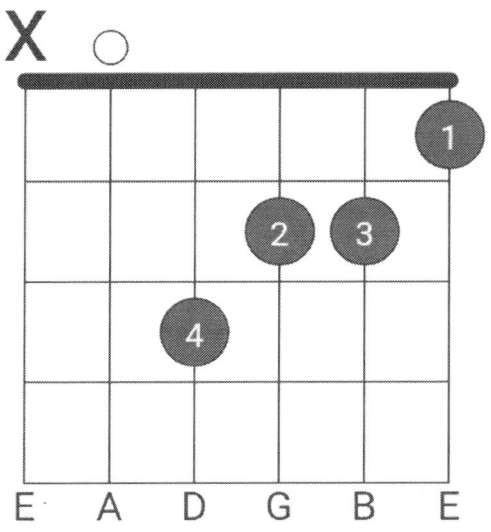
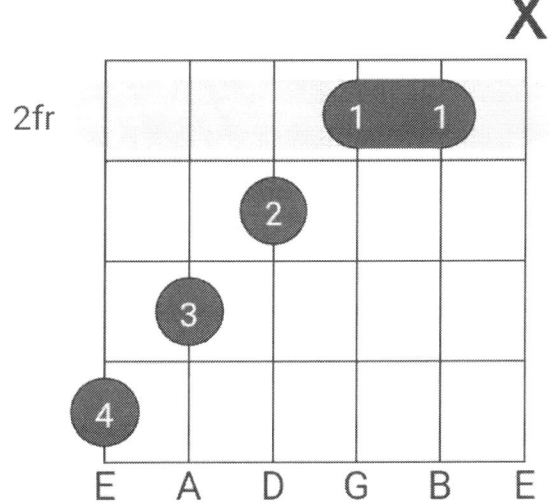
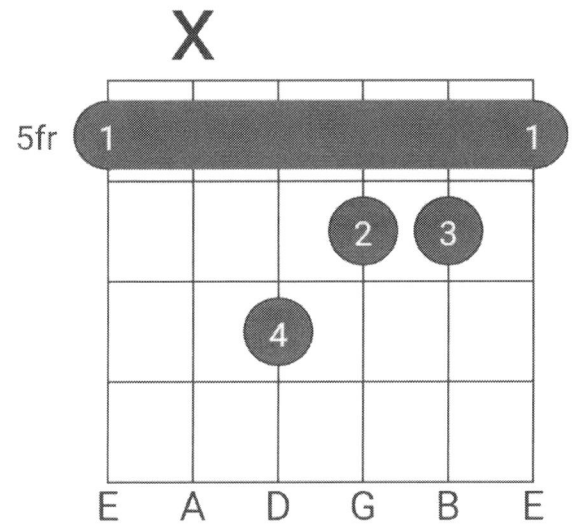
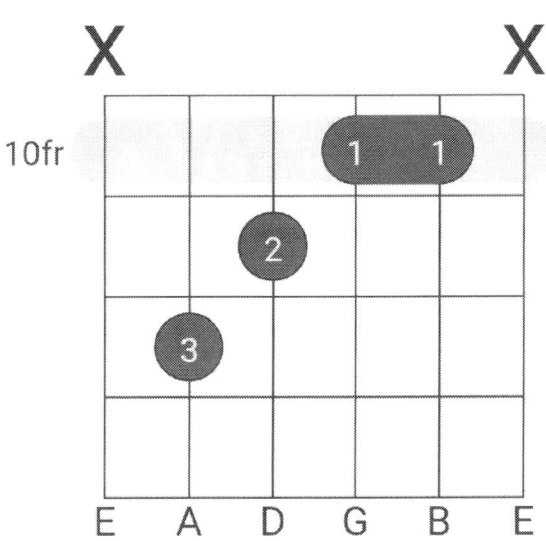

# A7

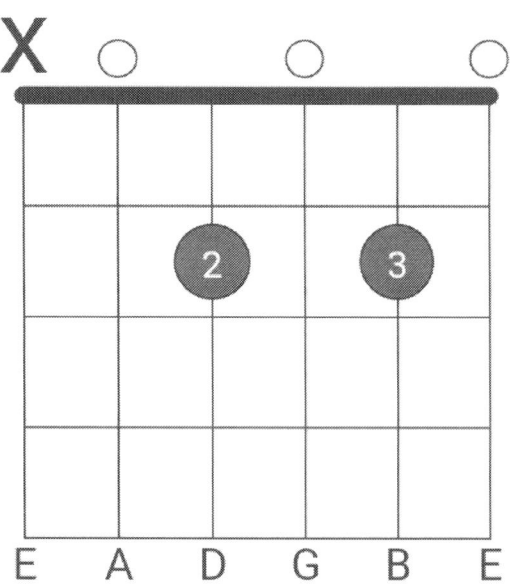
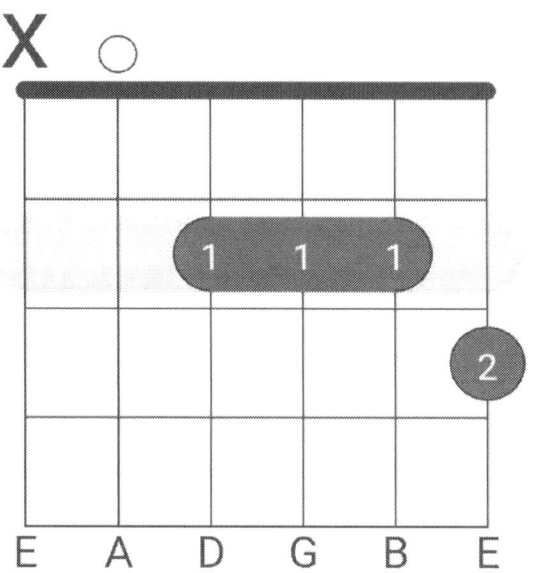
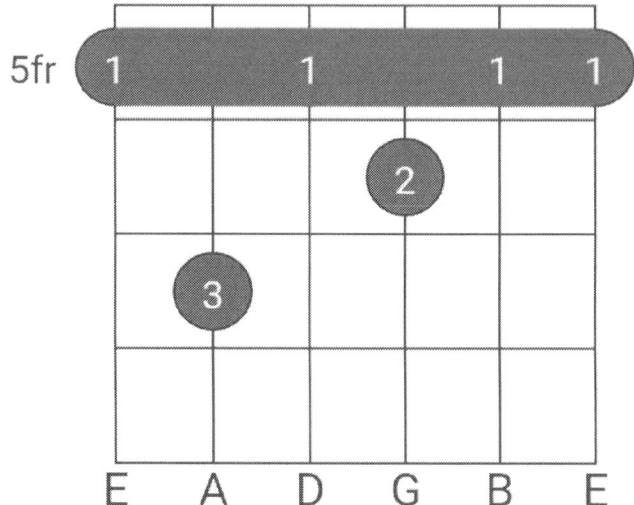
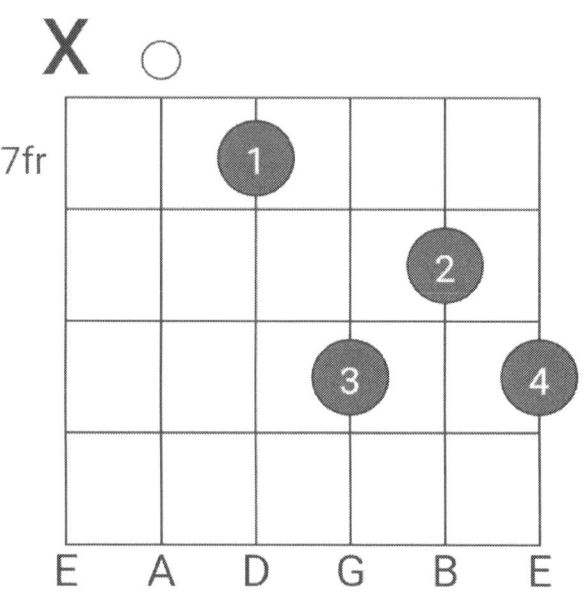

# A maj7

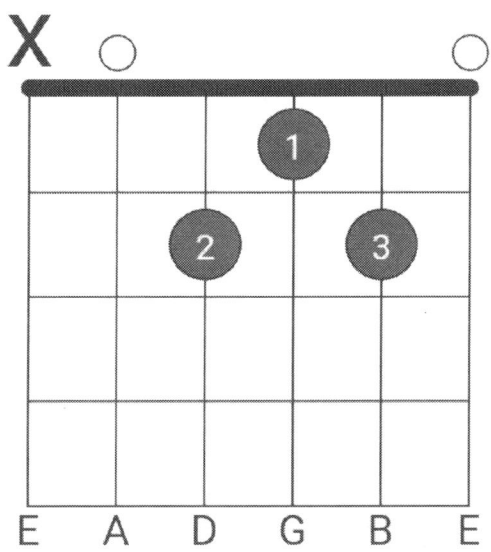
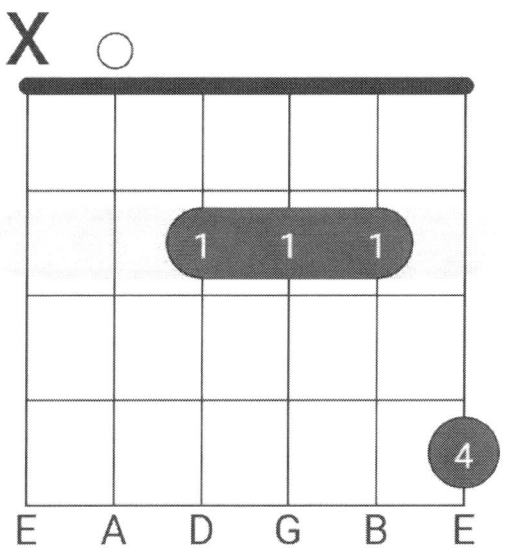
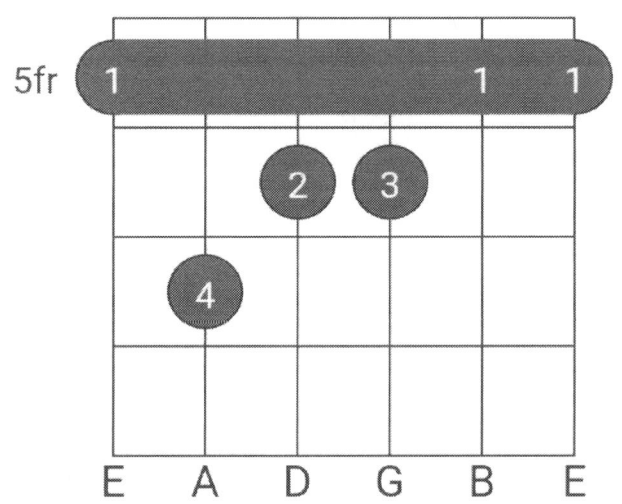
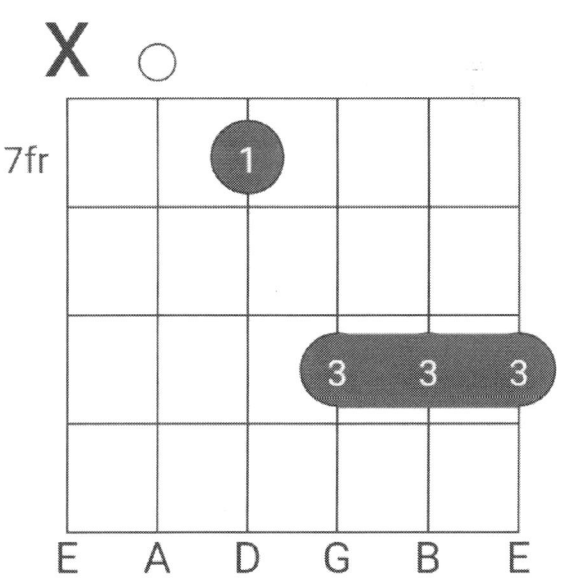

# Am7

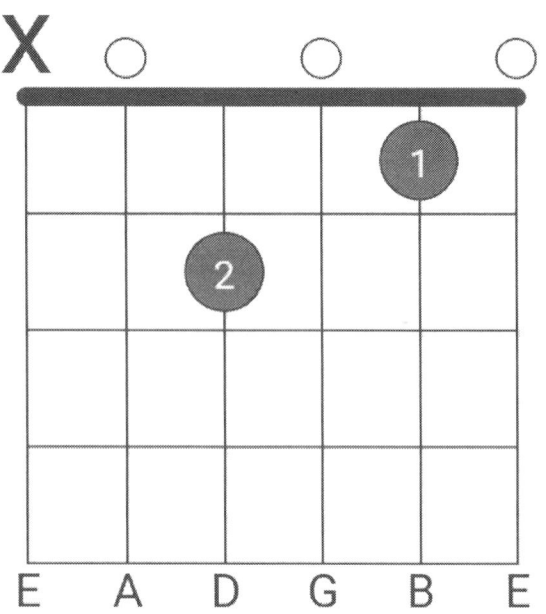
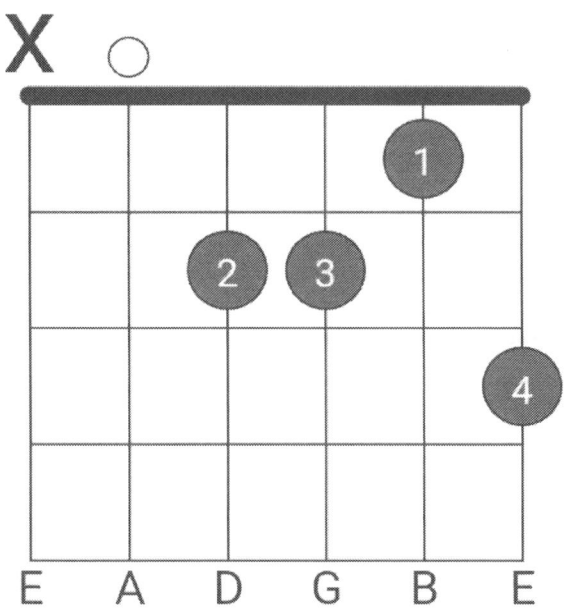
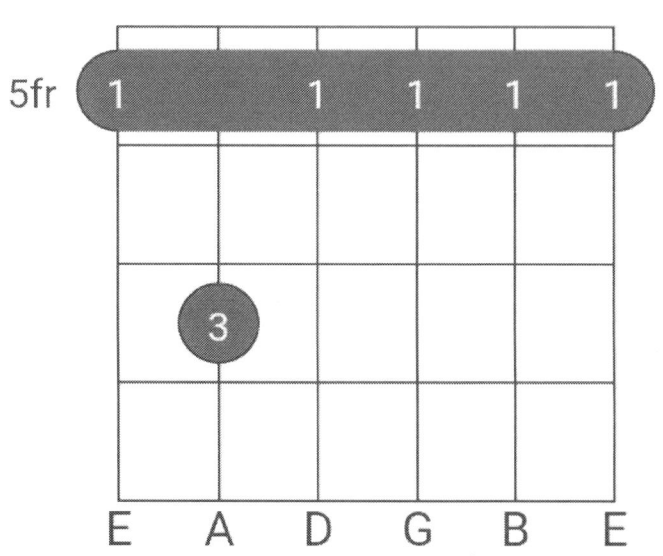
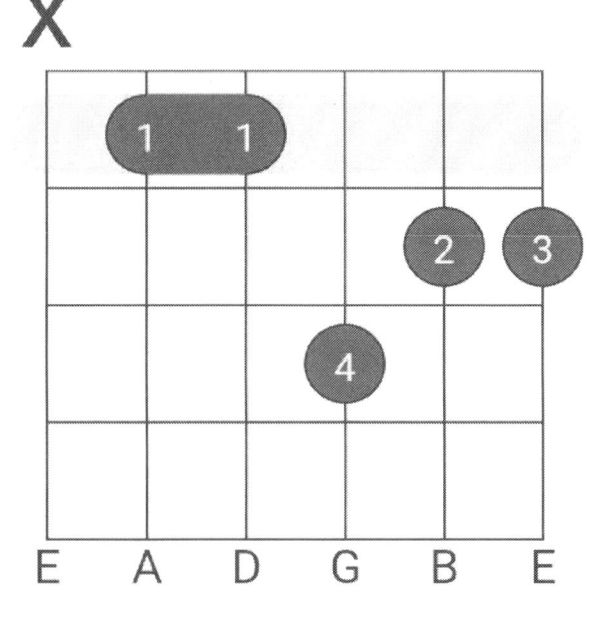

# A# / Bb Major

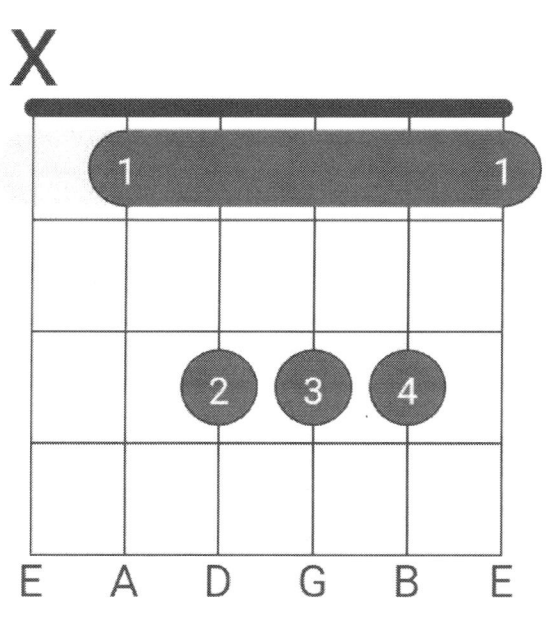
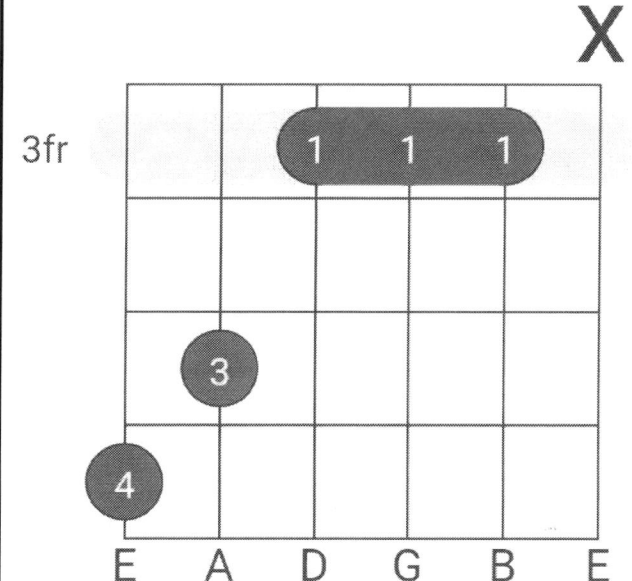
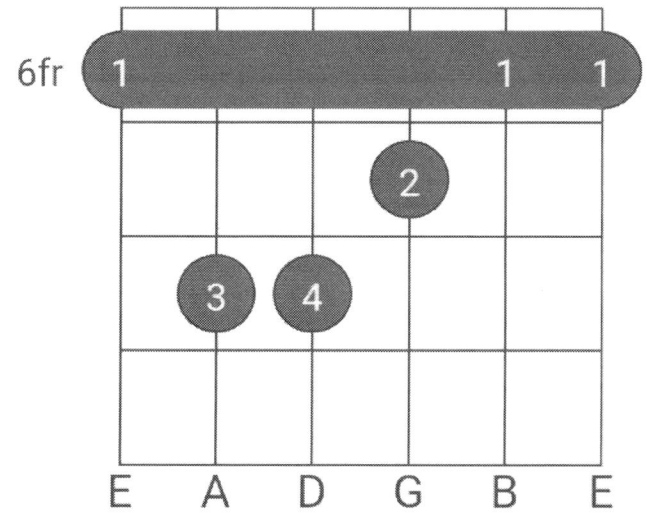
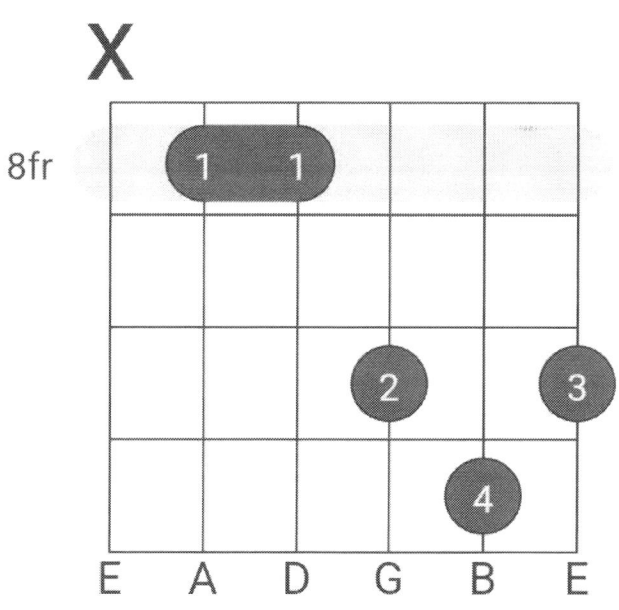

# A# / Bb minor

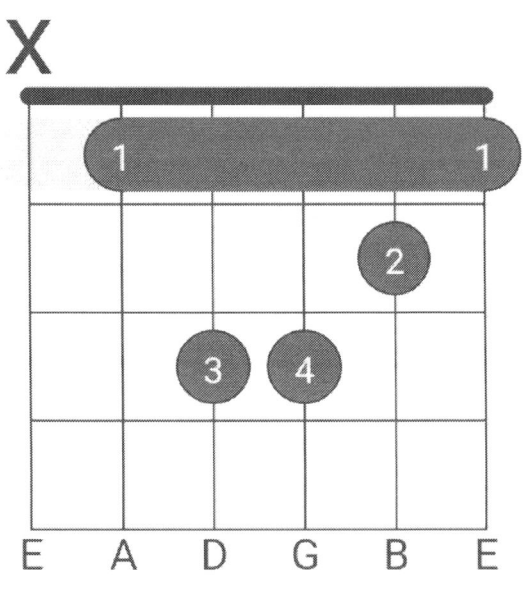
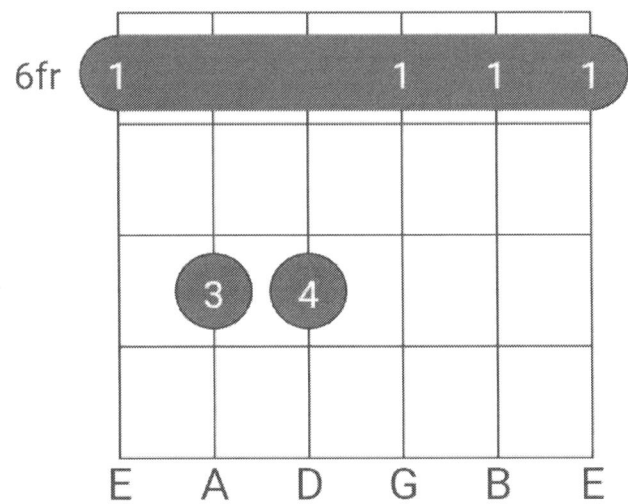
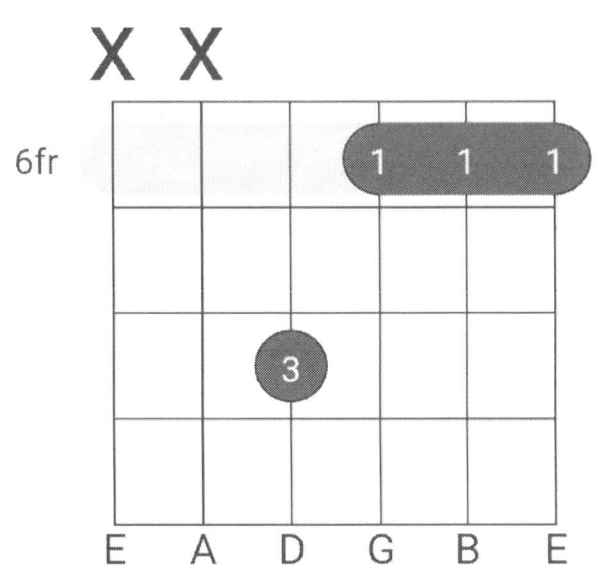
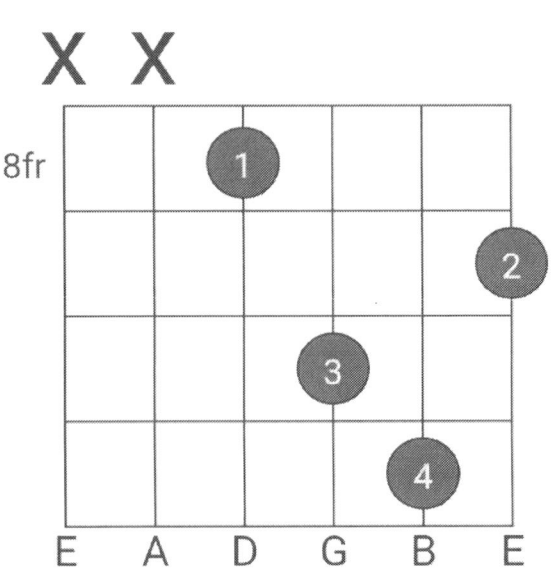

# A# / Bb dim

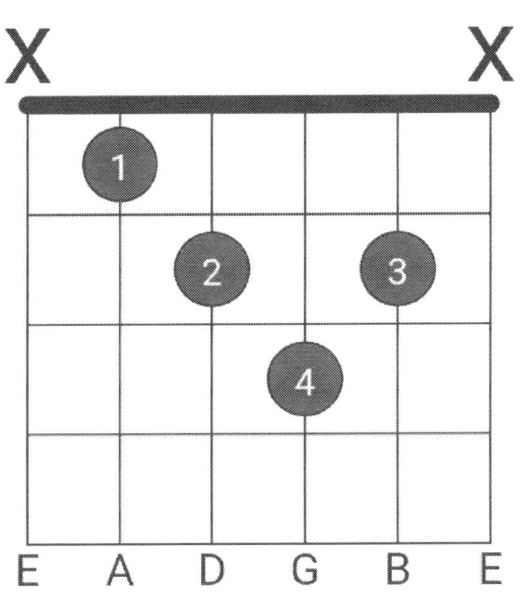
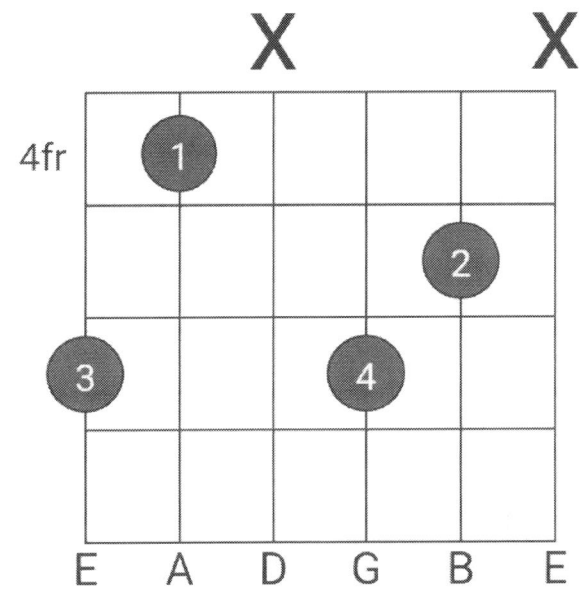
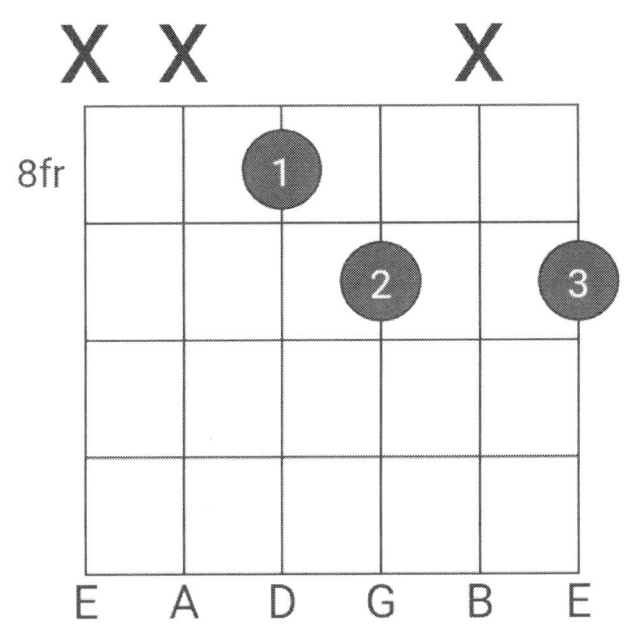
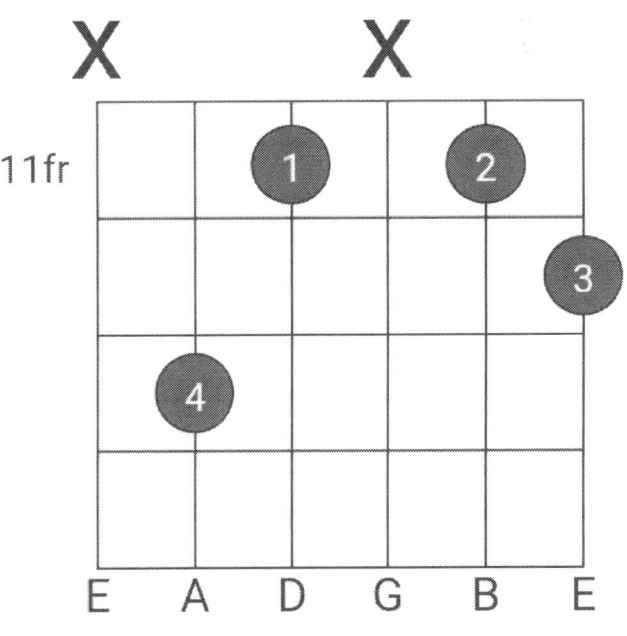

# A# / Bb Sus2

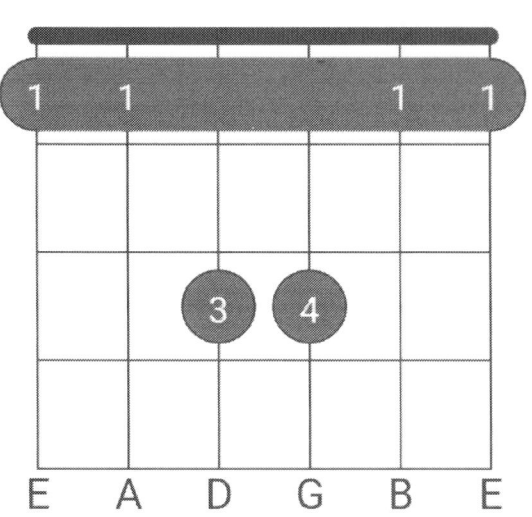
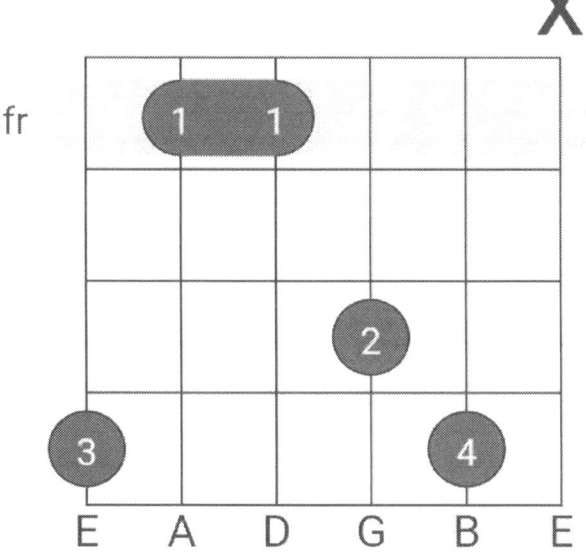
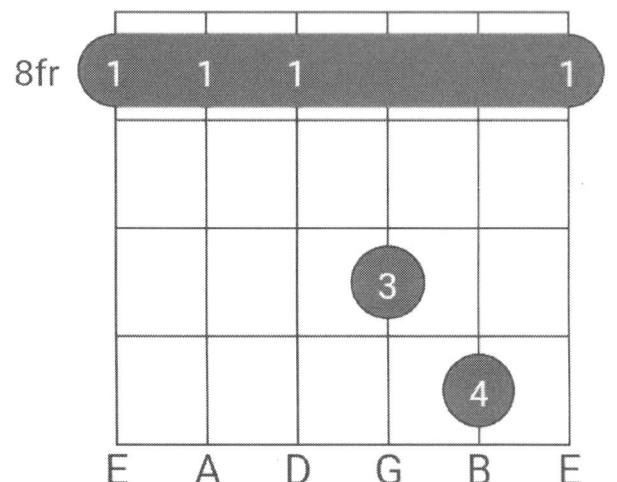
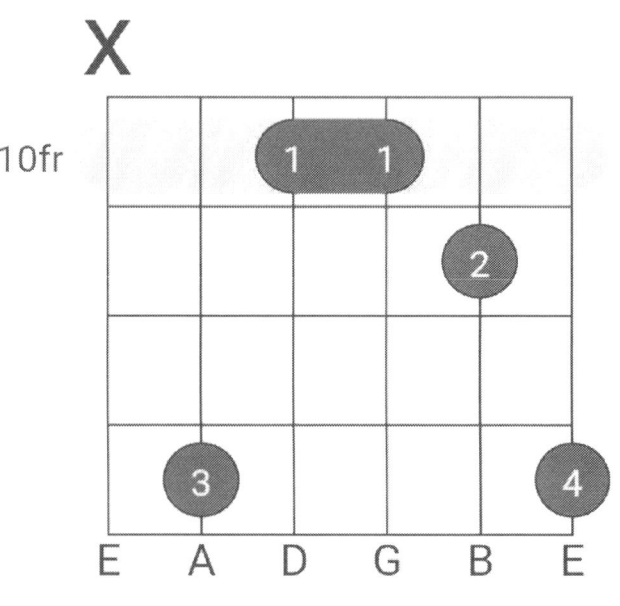

# A# / Bb Sus4

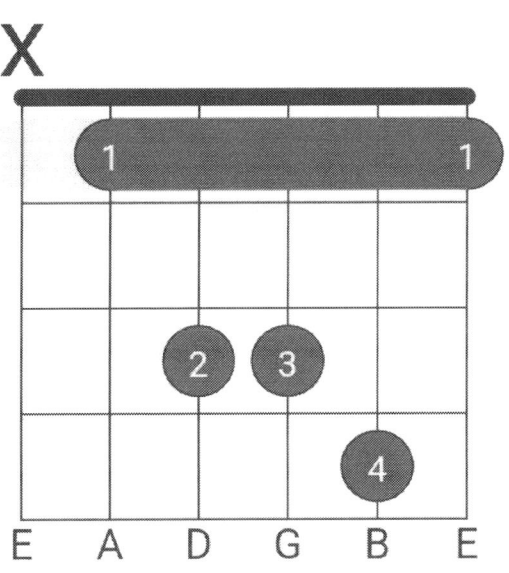
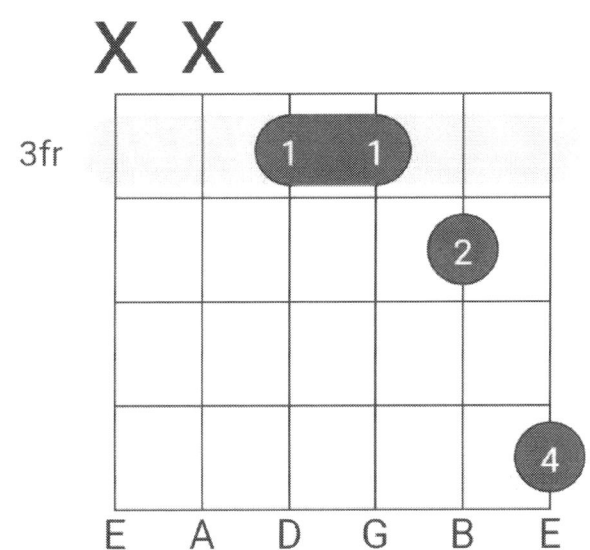
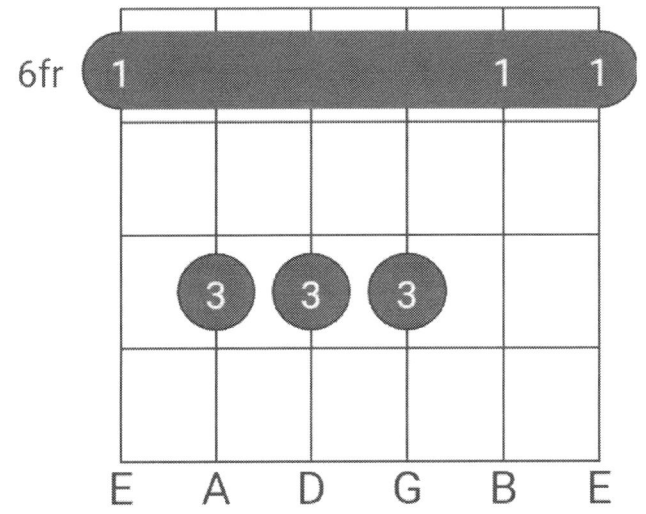
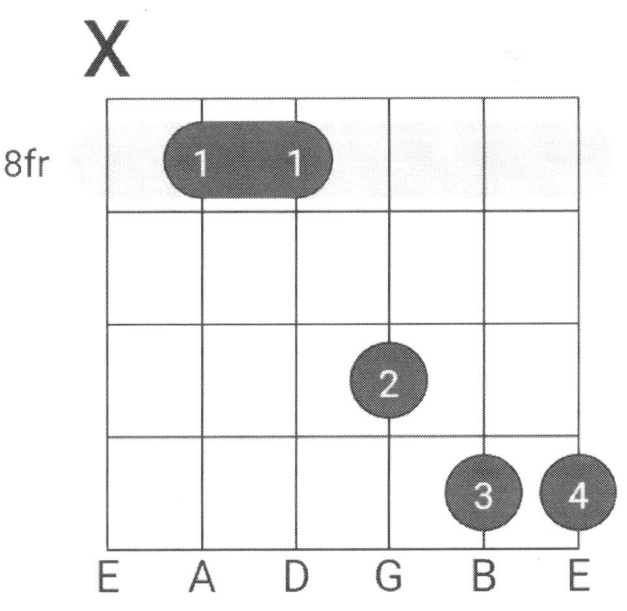

# A# / Bb aug

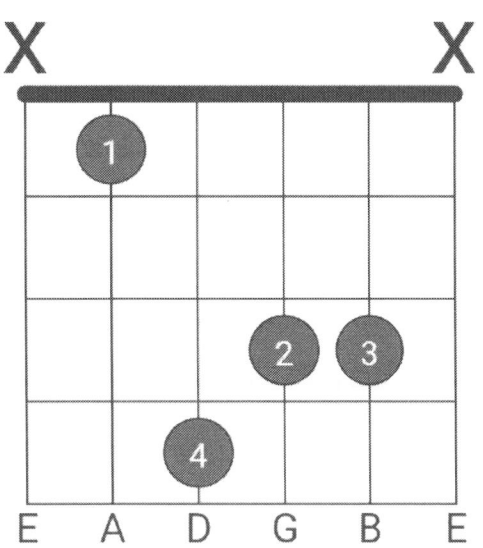
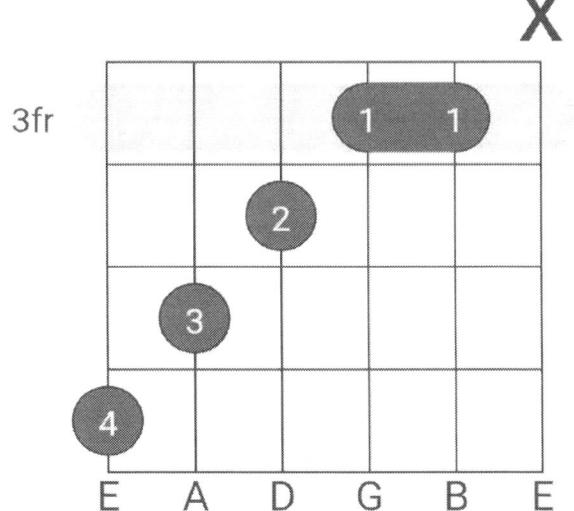
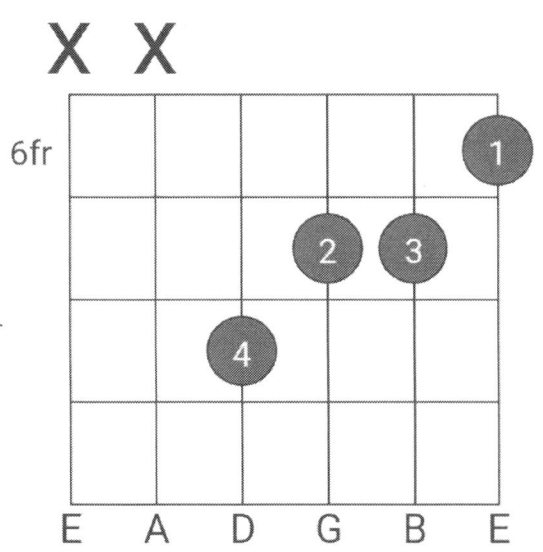
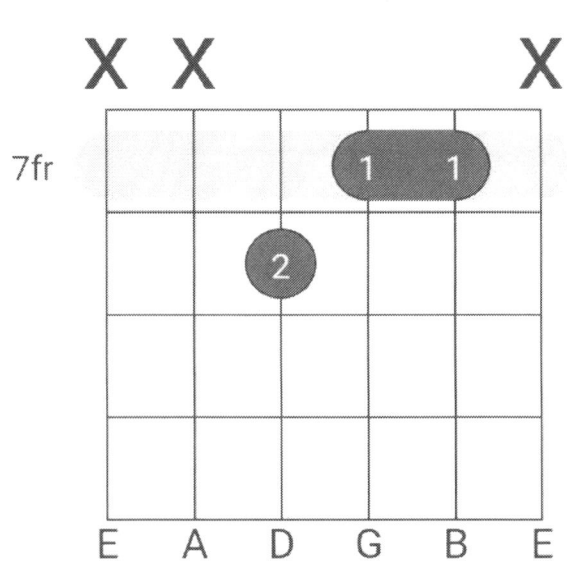

# A# / Bb7

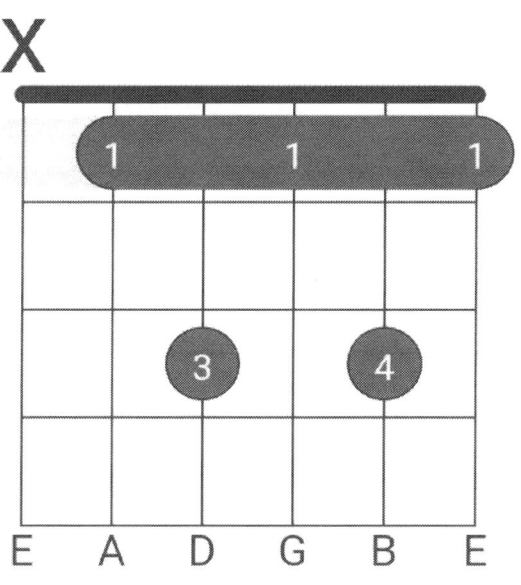
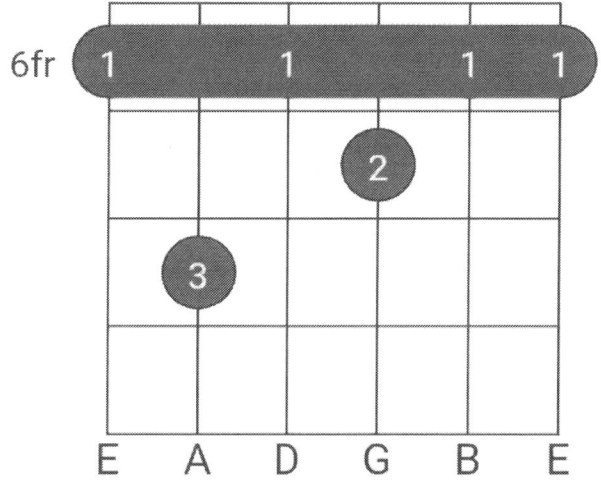
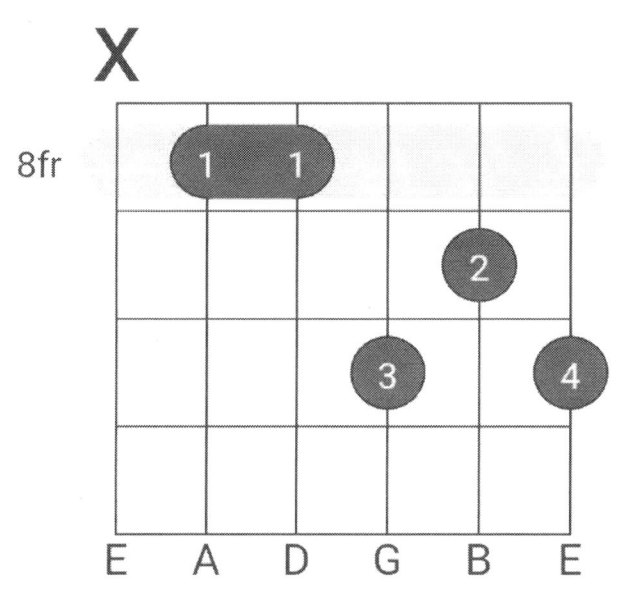
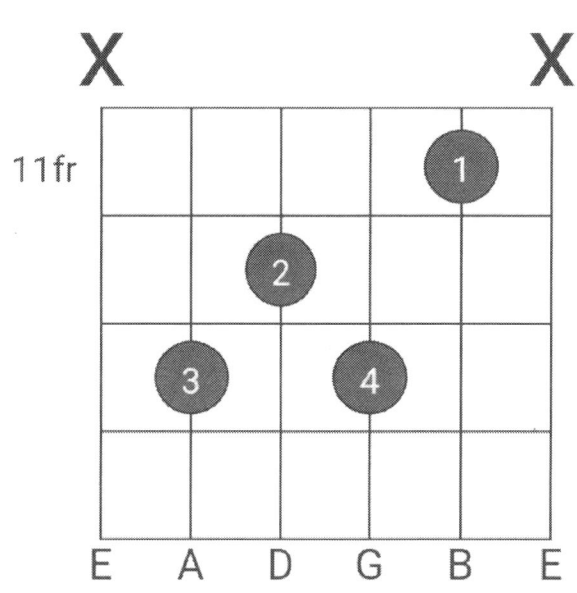

# A# / Bb maj7

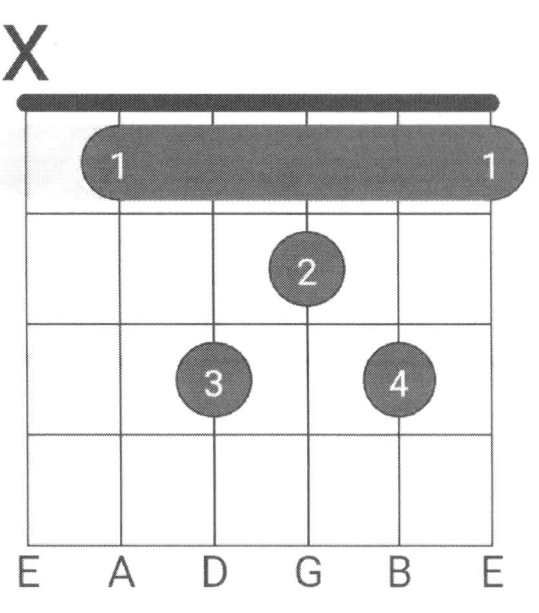
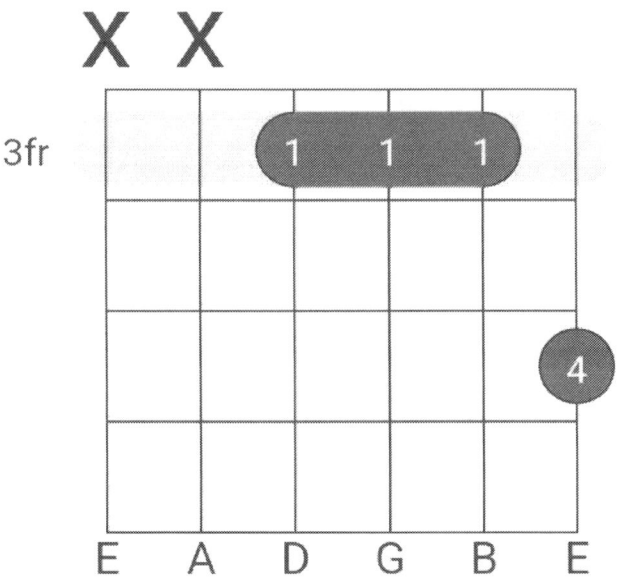
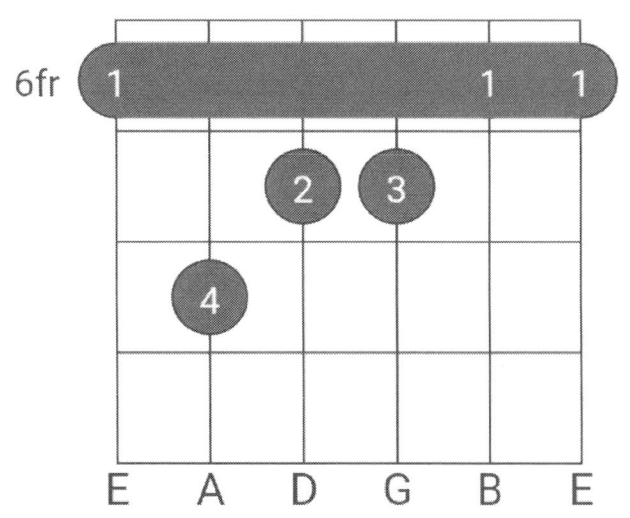
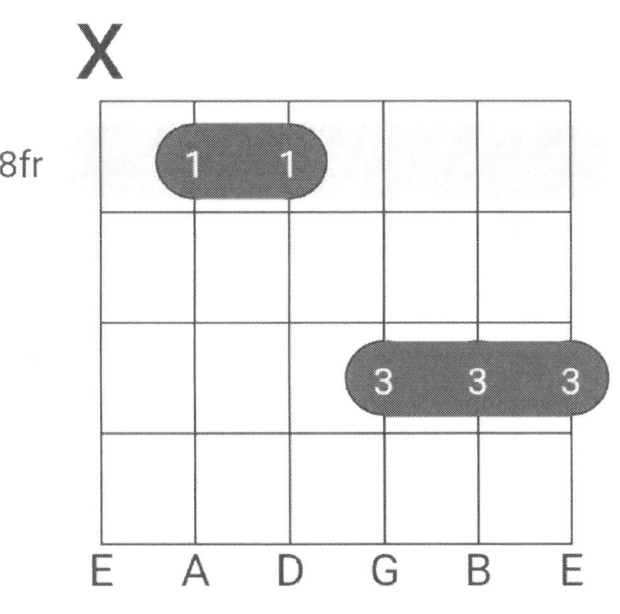

# A# / Bb m7

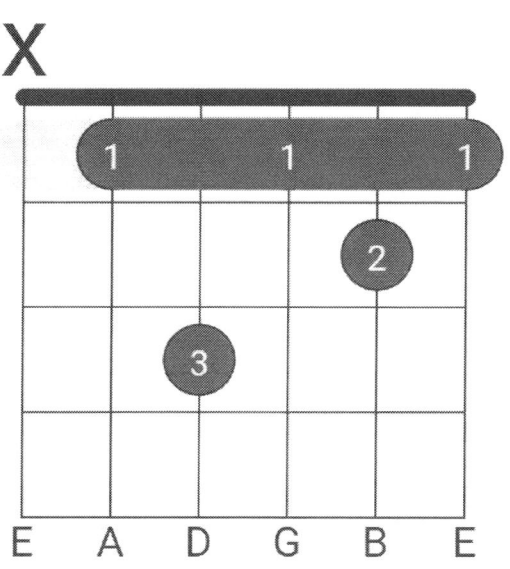
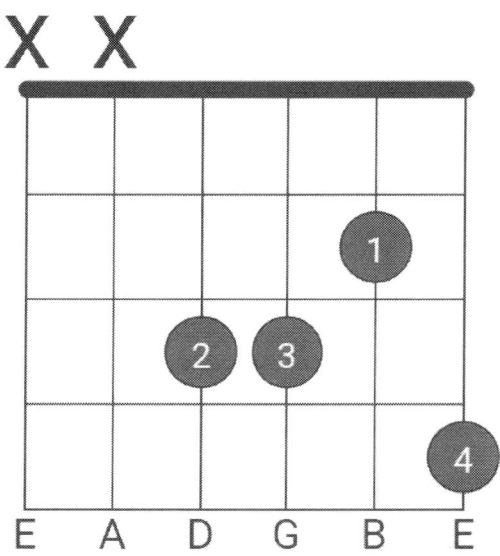
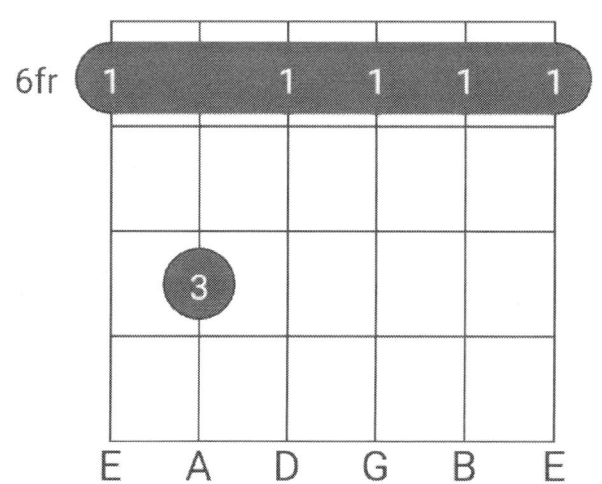
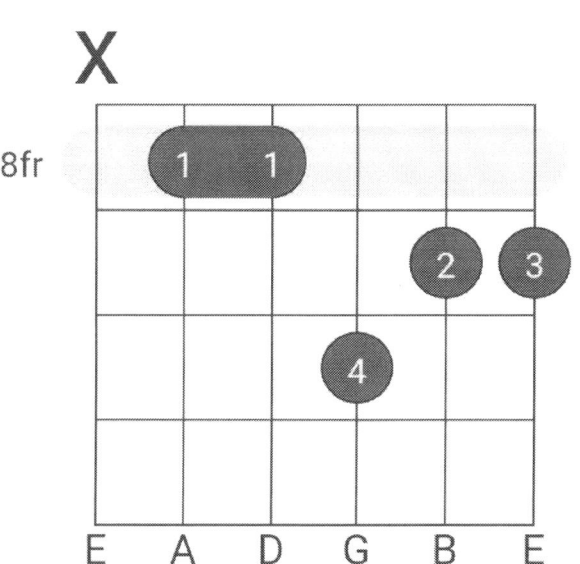

# B Major

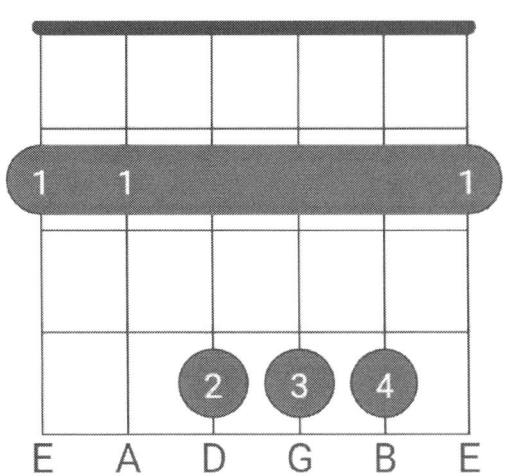
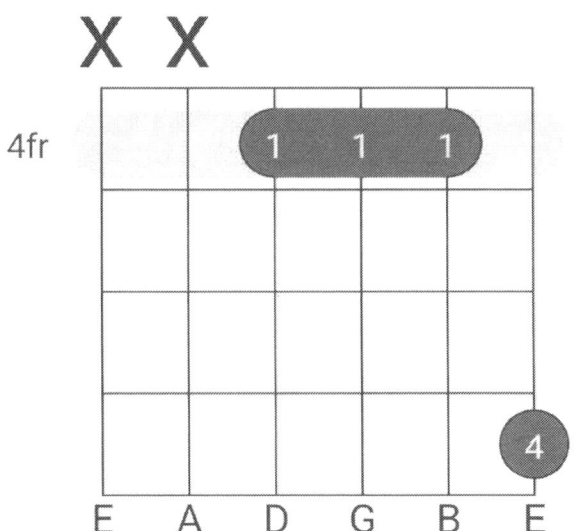
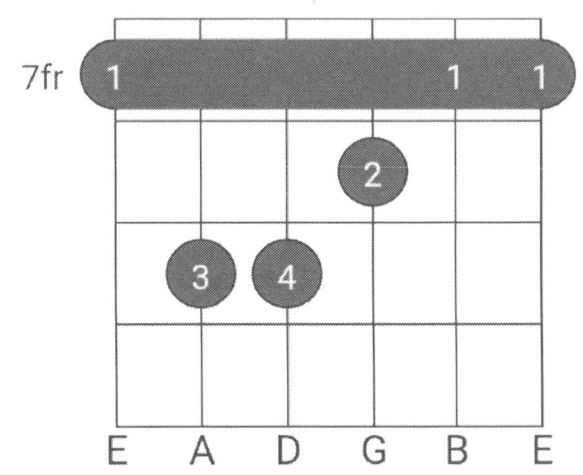
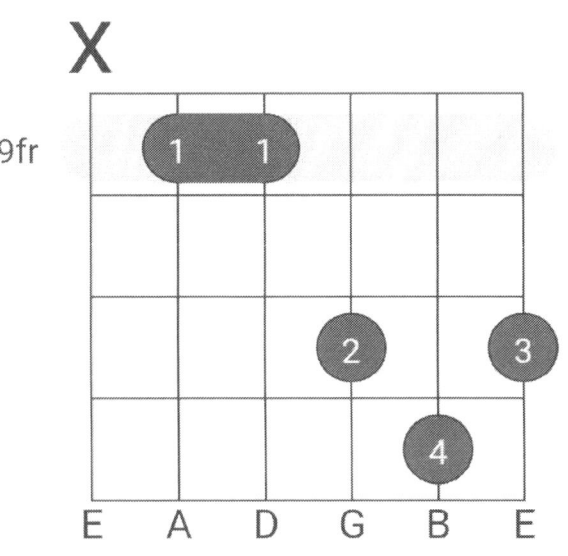

# B minor

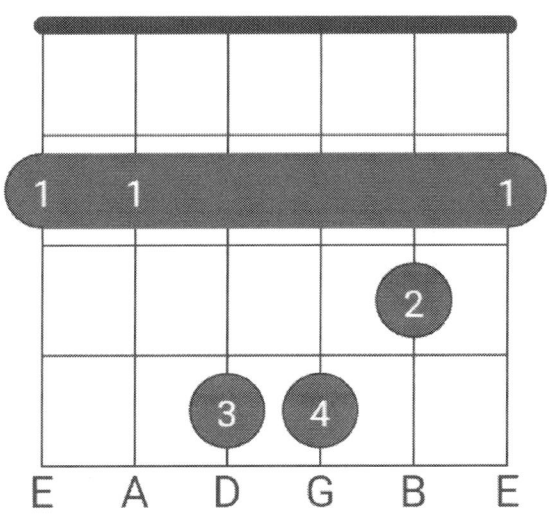
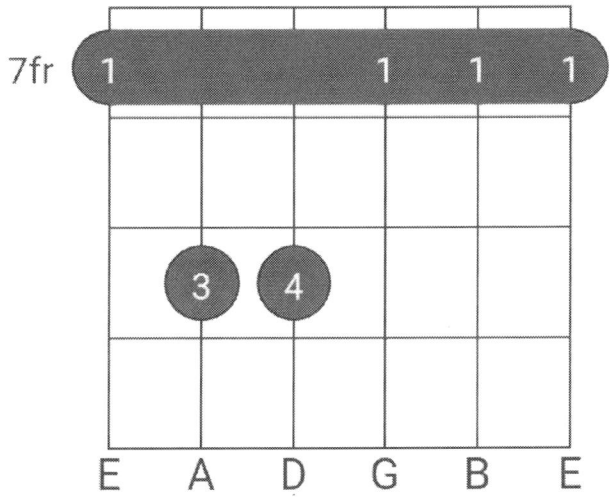
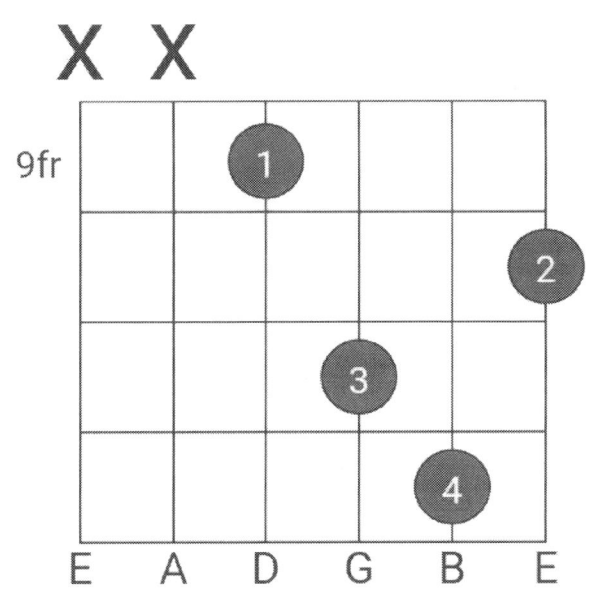
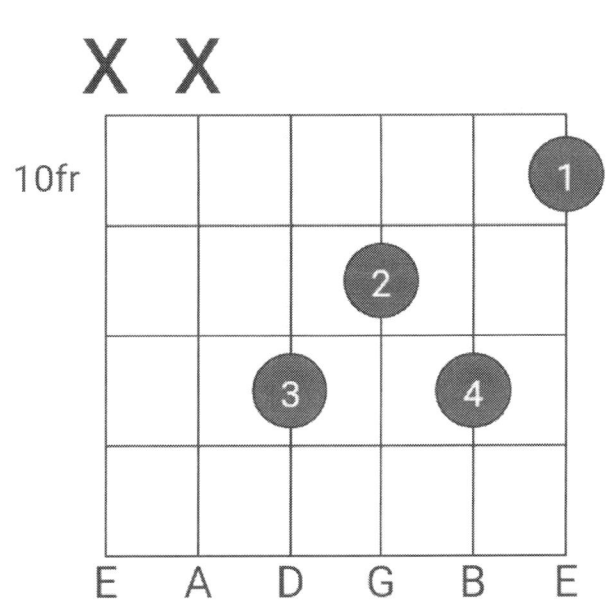

# B dim

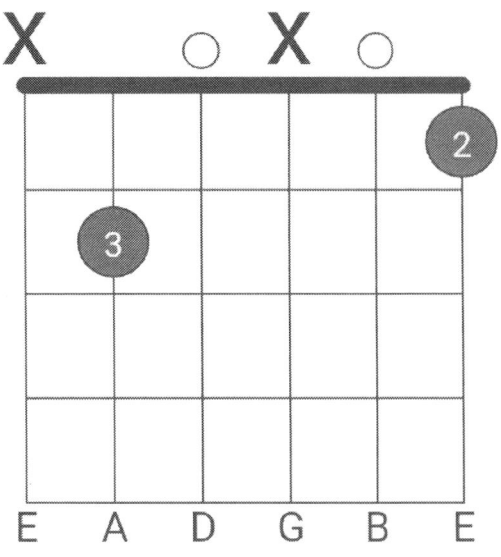
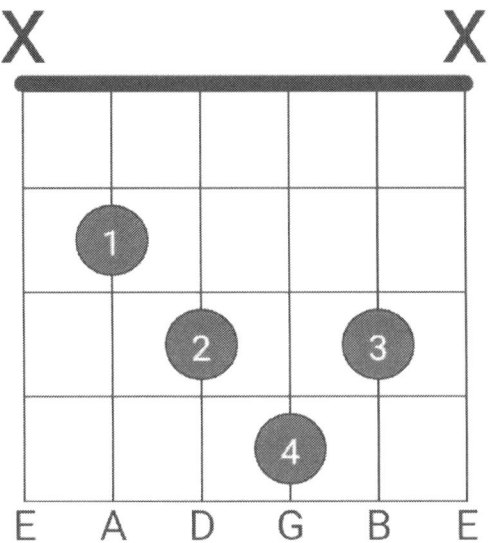
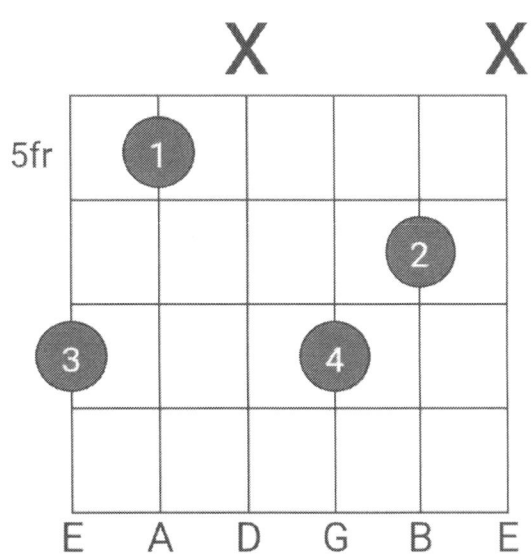
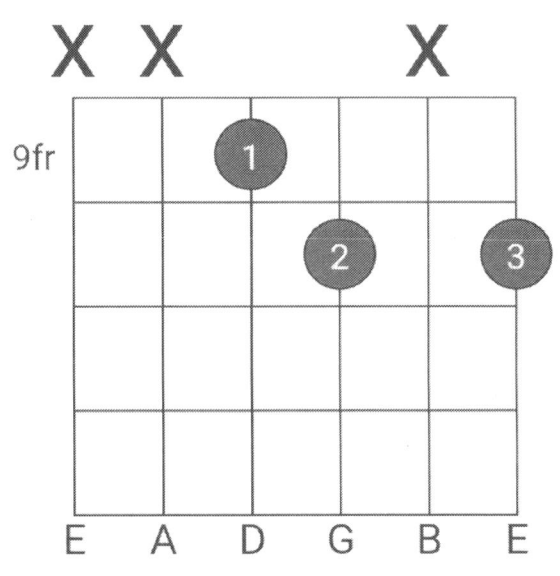

# B Sus2

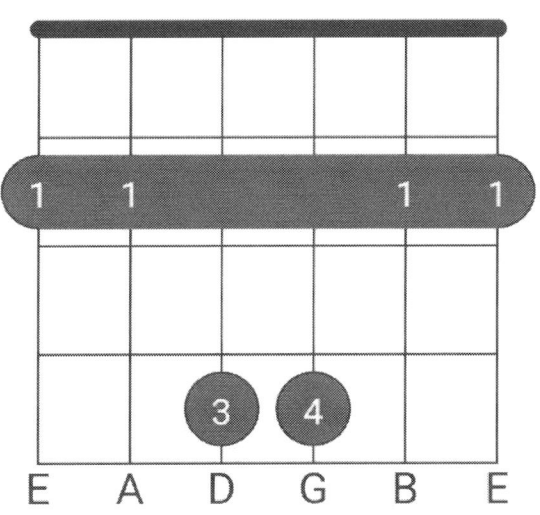
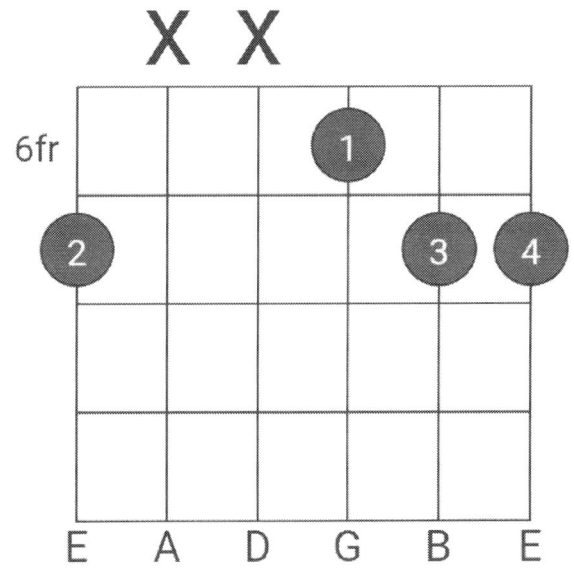
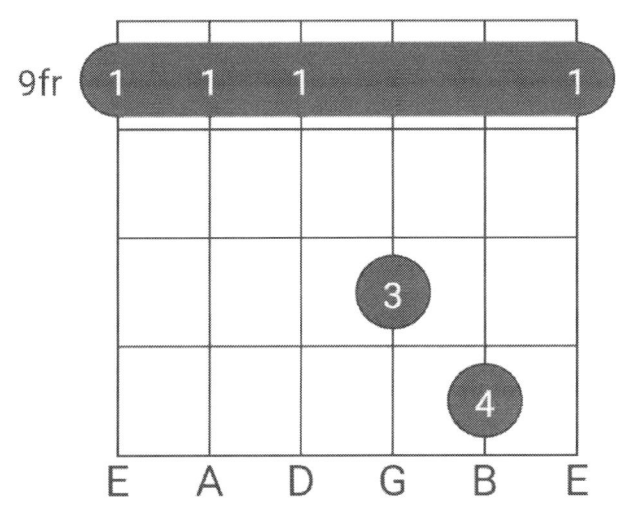
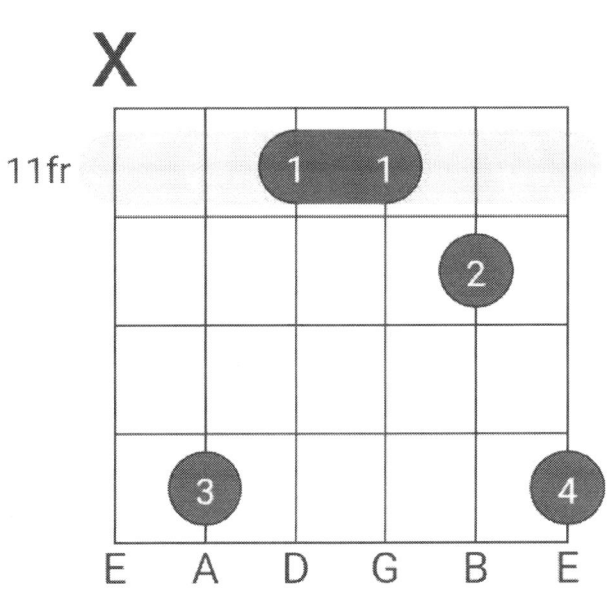

# B Sus4

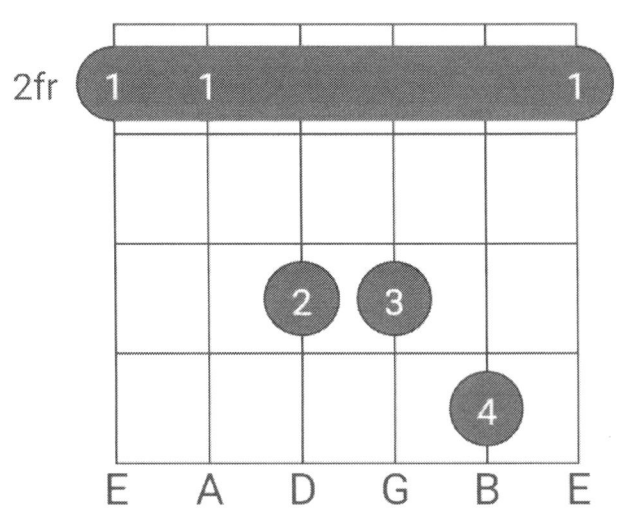
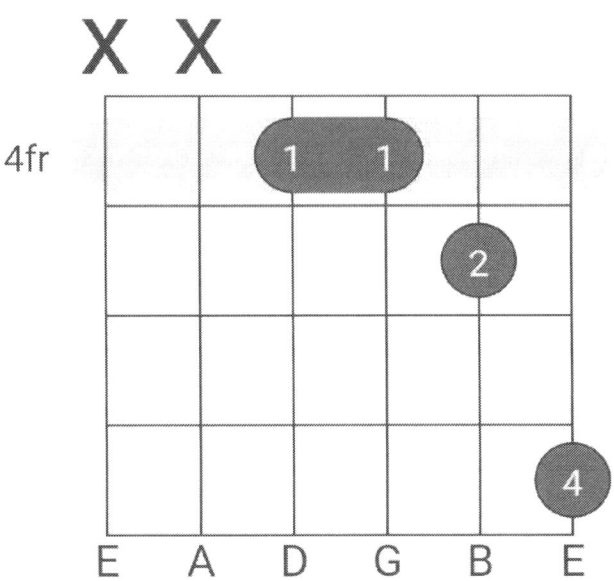
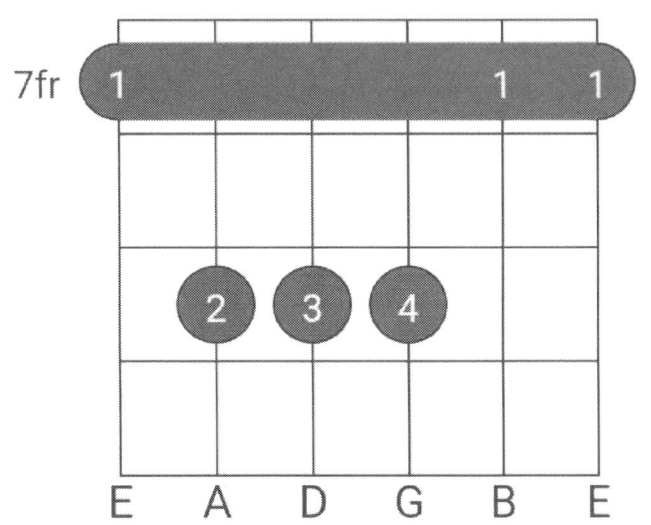
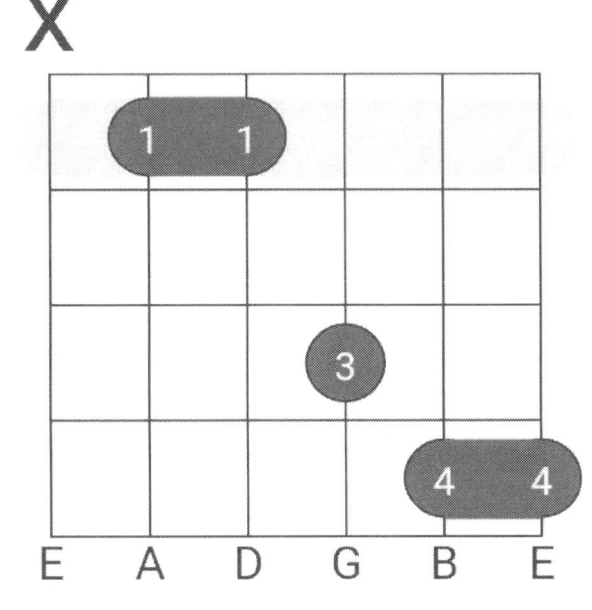

# B aug

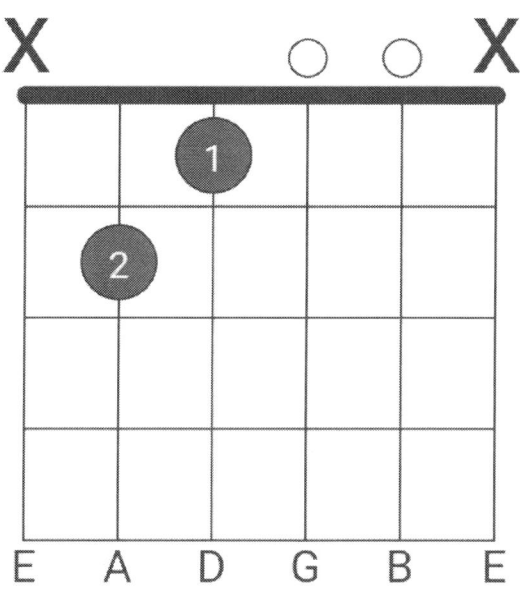
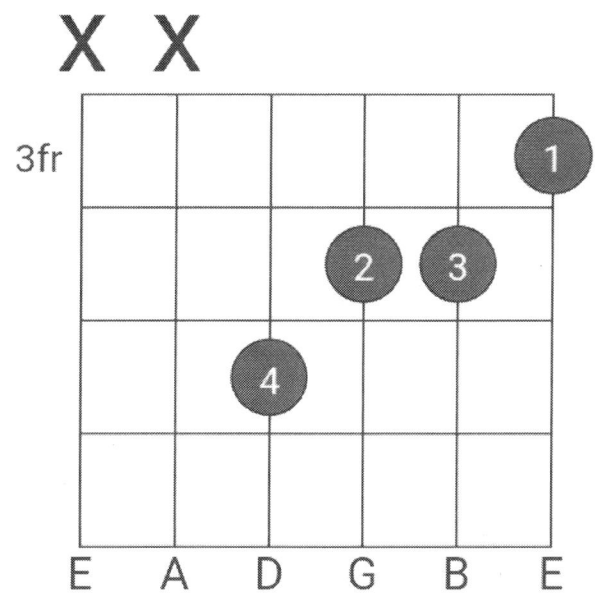
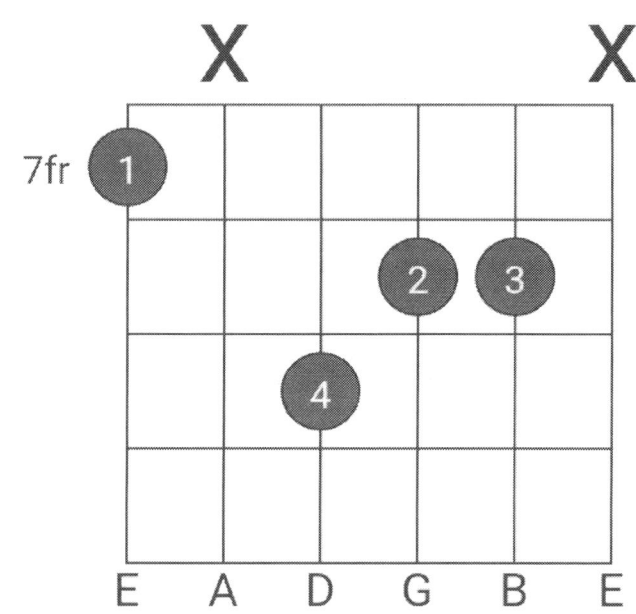
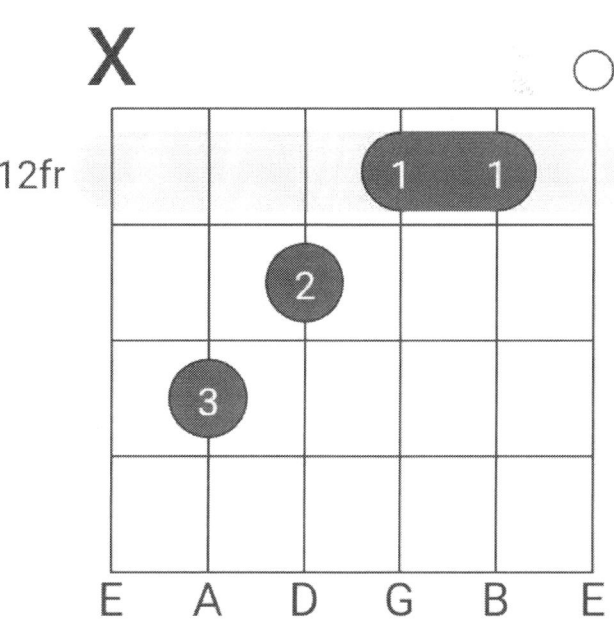

# B7

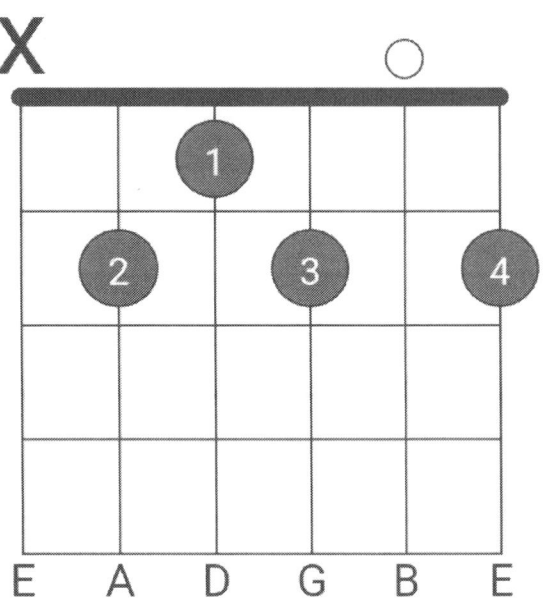
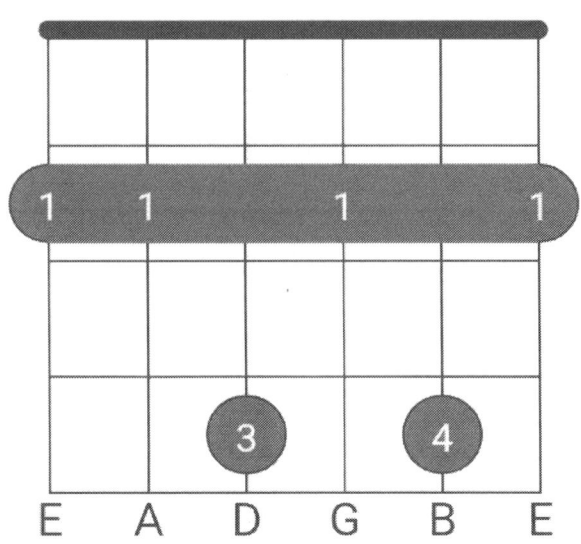
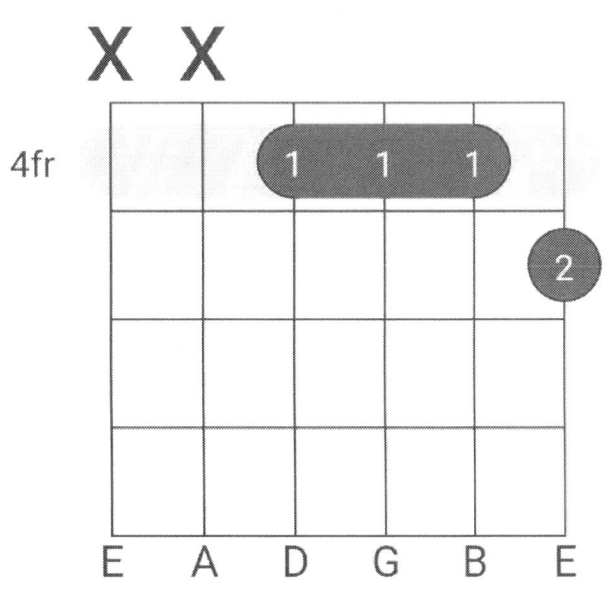
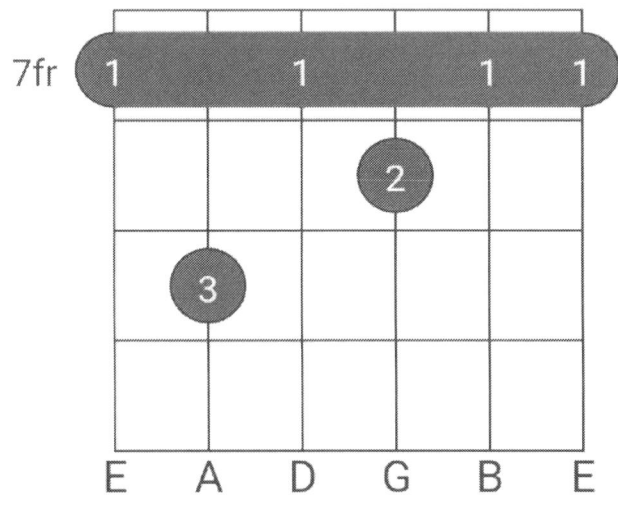

# B maj7

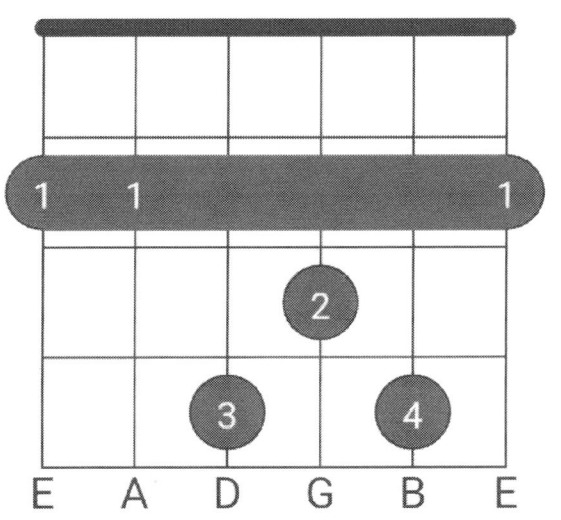
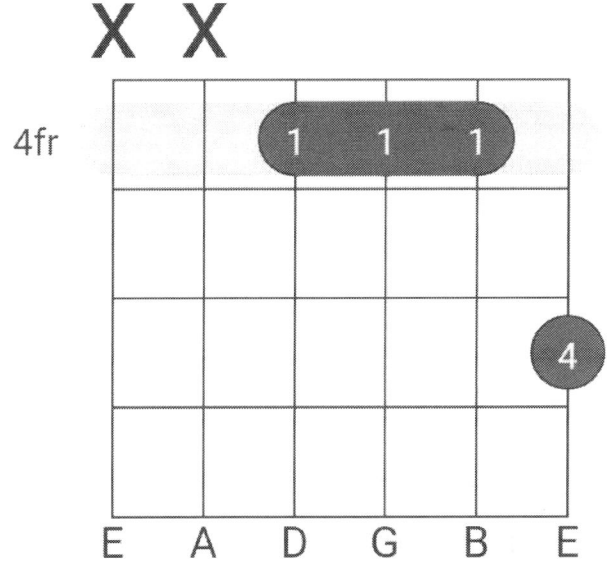
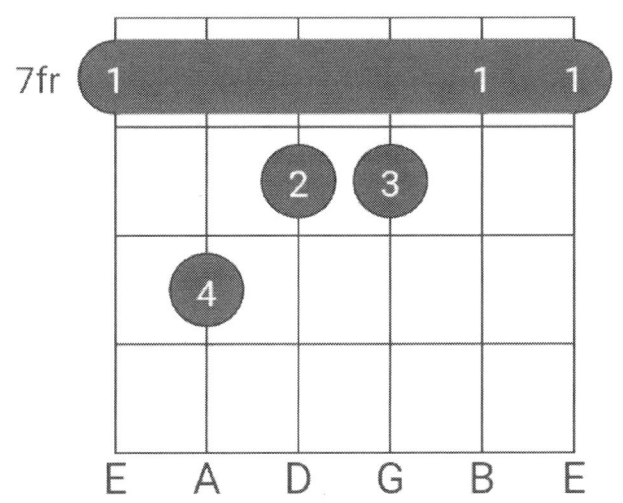
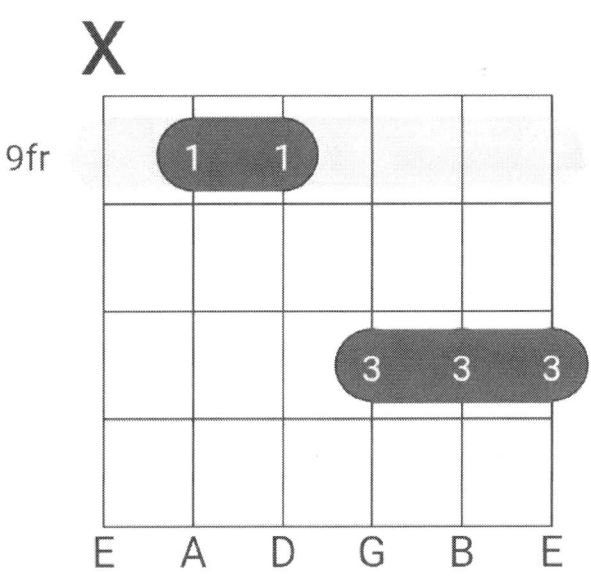

# Bm7

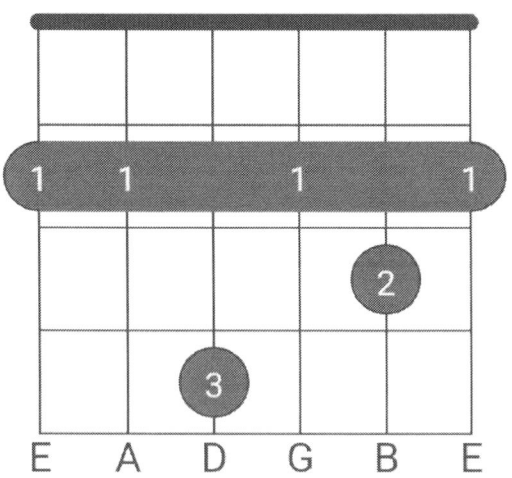
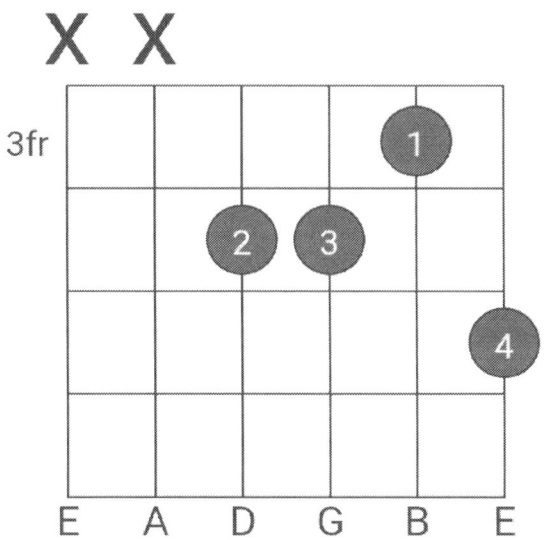
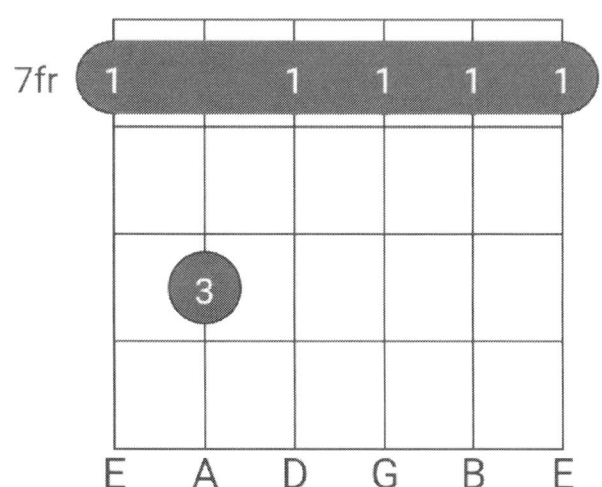
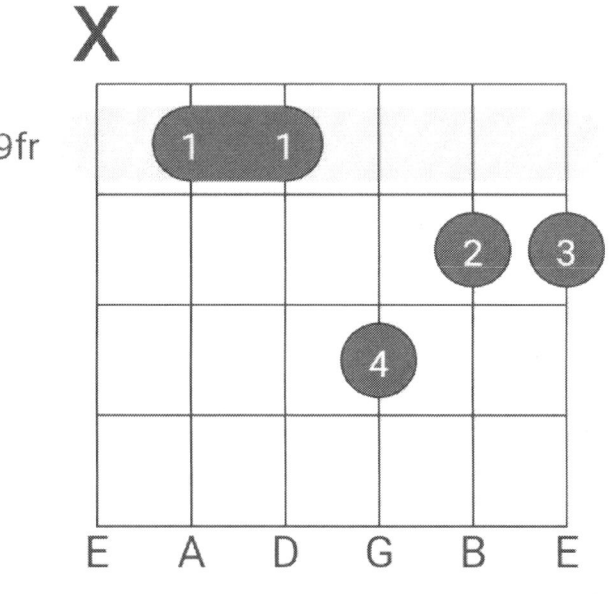

# Use QR codes and visit me:

He has been professionally involved in music for 16 years, teaching accordion and piano. Below you can see my work.

https://muzycznelekcje.pl/

All exercises have been done by me, so you can be sure that they are consistent and correct with the principles of music.
These particular exercises have a huge impact on the development of technique, which I noticed in myself and my students

Thank you for your purchase!
If you found the book helpful leave opinion under this product.

All Rights Reserved **2021**

Printed in Great Britain
by Amazon